CRITICAL THINKING,
LOGIC,
and ARGUMENT

ERIC DAYTON
University of Saskatchewan

Pearson Canada
Toronto

Library and Archives Canada Cataloguing in Publication

Dayton, Eric, 1946–
    Critical thinking, logic, and argument / Eric Dayton.

Includes index.
ISBN 978-0-13-502608-3

1. Critical thinking—Textbooks. 2. Logic—Textbooks. 3. Reasoning—Textbooks.   I. Title.

B809.2.D39 2010   160   C2008-908126-9

ISBN-13: 978-0-13-502608-3
ISBN-10: 0-13-502608-3

Vice President, Editorial Director: Gary Bennett
Editor-in-Chief: Ky Pruesse
Editor, Humanities & Social Sciences: Joel Gladstone
Signing Representative: Duncan MacKinnon
Executive Marketing Manager: Judith Allen
Developmental Editor: Rema Celio
Production Editor: Richard di Santo
Copy Editor: Dianne Fowlie
Proofreaders: Susan Bindernagel, Sally Glover
Production Coordinator: Avinash Chandra
Composition: Macmillan Publishing Solutions
Art Director: Julia Hall
Cover Design: Miriam Blier
Cover Image: Getty Images/Dorling Kindersley

1 2 3 4 5   13 12 11 10 09

Printed and bound in the United States of America.

To Emer, the light of my life

Brief Table of Contents

Detailed Table of Contents

7 Sentence Logic and Consistency   173

Preface

This text is about critical thinking: what it is, and how to become a critical thinker. It is aimed at helping students acquire a tool box of skills and an understanding of argument which will make them better at reasoning, more careful in their judgments, and more fully responsible for the beliefs they have. All of the skills are utterly practical and easily learned and as a package enhance the student's capacity for effective learning. It is the product of over 20 years' work teaching critical thinking.

My aim has been to produce a text that is short and to the point, that develops skills using numerous exercises (including answers), so that an instructor can use the book in its entirety in a half-year course. Because many instructors have their own views of critical thinking and have developed their own course materials, the text doesn't try to do absolutely everything, leaving room for instructors to add material should they wish.

The abilities to abstract (to see the general in the particular), to see patterns and models, and to make explicit the assumptions and presuppositions which guide inference so that one can discipline and take responsibility for one's own thinking processes are central to critical thinking and have immense practical application. It takes practice and experience with a variety of simple argument patterns applied in different contexts to acquire the ability to see a valid pattern of argument in a prose passage, or to discern fallacies that mar its conclusions. The text presents these issues in a broader context of basic philosophical distinctions into the nature of reasoning and the aim of belief, so that students are not only learning concrete skills but also gaining a general understanding of what reasoning is.

The text divides into three parts. Part I focuses on basic concepts, distinguishing arguments from non-arguments and premises from conclusions. We examine validity and soundness and look at some basic argument patterns, such as *Modus Ponens*, to see why they are valid. We consider what makes a premise acceptable, and discuss classification and definition, showing how good definitions will connect the meaning of a word with a set of necessary and sufficient conditions to produce a web or classificatory structure of meanings. We also look at arguments from definition, treating them as arguments with implicit premises which "everyone knows," and show how to make such arguments explicit so that they can be properly evaluated. This section concludes with a review which draws lessons for what an ideal critical thinker looks like and why method is of fundamental importance to sound reasoning.

Part II discusses informal reasoning and some of the dangers peculiar to it. A chapter is devoted to the dangers of ambiguity and circularity and the informal fallacies associated with these dangers. Another chapter looks at inductive and causal reasoning and includes a discussion of probability, Mill's methods, and the use of analogy in theory construction. The chapter discusses informal inductive fallacies and fallacies involving expertise, authority, and ignorance, which are symptomatic of failures to reason well. This section on informal reasoning concludes with a chapter on relevance and bias and the fallacies of emotional bias. Throughout the whole of Part II, the focus is on seeing fallacies as failed versions of informal argument forms which are normally successful. We treat the particular fallacies as diagnostic tools which reveal symptoms of error of one kind or another, such as inattention to relevant considerations or failing to consider alternative possibilities. The result is that the particular skills being developed are importantly connected to the larger project of reasoning well.

Part III focuses on deductive argument and has a chapter on categorical logic and a chapter on truth-functional sentence logic. Some instructors are reluctant to teach categorical logic on the grounds that it is old-fashioned and will not be used in later life. But I have found that there is great value in teaching it. The value lies not in the particulars of the formalization but in the insights students gain into logical structure and reasoning by disciplining their thought in these ways. The same applies to truth-functional logic. Students explore artificially explicit patterns of valid argumentation and practise the technique of translating ordinary arguments into a form that reveals those patterns. Experience of this artificially highlighted emphasis on form gives the student an increased sensitivity to the logical structure of ordinary prose and the role context plays in the meaning of ordinary sentences.

It is my view that the skills learned in examining informal reasoning and it fallacies, and the skills learned in translating ordinary prose into a formal vocabulary, and then evaluating the formally stated arguments for validity, are deeply and mutually supportive. Each skill set in its own way encourages clarity of thought and care in the formulation of beliefs, and encourages responsible belief formation; together, they provide powerful, practical tools for thinking critically. Along the way, students learn a great deal about the nature of reasoning and argumentation.

ACKNOWLEDGEMENTS

I would like to thank the following reviewers, whose comments and suggestions on drafts of this text were much appreciated: Kenneth Boyd, Athabasca University; Darcy Cutler, Douglas College; Bruce Howes, Okanagan College; and Mikal A. Radford, Sheriden College.

I would also like to thank Anthony Jenkins for helpful advice on categorical logic, and George Williamson and Derek Postnikoff, who taught sections of critical thinking using earlier versions of this text and had helpful comments. A debt of gratitude also goes to the very large number of authors whose books I read or used during more than 20 years of teaching critical thinking. And lastly, I would like to thank the helpful people at Pearson Education Canada who helped bring this book out—Christine Cozens, Joel Gladstone, Rema Celio, and Richard di Santo—as well as Dianne Fowlie, Susan Bindernagel, and Sally Glover for their commitment to this project.

ABOUT THE AUTHOR

Eric Dayton teaches in the Philosophy Department at the University of Saskatchewan. He works in epistemology, logic, practical reasoning, and aesthetics, as well as the history of American Philosophy; he is the editor of *Art and Interpretation* (1999), an anthology in the philosophy of art. He is also editor of *Dialogue: The Canadian Philosophical Review*, the journal of the Canadian Philosophical Association.

Part I
Critical Thinking and Argument

INTRODUCTION

In the two chapters of this section we look at basic logical concepts and the relation of argument to belief. In **Chapter 1**, inference as reasoning is distinguished from argument as a reasoned social interaction between one or more individuals that aims at **truth**. This broad conception of argument is then distinguished from logical argument narrowly considered, and some basic distinctions are introduced. We examine the distinction between valid and invalid arguments and introduce some familiar valid patterns of argumentation.

In **Chapter 2**, we look at classification and definition, and information that we implicitly appeal to in ordinary reasoning in order to show that we can frequently clarify and strengthen an argument by making these assumptions explicit. The chapter concludes by unpacking some consequences of regarding critical thinking as a kind of thinking that is disciplined so that it aims at the truth. Conditions of cogency in argument are stated and the idea of fallacies as failures to respect cogency is introduced.

Chapter 1
Introduction to Inference and Argument

INTRODUCTION

THIS BOOK IS ABOUT **CRITICAL THINKING**: WHAT IT IS AND HOW TO GET BETTER AT IT. Being able to think critically is to possess a tool kit of cognitive skills. This book will help you learn to use those tools skilfully so that your ability to think clearly and well improves. Human beings, unlike most other conscious creatures, have the capacity for critical thinking. Not only can human beings learn from their experience, they can learn from the experience of others. Because human beings can engage in reasoning together, they can benefit from the testimony of others and engage together in the evaluation of claims. As a result, human beings can learn how to learn more effectively. In this sense, critical thinking is thinking that is *disciplined,* in the sense of deferring to and being guided by methodological principles. Critical thinking rests on the search for good methodological principles that are able to pass public scrutiny. So in this course we will need to direct our attention to questions about what beliefs are like, how thinking can be disciplined by reasonable methods, what makes methods good, and what makes arguments successful vehicles for disciplining thought.

In this first chapter we will begin with some very general reflections on thinking, starting with the question of how to distinguish **reasoning** from mere thinking. We will then move to discuss argument and draw some distinctions that will be important throughout this course. Thinking critically is a complicated business but it is also an important business. It involves acquiring a variety of problem-solving skills, learning how to think clearly and objectively, and putting them together in real-life contexts. Some of the skills one needs to think critically will depend on the subject matter one is thinking about, but other skills have very broad application and help one think more clearly and productively about almost everything. It is on these latter skills that this book focuses: skills aimed at how to reason well, understand arguments, and manage one's beliefs to reduce error and increase understanding. In this chapter we will introduce the important distinction between inference, or reasoning, and argument. We will look at the role of

critical thinking is thinking that is disciplined by being guided by principles of good method both in the production and evaluation of beliefs. We will then turn our attention to various kinds of arguments broadly taken and distinguish them from argument in a narrower sense, which we will call logical argument. Let us start by considering what reasoning is and how it differs from mere thinking.

One way to approach the question of how reasoning is different from mere thinking is to ask, "When is a person responsible for what he or she believes?" If we reflect on this question, certain difficulties present themselves. For one thing, it suggests that you have choice about what to believe. But if you do have choice about what to believe then what guarantees that you will opt for the most reasonable or true belief? One might think that if you knew what was true then you could choose to believe that, but this just obscures what is at issue. If you know something to be true then you already believe what you are apparently opting for, so you don't really have any choice after all.

Let's consider a different tack. Consider a case where you don't know what is true. Then on what basis can you choose whether to believe or not? Should you choose to believe on the basis of the evidence you have? Well, in one sense, the evidence you have is just further belief, and so we might ask whether you should believe the evidence and thus end up back where we started. But let us ignore that worry and ask what kind of evidence we have. Suppose the evidence is sufficiently strong that it dictates what you should believe; in that case it seems that you have no real choice, or at least you don't if you are rational. For example, if all the evidence points to rain but you want to have a picnic and so "decide to believe" that it will be sunny, you have only yourself to blame when you get wet at the beach. In cases like this, talk of choosing what to believe just sounds silly.

But suppose the evidence isn't that strong, that it doesn't fully dictate what to believe. Then in what sense do you have a choice about what to believe (as opposed to hoping or wishing something to be true)? Suppose that you have bet on a horse at the track and you want it to win but the evidence you possess doesn't dictate what you should believe about which horse will win. If you choose to believe that your horse will win when the evidence doesn't support the belief, it appears that you would be a fool. And if you borrow the family rent money to bet on the horse you are worse than a fool; you are a cad. Believing without evidence or against the evidence or just plain believing on inadequate evidence is irresponsible and wrong. It appears, then, that you never have a choice about what to believe, and without choice it appears that you cannot be responsible for what you believe. But this would be an unfortunate result. After all, we do hold people responsible for what they believe and we demand good reasons from them; in fact, we hold ourselves responsible for what we believe.

Let us momentarily take up another line of thought. As a human being, you are part of the causal fabric of the universe. You have a body and sense organs that are sensitive to certain phenomena in the world (and not to others)—for example, you can tell what colour a thing is just by looking at it (at least if there is available light and so on) but you cannot smell carbon monoxide even if it is present in quantities sufficient to kill you. Whatever the causal story is about how your eyes and brain work, such that you can tell the colours of things just by looking, you are by and large stuck just trusting that your eyes are working normally. It is not as though your eyes give you evidence and then you make a judgment—typically you *just see* how things look. Your beliefs about the colours of things are caused in you by processes that work whether or not you know anything about how they work. And it is the *reliability* of those causal processes and the *normality* of the environment in which you find yourself, and not the choices you make, that dictate what you believe. You can see red and thus have beliefs about what things are red because a part of your consciousness is, in effect, a red-detector that functions normally.

More general beliefs are, of course, a different story. You cannot explain the acquisition of all beliefs on a perceptual model. Nonetheless, what we have seen here is that you have at least some of your beliefs because they are caused in you by processes to which you have no access and to which you do not need to have access in order for them to work. And isn't this true of all your beliefs at least to some degree? After all, turnips and rocks don't think at all and you do, and furthermore, how well you think doesn't depend on your knowing how you think. Indeed, is it not reasonable to believe that all of your mental processes are simply caused in you, and so isn't it reasonable for you to believe that what you believe, and whether or not you believe it, is just a matter of what beliefs are caused in you? And doesn't this make the idea that you choose what to believe (and are thus responsible for what you believe) an absurd thought?

We have just looked at two arguments that the idea of choosing what to believe is absurd. But isn't there something wrong with these arguments? Let's spend a moment thinking about where these arguments lead and whether their consequences are true. First of all, if you were not, indeed could not be, responsible for what you believe then it wouldn't be any kind of mistake to believe things without evidence or to believe things merely because you wanted to. But, as we have already said, we are committed to the idea that believing on inadequate evidence is irrational and wrong to do. And so we do seem committed to the idea that you can choose what to believe at least in the sense of choosing to have beliefs that merit belief because they are better (in the sense of being more belief-worthy). Without that, the whole idea of a critical thinking course wouldn't make any sense; indeed the whole idea of education wouldn't make sense. In order to give any usefulness to the idea of critical thinking, we need to think of *thinking as a process that can be evaluated for reasonableness*. We need to be able to imagine different lines of thought that would end in different beliefs. As well, we need to see belief as *aiming at truth*. Let us return to the vision example for a minute. You are caused to see things as having the colours you see: You look at a red piece of paper and believe it is red. But if you notice that a red light is shining on the paper, realizing this will just block you from forming the belief that the paper is red. If you have taken a piece of white paper and placed it in the red light, the case will be even clearer since you already know that the paper is white. If you are near sighted and without your glasses things look fuzzy, you won't be caused to believe that the things you see really are fuzzy. Similarly, if looking over the edge of your glasses at someone shows you two heads, you are not led to believe that the person has two heads! Examples like these show that even though vision is an automatic process that just causes visual beliefs, the visual beliefs that are formed are almost always automatically adjusted to cohere with other beliefs you already have. There is an important lesson in this. There is no necessary conflict between the *causal* character of belief-forming processes and what a person believes because it is *rational* to do so given other beliefs. On the other hand, and equally important, the relevance of other beliefs must be noticed or at least made suitably available for them to have influence.

In light of these considerations, let us make the following assumptions. Let us think of beliefs as the outcomes of pieces of reasoning, or as the products of thought processes. If a person has a number of different thought processes or pieces of reasoning that can be evaluated for successfulness in aiming at the truth, and if they can be analyzed for the principles that guide them in that aim, then we can compare those different principles with each other and determine which aim more successfully at the truth. We will talk more about these assumptions in a moment, but as a package they make human powers of reasoning into something impressive. Not every creature can reason. Chickens and dogs can learn from experience, but they cannot abstract general principles from past successes and failures and then apply them to new situations. But human beings, and quite possibly only human beings, can, at least to a limited degree.

In the remainder of this chapter we will unpack these ideas a bit. We started by asking how to distinguish reasoning from mere thinking. Let us return to that question and draw some distinctions. Human beings think a great deal. We do it all the time, in the sense that we think whenever we are conscious or aware of things. Thoughts constantly run through our minds. But the word "think" is ambiguous. On the one hand, it simply means to be in a conscious state; on the other hand, we use the word to refer to mental processes consisting of connected thoughts that fit together to form a piece of reasoning.

To tell someone what you are thinking in this second sense is to tell a story that has some kind of point or outcome. Sometimes the point of the story is entertainment, but often enough the point is to give another person reasons for believing something. In such cases the point of the body of the story is that it bears on the truth or reasonableness of the outcome. The thinking reported in stories of this sort can be evaluated or criticized according to *how well the body of the story bears on the truth of its outcome.* This course is about how to evaluate thinking in this sense. The stories we tell about our reasoning, particularly the stories we call arguments, are crucial in that evaluation. In spite of the fact that much reasoning is performed consciously and to a purpose, not all reasoning is conscious. Some, perhaps most, reasoning is unconscious reasoning. We know this because we sometimes find that we have worked out what we think about some matter without being aware of having done so. In such a case we have to *reconstruct* what our reasoning must have been like. In the process of reconstructing our thinking we also often reflect on what our reasoning *ought* to have been like. We will use the word "inference" to refer to a piece of reasoning, and when we say that a person infers something X we mean that they have engaged in a piece of reasoning with X as a conclusion. When we talk about reasoning in that way we assume that the piece of reasoning was guided by rules and that in virtue of that guidance it succeeded (or failed, as the case might be) in a certain aim.

INFERENCE AND ARGUMENT

INFERENCES AND ARGUMENTS ARE QUITE DIFFERENT THINGS, ALTHOUGH THEY ARE RELATED in an important way. An **inference**, or a piece of reasoning, is a kind of mental process. As such, reasoning and the inferences involved in reasoning happen in the privacy of the minds of the agents engaging in the reasoning. Reasoning is in this sense not public. Whether or not an agent's thought processes are disciplined by truth-conducive rules cannot be determined just by examining the conclusion an agent reaches. There is always more than one way to arrive at a conclusion and not all are equally good. When little Jimmy is trying to add 3 and 4 at the blackboard in grade one and writes "7" on the board, he gets the right answer. But if he writes "7" because it is his favourite number, or because he just guesses and is lucky, then his choice of 7 is only right by accident and isn't the right answer in the sense of being the product of the rules of addition. So it is important to distinguish thinking that reaches a conclusion for the *right reasons* from cases of thinking guided by subjective or merely personal or private rules (such as "write your favourite number as the answer"). When attempting to reconstruct our thought processes in order to become clear on our reasons, we make those reasons available for assessment. Often we can see just by reflecting that our reasons were inadequate, that they were, for example, hasty or ill-conceived.

Of course, I can invite you to engage in a piece of reasoning in hopes that you will make an inference or come to a conclusion that is guided by the right rules. I may do this by offering you an **argument**. If I do this I engage you in a public interpersonal reasoning process. *An argument in this broad sense is not a mental process but a social exchange between two or more persons.* Because inferences happen in the privacy of our own minds and may be largely unconscious or intuitive, they are hard to evaluate directly. Others have no access to them at all and our own access is limited by the unreliability of memory, the weakness of our self-analytical skills, and the fact that some aspects of our reasoning may not be available to consciousness. Most of us are not very skilled at evaluating the adequacy of our own thinking just by reflecting on it. Even though we have direct access to our thoughts, we typically lack the methodological skills necessary to evaluate the processes producing them. In contrast to this, arguments (in the broad sense) are public events typically involving a number of participants. The participants in an argument present claims that they offer as premises in favour of other claims or conclusions, which they assert can be *concluded* from the premises on the strength of a set of rules or principles. The participants in an argument and any observers who are present are all positioned to make judgments about how well the argument goes, for example, about whether the offered conclusions really do follow from the premises offered by the rules of inference in question. When we give verbal expression to our thoughts they become, so to speak, public property. Once a thought is spoken anyone hearing it can criticize it. The word "criticize" means several different things in ordinary usage; for example, it often means to express a *negative* assessment. But in this text we will use the word "criticize" in a somewhat technical way to mean *to evaluate by offering reasons*; when we use the term it will *not* mean *to* *express disapproval.* When we criticize the verbal expression of a thought, we bring rules to bear on it, and evaluate it. Sometimes our evaluation is negative and sometimes it is positive, but whether it is negative or positive will not depend on our attitude or bias but on what the rules we bring to bear have to say on the matter. Because we respond to claims with criticism, an argument is not only a public event, it is in addition a process that is governed by rules that regulate and guide its aims.

Finally, it is important to see that arguments are not guided by just any aims nor governed by just any rules. We have already seen the need to distinguish between the public rules of correctness from purely private rules. We also need to distinguish between the *aim or purpose* of argument as a public process and the purely private aims a person may have for engaging in an argument. Because arguments are public processes, the participants in arguments may have a variety of personal reasons for engaging in them. Some people pick arguments with others to annoy them or to show off or express hostility. But none of these purposes have anything to do with what arguments are really for and thus nothing to do with what sorts of rules regulate correctness in argument. An argument is a kind of exchange between an arguer and an audience *that aims at truth or reasonableness.* Of course, the arguer and the audience may turn out to be the same person, as is the case when you give an argument to yourself, so even when you give yourself an argument your reasoning should be guided by public rules of assessment. A good argument *ought to be persuasive* in the sense that it *would persuade a rational or reasonable agent* who heard it. Arguments are a kind of performance, then, that aims to persuade because—and only to the extent that—it provides good reasons. Of course, arguments are used in ordinary contexts to do a great number of different things, but as they bear on the task of critical thinking they have a structure in which the arguer

1. asserts the premises (claims them to be true or acceptable, even if only hypothetically or for the sake of the argument)
2. asserts that *if* the premises are true (or acceptable) *then* the conclusion is true (or acceptable) and thus
3. asserts the conclusion

Argument has a *public aim*, which is independent of the private purposes of arguers, and it has *public rules*, which are independent of the thought processes actually occurring in reasoners.

We will define a **cogent argument** to be one that meets the following conditions:

1. A cogent argument must be grounded in premises that are accepted or are rationally acceptable to a reasonable audience. The arguer's assertion of the premises cannot therefore be silly or arbitrary.
2. The premises must be relevant to the conclusion; they need to make a rationally grounded connection to the conclusion.
3. The premises must provide sufficient or strong rational grounds for asserting the conclusion.

As we will see in the next chapter, the real aim of argument is a consequence of the purpose of belief and the function of good method, each of which aims at the truth. In the next section we will define a narrower sense of argument than the broad characterization given above of arguments as public social exchanges that aim at truth—which we will call *logical argument* or *argument narrowly considered*—and discuss their essential features.

LOGICAL ARGUMENT

A LOGICAL ARGUMENT, OR ARGUMENT IN THE NARROW SENSE, IS A **CLAIM** PUT FORWARD together with the presentation of reasons in support of the truth of that claim. The public social exchanges we call arguments in the broad sense typically *contain* arguments in this narrower sense. A logical argument has as its objective to show some statement or position to be true or reasonable. We call *what is to be shown* the **conclusion** of the argument. Typically the conclusion is based on its logical relationship to certain statements or sentences in the body of the argument; we call these the **premises**. Often there are certain intermediate steps, which may add no new information to the premises but have the function of showing more clearly how the premises offer support to the conclusion; we will call these intermediate steps. The intermediate steps are not essential to the logical quality of the argument, but they are important devices for focusing attention on the relationship between the premises and the conclusion, and so help reasoners to evaluate the argument. And frequently we do not state all the premises that are needed for an argument to follow because they are obvious.

A moment ago we said that in an argument a claim is made or asserted—the conclusion—on the basis of other claims or assertions—the premises. When you use a sentence to make a claim or assertion that some state of affairs is true, you make a truth claim or **statement**. Not every sentence can be used to make a statement; for example, the sentence "What is your name?" *A statement is the use of a sentence to make a claim that can be true or false*. The answer "My name is Keith" (to the question "What is your name?") is a statement because it can be true or false: It is true if my name is Keith and false if it is not. Our language contains many different kinds of sentences, which are used for a great variety of purposes.

Austrian philosopher and mathematician Ludwig Wittgenstein called these purposes language *games* to highlight the fact that speaking a language is part of an activity or form

Ludwig Wittgenstein

Ludwig Wittgenstein (1889–1951), born in Vienna, was one of the most influential philosophers of the 20th century. He spent most of his career at Cambridge and is widely considered the founder of ordinary language philosophy.

of life. Making statements or asserting and denying claims is only one language game. Here are some others. We ask questions and answer them, make proposals or requests, read out loud, tell jokes, offer greetings, pray, curse, speculate or wonder out loud, thank people and acknowledge the thanks of others, give orders and obey them, express pain or fear, give verdicts, and so on. Language games are characteristic forms of human activity and we learn how to engage in them by learning the language. The sentences we use in these different language games are of different kinds and only some of them can be true or false. As we just saw, questions are neither true nor false, though answers are. If we think of giving an argument as a kind of language game, we see that it is one that involves making claims and supporting them with other claims and thus requires the use of statements.

To sum up, we may define an argument (in the narrow or logical sense) as a sequence of statements $(p_1, p_2, \ldots p_n, c)$, where the statements p_1 to p_n are the premises and c is the conclusion. For example, the argument "*You are tired and tired people should sleep so you should sleep*" contains two premises: p_1 = You are tired, and p_2 = Tired people should sleep, and the conclusion, c = You should sleep.

In order to make the structure of a logical argument clear, we put it in a **standard form**. To do this, we identify all the premises, making implicit premises visible, and identify the conclusion, listing the premises in a vertical stack with a line below it and placing the conclusion below the line. There are two major types of argument: **deductive**, or formal, arguments and **inductive**, or informal, arguments. In a good deductive argument the truth of the conclusion follows inescapably from the truth of the premises. In a good inductive argument the truth of the premises makes the conclusion probable or likely. Good deductive arguments depend upon their logical structure alone. As a result they are quite independent of what is actually true. Inductive arguments, however, depend in complex ways on empirical facts about the world. Accordingly, they cannot be studied in abstraction from the facts as we believe them to be. In the first section of the book we will focus on informal, or inductive, arguments and in the second section we will focus on deductive arguments. For the moment and for the rest of this chapter, we will primarily focus on deductive arguments.

The standard form of a logical argument:

Premise 1
Premise 2

.

.

Premise n
Conclusion

When we put an argument into standard form we put the conclusion *at the end*. But the conclusion of an argument is not always stated at the end. Consider these three sentences:

1. You are tired and tired people should sleep so *you should sleep*.

2. *You should sleep* because you are tired and tired people should sleep.

3. Tired people should sleep so *you should sleep* because you are tired.

They all state the same argument, which has the standard form

Premise 1   You are tired
Premise 2   Tired people should sleep
Conclusion You should sleep

What makes "You should sleep" the conclusion is not where it appears in the argument, but the *logical relation it has to the other parts of the argument.* In 2, the conclusion comes first and the word "because" signals that the other claims may support it; in 1 the conclusion comes at the end and the word "so" functions to connect it to the other claims as following from, or being supported by, them. An important part of recognizing an argument is seeing the relationships of support and dependence that the component claims have to each other; it is these relations that give the argument its force, by showing reasons that the conclusion should be accepted.

STUDY SETS 1

Part A. Which of the following sentences can be used to make statements? Since a statement is the use of a sentence to make a claim that can be true or false, this means that you should determine which of these sentences can make a claim that can be true or false.

1. It is nine o'clock.

2. What time is it?

3. Please come to dinner at seven.

4. I hate you.

5. Tell me when you can come to dinner.

6. Either Rome is the capital of Italy or it isn't.

7. The Pope is an old man.

8. Pay attention, you lazy lout!

9. Germans have big heads.

Part B. Determine whether these are arguments. If they are arguments, identify the premises and the conclusion, and place them in standard form by writing the premises and then the conclusion with a line separating them.

1. God can perform miracles but not contradictions—not because his power is limited, but because contradictions are not genuine possibilities.

2. The moral law demands that we pursue, and ultimately attain, moral perfection. But we can't reasonably expect to reach moral perfection in this life. Therefore, we must postulate, or suppose, that there is another life in which this demand of the moral law can be met.

3. Pain is pain wherever it occurs. If your neighbour's causing you pain is wrong because the pain hurts and hurting is bad, then the pain a dog feels when you mistreat it is wrong as well.

4. Martha bought vodka and Frank bought wieners. Between them they bought vodka and wieners.

5. No scientific hypothesis can be conclusively confirmed because no evidence we could ever find could rule out the possibility of contrary evidence in the future.

6. No computer can think. To think requires one to understand the meanings of statements. To understand the meanings of statements one needs to be conscious. But no computer could be conscious.

7. If we understood what good was we would naturally be moved to bring it about. But we often bring about evil and unhappiness, so we are ignorant of the nature of good.

8. The secretary isn't answering the phone and that is part of her job. So either she isn't there or she isn't doing her job.

9. A plus B equals C and C minus A equals D, so A and D are the same.

10. If I have a headache I take Aspirin. I only take Aspirin with food in my stomach. And if I eat Mary will eat, too. But Mary doesn't eat. So I don't have a headache.

11. He must be home. He never goes anywhere without his car and his car is sitting in the driveway.

VALIDITY, SOUNDNESS, AND SOME BASIC ARGUMENT PATTERNS

LET US NOW DEFINE TWO IMPORTANT CONCEPTS: *VALIDITY* AND *SOUNDNESS*. VALIDITY AND soundness are technical notions describing properties of some deductive arguments that make them good arguments.

The goodness of a good deductive argument is called **validity**. A **valid** deductive argument is such that *in any situation in which the premises are true the conclusion must also be true. Invalidity* is the failure of this relation. So an argument is **invalid** if and only if it is possible for the premises to be true and the conclusion to be false. Validity and invalidity are thus not about the truth or **falsity** of the premises or conclusion in the actual world. Instead they deal with the formal relationship between premises and the conclusion, no matter what the facts of the world are. An argument is **sound** if and only if it is valid and its premises are true.

An argument is **valid** if and only if it there is no possible situation in which the premises are true and the conclusion is false.

An argument is **sound** if and only if it is valid and its premises are true.

Logical arguments usually occur in characteristic *patterns*. These patterns represent the relationships the premises have to each other in light of which they support the conclusion. We will look at a large number of **argument patterns**, some very informal and some highly structured, with the aim of making you a better reasoner. We will put special emphasis on deductive or formal arguments in the next few pages, because they are clearer and easier to understand. In the two final chapters we will look at two kinds of deductive arguments in detail and characterize validity very precisely. Deductive arguments are important for critical thinking because the correctness of a deductive argument is entirely a matter of its form, or the argument pattern it exemplifies. Even when we look carefully at informal arguments, it is useful to make their form as clear as possible. There are some simple basic deductive forms that we will come across repeatedly in the course. We will first look at five valid deductive argument patterns and then expand our discussion to several other forms. We present them in a general form using capital letters "P" and "Q" and so on to represent statements, and then give examples.

MODUS PONENS	*MODUS TOLLENS*	HYPOTHETICAL SYLLOGISM
if P then Q	if P then Q	if P then Q
P	not Q	if Q then R
∴ Q	∴ not P	∴ if P then R

DISJUNCTIVE SYLLOGISM	CONSTRUCTIVE DILEMMA
P or Q	if P then Q
not P	if R then S
∴ Q	P or R
	∴ Q or S

Here are examples of those patterns:

Modus Ponens *If* we live in Saskatoon *then* we live in Saskatchewan
We live in Saskatoon
therefore we live in Saskatchewan

Modus Tollens *If* we live in Toronto *then* we live in Ontario
We don't live in Ontario   or *not* [We live in Ontario]
therefore We don't live in Toronto   or *not* [We live in Toronto]

Hypothetical Syllogism	*If* we drink too much *then* we fall down a lot
	<u>*If* we fall down a lot *then* we miss Eric's exciting lecture</u>
	therefore if we drink too much *then* we miss Eric's exciting lecture

Disjunctive Syllogism	*Either* we live in Saskatoon *or* we live in Toronto
	<u>We don't live in Toronto</u> or *not* [We live in Toronto]
	therefore we live in Saskatoon

Constructive Dilemma	*If* we drink too much *then* we fall down a lot
	If we smoke dope *then* we get spaced out
	<u>*Either* we drink too much *or* we smoke dope</u>
	therefore either we fall down a lot *or* we get spaced out

In each of these examples the argument is valid because of the formal relationship between the premises and the conclusion. In each case, the premises cannot both be true without the conclusion also being true. The truth of the conclusion is necessitated by the truth of the premises. I have italicized the logical words that appear in the patterns in the box. The sentences, such as "We live in Saskatoon" and so on, appear in the patterns as Ps and Qs. You could replace those sentences with any other sentences you like, as long as you use the same sentences for each different letter in the pattern, and you would always get valid arguments.

Of course, not all argument patterns are valid. In Chapter 2 we will look at a variety of informal argument patterns, called *informal fallacies*, which involve ways in which informal reasoning goes wrong. But there are *invalid* deductive argument patterns, too. Here are two common INVALID deductive argument patterns:

DENYING THE ANTECEDENT	AFFIRMING THE CONSEQUENT
If P then Q	If P then Q
<u>Not</u>	<u>Q</u>
4 not Q	∴ P

Here are examples of those patterns. First, *denying the **antecedent***:

Denying the Antecedent	*If* we live in Saskatoon *then* we live in Saskatchewan
	<u>We don't live in Saskatoon</u> or *not* [We live in Saskatoon]
	therefore we don't live in Saskatchewan or *not* [We live in
	Saskatchewan]

This is clearly an invalid argument. If, for example, we live in Regina, then the two premises are made true by that fact, but since if we live in Regina we also live in Saskatchewan, the conclusion is false and so the falsity of the conclusion is consistent with the truth of the premises. This means that the argument in invalid. The claim that we live in Regina is thus a **counter-example** to the argument; it is an example that makes the premises true and the conclusion false.

Here is an example of *affirming the* **consequent**:

Affirming the Consequent	*If* we live in Regina *then* we live in Saskatchewan
	We live in Saskatchewan
	therefore we live in Regina

This is also clearly an invalid form of argument. The claim that we live in Saskatoon is a counter-example to this argument: If we live in Saskatoon, then both the premises are true but the conclusion is false and so the argument is invalid.

In a valid argument, the truth of the conclusion follows as a matter of form from the truth of the premises, so *a valid argument cannot have a counter-example*. There is no way to make the premises true and the conclusion false in a valid argument, so finding a single counter-example **refutes** an argument and shows that it cannot be valid. In both of these cases, we showed the argument to be invalid by producing a counter-example: We imagined a circumstance or possible situation in which the premises are true and the conclusion is false. It doesn't matter whether the possible situation imagined in the counter-example is actually true. It must merely be possible or consistently thinkable. The validity of an argument doesn't depend merely upon what is actually true or false—a valid argument is valid in every *possible* circumstance. That means that every possible circumstance that makes the premises true must also make the conclusion true. Finding a single counter-example refutes an argument's claim to validity and thus refutes its claim on rational persuasion.

We can demonstrate this by means of a model showing all the logically possible circumstances of truth and falsity of the premises. Let us compare the formally valid argument pattern Modus Ponens with the formally invalid pattern Affirming the Consequent using a graphic diagram (Figure 1.1) of the four possible situations generated by two sentences and their **negations**.

Consider the two sentences A = *The cat is on the mat* and B = *It is raining*. Since each sentence is either true or false there are four possibilities for truth and falsity that combine the two sentences:

Possibility 1	Possibility 2	Possibility 3	Possibility 4
A is true	A is true	A is false	A is false
B is true	B is false	B is true	B is false

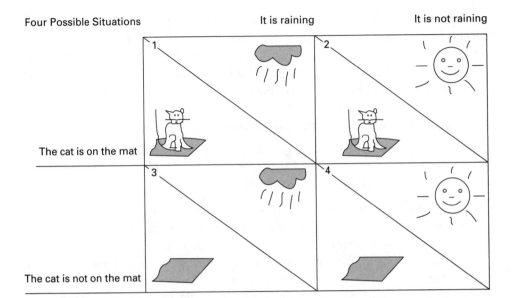

Four Possible Situations   It is raining   It is not raining

The cat is on the mat

The cat is not on the mat

Figure 1.1 exhibits the four possible situations (labelled 1–4).

The pictures represent the facts that make the sentences true or false. In situation 1 the cat is on the mat and it is raining; in situation 2 the cat is on the mat but it is not raining. In situation 3 the cat is not on the mat but it is raining, and in situation 4 the cat is not on the mat and it is not raining either. These four situations exhaust the logical possibilities for truth and falsity of these two sentences; there just aren't any other possibilities.

Here is an example of the argument pattern *Modus Ponens* using the two sentences represented in our model as components in its premises:

Premise 1   *If* the cat is on the mat *then* it is raining
Premise 2   <u>the cat is on the mat</u>
Conclusion   ∴ it is raining

We can see that this argument is VALID by examining the model because

■ premise 1 rules out possible situation 2, because in that situation the cat is on the mat but it isn't raining, which is inconsistent with the claim made in premise 1;

■ premise 2 rules out situations 3 and 4, because in those situations the cat is not on the mat, which is inconsistent with the claim made in premise 2;

■ as a result the two premises taken together rule out three of the four logical possibilities. This means that the only way for the two premises to be true together is for situation 1 to be the one that obtains, since at least one situation must obtain and it is the only situation *not ruled out by the premises*. When we examine situation 1 we see that its conclusion is true (it *is* raining in situation 1). This means that *if* the premises are true *then* the conclusion is true as well. The only situation consistent with the truth of both premises is one in which the conclusion is also true. The argument is **valid**.

Here is an example of the fallacious argument pattern Affirming the Consequent using the two sentences represented in our model as components in its premises:

Premise 1   If the cat is on the mat then it is raining
Premise 2   <u>It is raining</u>
Conclusion   ∴ the cat is on the mat

We can see that it is INVALID because

- premise 1 rules out possible situation 2, because in that situation the cat is on the mat but it isn't raining, which is inconsistent with the claim made in premise 1;

- premise 2 rules out situations 2 and 4, because in those situations it is not raining, which is inconsistent with the claim made in premise 2;

- this leaves two situations that are consistent with the premises, situations 1 and 3. The conclusion is true in situation 1 but it is false in situation 3, so *the truth of the premises is consistent with the falsity of the conclusion* and the argument is **invalid**.

The important thing about the patterns of valid arguments we have seen is that many, many different arguments fit each pattern. Our example of *Modus Ponens* was

If we live in Saskatoon *then* we live in Saskatchewan
<u>We live in Saskatoon</u>
therefore we live in Saskatchewan

But so are:

A   *If* Canada is in North America *then* Canada is in the Western Hemisphere
     <u>Canada is in North America</u>
     therefore Canada is in the Western Hemisphere

B   *If* dogs are telepathic *then* cats can fly
     <u>Dogs are telepathic</u>
     therefore cats can fly

and

C   *If* dogs are telepathic *then* Toronto is a city
     <u>Dogs are telepathic</u>
     therefore Toronto is a city

All of these examples of *Modus Ponens* are valid for exactly the same reason as the original example and you should be able to confirm this for yourself. Notice that A has true premises, so it is not only valid but also *sound*. B, on the other hand, has false premises and a false conclusion: Dogs are not telepathic and even if they were it wouldn't make it true that cats can fly, so B is valid but it is not sound. C, finally, has false premises but a true conclusion; like B, it is valid, but because it has false premises is also unsound.

THE SYLLOGISM

A **SYLLOGISM** IS A VERY GENERAL ARGUMENT PATTERN THAT INVOLVES TWO PREMISES AND a conclusion and three terms. There are many varieties of the syllogism pattern; here are a couple of examples:

1	2	3
Bill is older then Fred	Regina is in Saskatchewan	9 is greater than 7
Fred is older than Joe	Saskatchewan is in Canada	7 is greater than 4
so Bill is older than Joe	so Regina is in Canada	so 9 is greater than 4

You can easily tell that all three of these arguments are valid. If the premises are true then the conclusion must be true. Let's spend a few moments to talk about what makes them valid.

- In each line there are two *terms connected by a relation*. For example, in the first premise of the first argument, the terms "Bill" and "Fred" are connected by the relation "___ is older than ___"; in the second argument the relation is "___ is in ___"; and in the third argument the relation is "___ is greater than ___."

- The two premises *share a "middle term."* For example, in syllogism 1, "Fred" appears in both premises.

- The relation *is transitive*. Transitivity is an ordering relation. A transitive relation, R, has the property that for every three things a, b, and c to which R applies, if a is R to b and b is R to c then a is R to c.

- Finally, the three terms are in the right places in the relation to make the conclusion valid. That is, two premises take the form "*a is R to b*" and "*b is R to c*" and the conclusion has the form "*a is R to c*" (notice that "*b*" is the middle term).

Many relations are transitive. Here are some examples:

____ = ____ (is equal to),

____ > ____ (is greater than),

____ ≤ ____ (is smaller than or equal to),

____ ≥ ____ (is greater than or equal to),

if ____ then ____,

____ is a species of ____,

____ is fatter than ____,

____ is heavier than ____,

____ is poorer than ____.

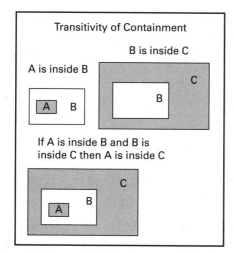

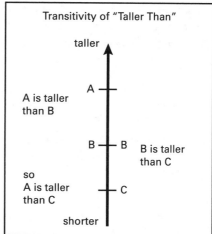

Figure 1.2

The diagram in Figure 1.2 illustrates the transitivity of two relations, *containment* (or "__ is inside __") and *relative height* (or "__ is taller than __").

You can *see* that *containment* is transitive in the diagram because you can see that if A is inside B and B is inside C, then A must be inside C. Similarly, with the relation "taller than": We may not know how much taller A is than B, but if A is taller than B then A is somewhere above B on the height arrow and, if B is taller than C we may not know by how much but in any case C will be below B on the arrow. If A is above B and C is below B then A must be above C.

Of course, *not every relation is transitive*, and *not every syllogism using a transitive relation is valid* because the terms may not be in the right position in the argument. Here are two examples of the syllogism pattern that are **not** valid:

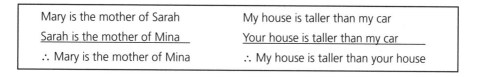

In the first example the problem is that the relation "__ is the mother of __" is not transitive: The mother of your mother is not your mother. In the second example "is taller than" is transitive but the terms are not in the right place for the relation "__ is taller than __" to order them with *respect to each other*. We know that both your house and my house are taller than my car but that is all we know about how tall our houses are, and since we do not as a result know which of our houses is taller than the other, the argument cannot be valid.

In Chapter 5, we will spend some time looking at the traditional **logic** of terms, also known as categorical logic. The syllogism pattern figures prominently in that logic in the form of the *categorical syllogism*. Here are two examples that are easily seen to be valid:

All ducks are birds	No humans are gods
All birds are living creatures	Prime Minister Harper is human
∴ All ducks are living creatures	∴ Prime Minister Harper is not a god

We can see that both arguments are valid because of the transitivity of containment, which we saw above. Figure 1.3 shows how these examples work. In the first case we can imagine drawing a circle around all the ducks and a larger circle around all the birds. If all ducks are birds then the duck circle will be *inside* the bird circle. Similarly for all living creatures, the bird circle will be inside the circle around all the living creatures and the duck circle will be inside that. In the second argument, once you realize that to say that *no human are gods* is the same as saying that *all humans are non-gods*, you can see that Harper will be inside the circle around all the humans and that circle will be inside the circle containing all the non-gods.

Here is a second way to think about why these two arguments are valid: First of all, to say that all ducks are birds is tantamount to saying that *if something is a duck then it is a bird*, and to say that all birds are living creatures is tantamount to saying that *if something is a bird then it is a living creature*. In short, we can rewrite the argument so that it has the form of a *Hypothetical Syllogism*:

If something is a duck *then* it is a bird	(in short, If P then Q)
If something is a bird *then* it is a living creature	(If Q then R)
∴ *If* something is a duck *then* it is a living creature	(∴ If P then R)

Figure 1.3

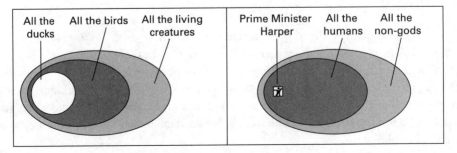

In the second argument we see that since Harper is human and all humans are non-gods then Harper must be a non-god, which we can put as *Modus Ponens:*

Harper is human	(in short, P)
<u>*If* Harper is human *then* Harper is not a god</u>	<u>(If P then Q)</u>
∴ Harper is not a god	(∴ Q)

If you think about these examples you should be able to see how syllogisms can be represented by argument patterns we have already seen, such as *Modus Ponens, Modus Tollens* and the like.

STUDY SETS 2

Part A.

1. Write down the argument forms *Modus Ponens, Modus Tollens,* and Disjunctive Syllogism. Give an example of each pattern that has true premises (and so has a true conclusion) and an example that has false premises.

2. Make up a valid syllogistic argument that relies on transitivity of containment or one of the other transitive relations mentioned above: "is equal to," "is greater than," "is smaller than or equal to," "is greater than or equal to," "if ____ then ___," "is fatter than" and so on.

3. Think of some other transitive relations and construct arguments using them.

Part B. For each of *Modus Tollens* and Disjunctive Syllogism, make a square representing the four possibilities for truth and falsity of the component sentences of your examples, and show that each is valid by crossing out each possible situation that is ruled out by a premise and determining that the conclusion is true in any possibility consistent with the truth of the premises. Use the example in Figure 1.1 on page 16 as your model.

Part C.

1. Write down some examples of the invalid forms Denying the Antecedent and Affirming the Consequent. Give an example of each that has true premises and a true conclusion, and using the method of Part B, show why it is still invalid.

2. Give a few examples of invalid syllogistic argument patterns that are invalid because a) the relation is not transitive or b) the terms are not in the right order.

Part D. All of the following arguments reflect patterns we have seen in this section. Identify the pattern of each argument and put it in standard form for that pattern.

1. The eggs are spoiled because they are six months old and if eggs are six months old they are spoiled.

2. If Ottawa is in Manitoba then it is near Brandon. Ottawa isn't in Manitoba because it isn't near Brandon.

3. All Calgarians are Albertans and all Albertans are Canadians, so Calgarians are Canadians.

4. The Senators play in either Ottawa or Montreal. They must play in Ottawa because they don't play in Montreal.

5. If eggs are six months old they are spoiled and the eggs are spoiled so they must be six months old.

6. If you are tall you can reach the cookies and you can eat some if you can reach them so if you are tall you can eat some cookies.

7. In Vancouver either it will rain or it just rained. You will get wet if it is going to rain and if it just rained then you are wet, so in Vancouver either you are wet or you will be.

RELEVANCE IN ARGUMENTS

WE HAVE JUST LOOKED AT VALIDITY AND SOME OF THE FORMAL PATTERNS THAT VALID arguments have. But arguments can be good without being formally valid and we use arguments for much more than merely to demonstrate universal formal truths. In ordinary life we must evaluate arguments broadly. We use arguments to do many things: to show, suggest, convince, persuade, and explore ideas with and to others. In this broader communicative context, arguments must meet additional criteria beyond mere validity and soundness. When we introduce considerations to another person that are directed toward influencing their beliefs and opinions, the considerations we introduce should have some **relevance** to that person. Since the aim of logical argument is to offer rational considerations for belief, a premise in an argument is relevant to the conclusion if accepting it provides the recipient of the argument with some reason to believe the conclusion. When we look at the informal fallacies in Part 1, we will see that most informal fallacies violate some consideration or another of relevance. In some respect or another they offer the appearance, but not the substance, of a reasonable argument. Of course, people can and sometimes do use arguments to deceive, humiliate, and dominate others; in short, they use arguments in ways that are not aimed at truth. But we will not consider these uses at all in this book; our interest is directed toward methods that are good in the sense of aiming at truth and thus relevant to thinking, which is critical.

If an argument is to be rationally convincing to its audience, it needs to have more than a reasonable form; its premises must also be *dialectically acceptable*. So what does it mean to say that a premise is dialectically acceptable? We formulate arguments both to clarify our own thinking about a matter and to convince others to accept our thinking as reasonable or true. Sometimes we try to convince others of the incorrectness of an opinion that they hold dear. To do this, we must get them to change their minds, to come to believe something inconsistent with what they presently believe.

But in such cases we cannot always appeal to premises that they already believe. Instead we may need to suggest to them that they *ought* to accept as premises claims that they presently think are false or dubious. To do this, we need to be able to show that they have *some reason for accepting these premises*, even if only provisionally, and thus that *they will accept or at least consider them if they are reasonable*. If they accept the premises and the argument is good, then, if they are rational, they will be moved to accept the conclusion.

It turns out to be very difficult to state precisely when a premise is acceptable and when a person should accept or consider accepting a premise. To say that a premise is acceptable certainly does not mean that a person actually does accept it. Rather, it means something like *what a person ought to accept on the evidence presented, if they are reasonable, and so on*. Spelling out what "and so on" comes to is very difficult. On the other hand, there are uncontroversial examples of acceptable premises that can offer us some guidelines. Here are some examples of types of premises that are uncontroversially acceptable:

- claims that report our uncontested conscious experience (what we or others see and hear, for example)
- claims that reflect widely accepted and uncontroversial common knowledge (roughly "what everyone knows" or what is generally accepted)
- claims that are made by recognized experts in a given area that have not been called into question by other recognized experts in that area

In addition to examples like these, a statement that is the conclusion of another (good) argument that has acceptable premises ought to be acceptable as a premise. A statement may also gain acceptability if accepting it explains or renders understandable some other claim that people accept but which presently lacks support.

In short, for a premise to be acceptable, it must pass certain reasonable tests and survive controversy. This is why I have used the term "dialectically acceptable." To be dialectically acceptable is to be able to survive a dialogue or discussion about its acceptability, for it to be able to meet reasonable counter-arguments. If a reasonable listener using reasonable premises can question a statement, the person putting it forward must be able to meet those arguments with an adequate defence appealing to premises that are just as reasonable. When we come to look at the fallacies we will see that some fallacies violate the criterion of dialectical acceptability because they appeal to illegitimate authorities or depend upon inadequately defended premises. You should notice that even though the idea of dialectical acceptability is vague, it is vague because there are a great many ways that arguers can interact reasonably and it is impossible to state exactly when reasonable people will find a premise or conclusion to pass or fail the test of dialectical reasonableness. This does *not* mean that reasonableness is just a matter of personal opinion—quite the opposite is true; determining dialectical reasonableness, and relevance generally, requires careful consideration of alternatives, and openness to the views and arguments of others. In fact, to call something just "personal opinion" is to suggest that the claim will not survive rational scrutiny and informed discussion. Determining what is dialectically acceptable may require, on occasion, a good imagination. Seeing what is reasonable and what is not depends on a variety of critical thinking skills, which we will examine more fully in later chapters of the book.

Chapter 2
Classification and Definition

CLASSIFICATION

Clarity and precision are important for critical thinking. Using words or concepts in a loose or sloppy manner is an invitation to errors of many kinds. It is now time to talk about the importance for critical thinking of precision and clarity in our use of words and symbols. First we will discuss how words classify and what they refer to, and after that we will discuss the importance of definition. If we reflect on maps, it is clear that different maps or parts of maps may classify what they represent in different ways. Consider a road map of Ontario. Cities and towns may be represented by circles of different sizes, where the size of a circle represents population (e.g., • = under 1,000, ● = 1,000 to 5,000, etc.), but they could also be represented by squares representing the physical region of the urban area. Different ways of representing Ontario might be good for different purposes, and one can imagine specialized maps that identify cities and towns by economic activity, percentage of elderly people, ethnic composition, religion, quality of drinking water, or even the number of claimed UFO sightings.

Maps are just one sort of system of representing the relationships of objects classified in different ways. Our theories and hypotheses similarly vary in the way in which they classify the things they represent. The concepts we use do not simply list the things in the world but organize them into patterns; in fact, there is no way to list things without classifying them in some way. Here is an example. Suppose Karen, who lives in North Bay, has a black registered long-haired dachshund named Mabel that weighs 17 kg, likes corn flakes, and once bit the postal worker. Mabel may be known in the neighbourhood as "that black ratty thing," "Karen's pet," or "li'l porker," and each of these terms will function like a name, picking Mabel out from the other things in the neighbourhood. But when we classify Mabel as black or as a dog or as liking corn flakes, we are grouping her together with other things that are the same or similar in some respect. Mabel is one of the referents of the term "dog" and perhaps also one of the referents of the term "animal that has bitten the postal worker." In fact, there are indefinitely many terms that have Mabel as a referent ("weighs less than 1,000,000 kg," "is wingless," "cost more than $400," "lives in North Bay," and so on).

We classify things for many different purposes and so there are many possible **classification** schemes. By definition, *classification is a kind of division according to a rule*: A group of individuals is divided into subgroups by a rule that sorts them by a set of common properties. Imagine you have a pile of old toys and you want to sort them into groups so you can put them away on a set of shelves. You might put all the trucks on one shelf and all the dolls on another and all the blocks on a third. You could label each shelf ("the truck shelf," "the doll shelf," and so on) so you knew what to put there. A good classification scheme would divide the toys into a coherent set of groups, where each group went on a different shelf, and each and every toy was assigned to only one group so that every toy had a place on one shelf or another. Now imagine you decide to put trucks on one shelf and red things on another shelf and dolls on a third. If none of the dolls or trucks are red, this system might work well enough, but suppose one of the trucks is red. Now you have a problem: Your rules of classification would tell you to put the red truck on two different shelves, the shelf for trucks and the shelf for red things. Of course, you can't put it on both shelves at the same time. So your classification system would fail to tell you where to put trucks (or dolls) that are red. A good classification scheme won't do that.

Here are four rules for classification.

1. A classification scheme should be *exhaustive*. This means that each and every member of the whole group being classified should be put in some subgroup or another; the classification scheme *doesn't leave anything out* in the group being classified.

2. A classification scheme should be *exclusive*. This means that no member of the group being classified should be put into more than one group; groups don't overlap.

3. A classification scheme should be *clear*. The rules of classification should be sufficiently easy to understand and imply that it is clear to which group members belong.

4. Classification systems are developed to perform particular jobs, so a classification scheme should be *adequate for its purpose*.

The first two rules of classification, that a scheme should be *exhaustive* and *exclusive*, have the consequence that everything in the group being classified is put into a group and only one group; the other two rules are aimed at *usefulness*. Let's consider some examples. Suppose you are given the job of digging potatoes and given a large basket and a small one and told to put the big ones in the big basket, the tiny ones in the small basket and to leave the rotten ones in the field. These instructions divide the potatoes into three categories, and by reasonable implication you understand that you only put non-rotten in either basket. If a potato is rotten you don't worry about its size. Whether or not the big/small division is clear will depend on the circumstances; if there is continuous variation in potato size then you need a clear-cut boundary; if there are only very big ones and very small ones the distinction will be clear enough. So whether a classification scheme is clear will depend in part on what the things being classified are like.

Many things, particularly natural kinds and manufactured objects, come already classified in certain ways. Paper money, for example, comes only in certain denominations, new cars come in a finite number of models and colours, and metals are either iron, gold, or tin, etc. In Part II when we examine various fallacies, we will see many misapplications of classification systems, which produce faulty inferences.

DEFINITION

DEFINITIONS TELL YOU WHAT A TERM MEANS. THERE IS AN INTIMATE CONNECTION BETWEEN *definition* and *classification*. The meaning of a term in effect classifies what the term refers to. The meaning a term has is not a natural property of the term that could be discovered by investigation; a term has whatever meaning it has been given by the people using the term. Of course, some terms, for example "water" or "gold," refer to natural kinds of things, and the properties of those natural kinds *are* discovered by investigation. But this is a consequence of the kind of thing in question. The meanings of words are a function of social practice or are stipulated by users, so it is important for successful communication that all the parties in an argument are *using terms in the same way to mean the same thing.* On the other hand, there is a natural order that is independent of the meanings of terms that human beings use. Dogs, for example, exist quite independently of the fact that we have a word "dog," which we use to refer to them. The same is true of cats. Cats and dogs are both animals but they are different kinds of animals, and if we used one word to refer to both species they would still be different and we would need other words to distinguish them in thought. Of course, the meaning of a term does not stand alone; terms stand in relation to other terms that also have meanings. One of the principal uses of definition is to clarify the relationships *between* terms. When the dictionary defines "dog" as a "domesticated canine animal," it provides us with the meaning of the word "dog" by referring us to several other terms. If we know the meanings of those terms, we will know the meaning of "dog." If we looked those terms up and then looked up the terms those terms were defined by, and if we continued to look up terms in a dictionary, we would ultimately find a closed circle of terms—all of the terms we were looking up would be defined by using other terms we had looked up already. Since definitions classify or group things together that are the same or similar in some respects, the language as a whole functions as a giant classification system, or, more accurately, as a super set of classifications systems, which allow us to group the things in the world in a very great variety of ways depending on our interests and needs. Furthermore, the ways we can distinguish the things in the world from each other reflect real differences in things, facts about the world that are there for us to discover. As a result, there is an enormous amount of factual knowledge about the world that is embedded in word meanings, and we can gain access to that knowledge simply by paying attention to definitions. So knowing what words mean gives us a great deal of knowledge of what the world is like. This is one reason it is important to know what words mean and to have a large usable vocabulary.

Definitions have more than one function; we have mentioned one. Another use of definition is to tell us what is and what is not included in the reference of a term. Well-constructed definitions can do this because the terms we use classify things in systematic ways. In the definition of "dog" as "domesticated canine animal," for example, the term "domesticated" rules out the other members of the class of canine animals (wolves, foxes, etc.) because they are not domesticated, the word "canine" rules out other classes of animals (rodents, cats, etc.), and the word "animal" rules out other classes of beings (plants, minerals, etc.). Not all classification systems are equally orderly. But the careful use of terms that have systematic definitional connections with other terms makes using the terms in arguments much easier. This is because there are many truths that simply follow from the meanings of the words.

A good definition of a term will have a number of important features. Dogs are mammals—every single one of them is a mammal—so if we know that something is a dog then we know it will be a mammal as well. We can put this as: *Being a mammal is a **necessary or essential** condition for being a dog.* However, lots of non-dogs are mammals as well (cats and horses and sheep and humans . . .). So "being a mammal" is not an adequate definition of being a dog since it is *too wide*—while it does include all dogs, it also includes many animals in the definition that are not dogs. Poodles are dogs—every single one of them is a dog—so if something is a poodle we know it will be a dog as well. We can put this as: *Being a poodle is a **sufficient condition** for being a dog.* On the other hand, lots of non-poodles are dogs (dachshunds, boxers, shepherds, terriers . . .), so "being a poodle" isn't an adequate definition of a dog either, since it is *too narrow*—it would fail to include all the animals that are dogs. An ideally adequate definition of being a dog is one in which the parts of the definition are, when taken together, *jointly necessary and sufficient* so that every creature that is a dog is included in the definition (it is not too narrow) and no creature that is not a dog is included in the definition (it is not too wide). Another way of describing these relations is by way of the terms *genus* and *species* (which are here used in a more general way than they are in biology today). By "genus" we understand a broad concept that includes narrower concepts that pick out subgroups from all the referents in the genus. By "species" we understand a narrower concept included under some genus. A species picks out one type of that larger class. "Genus" and "species" are relative terms. For example, DOG is a species of MAMMAL, but DOG is a genus for POODLE.

With these terms in mind, we can give six rules for a good definition:

1. A good definition of a term "X" shouldn't be too broad (include too much).

    We can also put this as the requirement that the rule state the sufficient conditions that a thing must meet in order to be X. This means that it should include only things that ordinary usage calls X. (Example: "A horse is an animal" is too broad since being an animal is not enough to pick something out as a horse; it characterizes the horse by the genus it falls under rather than by its specific difference from other species falling under that genus.)

2. The definition shouldn't be too narrow.

    A good definition of a term "X" should state the necessary conditions of meeting the definition. This means that it should include in the definition all the things that ordinary usage calls X. (Example: "Person born in Canada" is too narrow a definition of "Canadian citizen" because being born in Canada is not a necessary condition of citizenship; it identifies only one species of citizen and excludes other species [for example, naturalized citizens] that fall under the genus "citizen.")

3. A good definition of a term "X" should avoid vagueness and obscurity.

    The point of definition is clarity; it shouldn't be harder for your audience to understand the definition of X than to understand the word X itself.

4. A good definition of a term "X" must not be circular.

A term cannot explain what its own meaning is. If I tell you that "podiatry" means the subject that a podiatrist practises but you don't know what podiatry is, then the definition is useless since it provides you with no information about how to use the term. If you already know what the term means then the definition doesn't add anything. We will look at circularity and its relation to critical thinking and argument in detail in Chapter 3.

5. A good definition of a term "X" should not be negative (unless absolutely necessary).

Negative definitions are usually either too broad or too narrow; they are also likely to be uninformative since they define a thing by what it is not rather than by what it is. If I tell you that a cat is a domesticated animal that is not a dog or a horse, I have not ruled out enough (e.g., donkeys), but more importantly I haven't said anything positive about what makes something a cat.

6. A good definition should not be slanted or biased.

Slanted definitions do not really state the necessary or sufficient conditions of a being X, but instead express the (positive or negative) attitudes or biases of the speaker toward the thing being defined. For example, if I tell you that politicians are professional liars who live off the public purse, I have not given you either necessary or sufficient conditions but instead have given a negative value judgment about politicians.

It is possible for a definition to be both too broad and too narrow at the same time. For example, the definition *a swimming pool is an enclosed artificially constructed area of water intended for public use* is both too broad and too narrow at once. It is too broad because it includes wading pools and fountains and other things that are not swimming pools. It is also too narrow because not all swimming pools are intended for public use; some swimming pools are privately owned.

Here is another example: A dog is a short-haired pet with four legs and paws rather than hoofs. This definition is too narrow in two different ways because it mentions two inessential characteristics. It excludes dogs with long hair, but it also excludes dogs that are not pets. Neither being a pet nor having long hair has anything essential to do with being a dog.

STUDY SETS 3

Part A. Evaluate these classification schemes. Are they exhaustive, exclusive, clear, and adequate to the task?

1. Put away all your toys. Very small things go on the top shelf. Large stuffed animals go in the box. The books go on the middle shelf and everything else goes in the closet.

2. Divide your marble collection into the multicoloured solids, the clear coloured, the clear colourless with swirls inside, the clear colourless without swirls inside.

3. Big animals, scary animals, smelly animals, animals named George.

4. Friends (be nice), people who can hurt you (be nice), everyone else (screw them).

5. My mom, my brothers and sisters, my parents, my friends, the people I hate, everyone else.

6. (Kinds of animals): Pets, vermin, game, work animals, food animals.

7. (Things I collect): Balls of string, pop bottle caps, rotten cheese, autographs by people named George, Coke bottle caps, large American cars, Elvis records, old buttons.

8. (Pre-season list for the coach): Last year's returning players, kids with attitudes, losers, kids who are promising but need more skills, kids I can't tell about yet.

Part B. Think of a number of different things that are small enough to put on a shelf. List 10 of these things picked at random. Now make a classification system that will sort and organize them onto three shelves by putting like things on like shelves. (Don't cheat by picking things that will clearly fit the classification system; pick the things first).

Part C. Evaluate these definitions. Are they, for example, too broad, too narrow, vague or obscure, circular, negative, or slanted?

1. The Conservative party is a political organization of patriotic, civic-minded citizens dedicated to preserving the cherished freedoms of all Canadians.

2. A kite is a toy consisting of a light frame with paper or other thin material stretched upon it, to be flown in a strong wind by means of a string attached and a tail to balance it.

3. "Democracy" means rule by the ignorant masses.

4. "Homophobe" means a person who has an irrational hatred or fear of homosexuality.

5. "Postmodern" means a chaotic and confusing mishmash of images and references that leaves readers and viewers longing for the days of a good, well-told story.

6. A paddle is a stout pole shaped into a wide and flat blade at one end held freehand and used to propel a boat through water.

7. A poem is a rhymed composition in verse.

8. "Rectangle" means a two-dimensional figure with four sides.

9. "Lawyer" means a scum-sucking scavenger who preys on the weak and powerless for a hefty fee.

10. "Cello" means a stringed musical instrument made of wood.

11. "Prestidigitator" means a person who practises the art of prestidigitation.

IMPLICIT PREMISES AND ARGUMENTS FROM DEFINITION

AS WE HAVE JUST SEEN, WHEN WE PROVIDE A GOOD DEFINITION OF THE MEANING OF A TERM we will state essential features that things must have in order for the term to apply to them. These features will usually be facts about the world that are quite independent of language, and this means that the meanings of words have knowledge about things embedded in them, knowledge that we can exploit when we make inferences and give arguments. When we reason and when we formulate arguments, we always rely to a certain extent on information that is *implicitly* available in the form of knowledge carried simply by the meanings of words. We also often rely on free-floating knowledge—what "everyone knows." Some of this free-floating "knowledge" is simply prejudice or overgeneralization, and when we examine fallacious forms of reasoning, especially in Chapters 4 and 5, we will look at a number of ways that reasoning can be damaged by such assumptions. But the vast majority of what "everyone knows"—that water is wet, that dogs are animals, that you can buy food to eat at a restaurant, and so on—is just knowledge that everyone has by virtue of being part of a culture and knowing a language. Here I want to talk about how a good *argument from definition* can contain **implicit** information that *if made explicit shows that the argument is valid.*

An **argument from definition** is an argument in which the conclusion is presented as following simply by definition or by the meanings of the words used in the argument. Consider "Bruce is my father so Bruce is a man"; here, the conclusion "Bruce is a man" is presented as following from the meaning of "father" and from the fact that a good definition of "father" will include the requirement that if someone is a father then that person is a man. A statement that follows "by definition" from a good definition of a term will capture a necessary or essential condition of the application of that term, and so the statement is made necessarily true by virtue of reflecting partly of the meaning of a term. Since a statement that is necessarily true is true in every possible circumstance, adding a **necessary truth** to an argument cannot make a valid argument invalid. A good argument from definition is therefore *implicitly valid* and can be shown to be valid by making the definitional connection **explicit**. We can see this for the argument from "Bill is a father" to "Bill is male."

A **proof** that an argument from (a good) definition is valid follows.
Consider the argument:

Bill is a father
∴ Bill is male

If one looks at the definition of "father" one finds it means "male parent." This means that the concept of being a father includes the concept of being male and the assertion that Bill is a father implicitly includes the assertion that Bill is male. To make the validity of the argument explicit, we need to make this information explicit.

1. Bill is a father. [The premise]

   However, since "father" *means* "male parent" and "Bill is a father" says the same thing as "Bill is a male parent," we can substitute one for the other, and so by substituting one for the other we can rewrite 1 as:

2. Bill is a male parent.

   Again, since "Bill is a male parent" says *both* that Bill is male and that Bill is a parent, we can replace it by these two claims, and so by substitution again we can rewrite 2 as:

3. Bill is male and Bill is a parent.

But if Bill is *both* a male and a parent then Bill is a male, so we can conclude from 3 that:

4. Bill is male. [The conclusion]

(This last move is acceptable because it is a necessary truth that if a statement "A and B" is true, then "A" is true and of course so is "B," which allows replacing the truth "A and B" with "A," or "A and B" with "B," without loss of truth.)

Since all the moves from 1 to 4 simply depend on making *explicit* "what is included" in 1, we may say that the conclusion was "included" in the premise, and it follows from it by the definition of the term "father." The argument is valid because the conclusion must be true if the premise is true.

Some caution is warranted in extracting information from definitions. Definitions are, after all, human creations, and to the extent that the terms are not fully defined we need to be cautious about argument from definition. On the other hand, the practice of defining your terms carefully imposes the clarity of structure on your arguments, and appealing to definitions held in common between participants in argument allows you to make explicit a body of agreement that makes reasonable inferences more rationally persuasive and secure.

Arguments from definition are not the only kind of argument relying on implicitly available information. Often enough when we give an argument we rely on our audience to share common knowledge with us, which we therefore do not need to state. Arguments that rely on this sort of shared knowledge are called **enthymemes**. An *enthymeme is an argument in which a required premise is not stated explicitly but is assumed implicitly as part of the argument.* Consider the claims like

1. "Dogs are animals so they are not machines" or

2. "*Huckleberry Finn* is a racist book so it should not be taught in schools."

In each case the arguer appears to appeal to something that "everyone knows" or at least something that can be assumed to be true for the purposes of argument. The implicit premise in 1 could be expressed in a number of ways but it is something like "animals are not machines" or "no animal is a machine" or "if something is an animal then it is not a machine," and so if we make the claim in 1 *explicit* then we get something like

1. "Dogs are animals and *no animal is a machine*, so they are not machines."

In 2, if we add the implicit premise that racist books shouldn't be used in schools we get

2. "*Huckleberry Finn* is a racist book and *racist books shouldn't be used in schools*, so it should not be taught in schools."

Some philosophers argue that every enthymeme is an incomplete argument because it is missing the explicit statement of a premise, and that all arguments with implicit premises can be made fully explicit. Other philosophers think that reasoning skills always appeal to implicit claims and that while any particular argument can be made explicit, we cannot make everything explicit. I will not try to settle the issue here. But notice that there is a great variety in implicit arguments. Here are four very different ones:

3. Seattle is south of Vancouver
   so Vancouver is north of Seattle

4. Prince George is north of Vancouver
   so Prince George is north of Los Angeles

5. There is no water on Venus
   so there is no life on Venus

6. People who love children make good teachers
   so Mary will be a great teacher

Argument 3 might be thought of as a kind of argument by definition; one could not understand "north" and "south" without seeing that they are interdefined and so being able to make the inference. Argument 4 reflects the assumption that "everyone knows" the relative positions of Vancouver and Los Angeles, and thus knows that Vancouver is north of Los Angeles. Given that assumption, one can infer that Prince George is also north of Los Angeles as soon as one learns that Prince George is north of Vancouver. In argument 5, an appeal is made to a "law of nature," something like "living things require water to live," which is widely believed but is perhaps not certain. Argument 6 assumes that we know who Mary is and what she is like, so—in the context of the discussion, say, between the friends and relations of Mary—it is (presumably) reasonable to assume (and thus not have to say) that Mary loves children.

Although these four kinds of enthymemes have implicit premises of different kinds, what they all have in common is that in a given context leaving the implicit assumption unstated is a reasonable thing to do. The trouble with enthymemes is that they assume that you will *notice* the implicit assumption or premise and fill it in and so get the point. But this doesn't always happen, even when the thing that you fail to notice is something you know well and that is, in another context, quite obvious. **Context** functions to highlight certain relevant considerations and so helps us to see what is relevant in a situation, but it can also make us blind to other considerations that are perfectly obvious but that the context does not highlight. So in order to evaluate arguments with implicit parts reliably, we need to be able to reconstruct them so that the implicit part is made explicitly visible. An important part of critical thinking is simply being careful, and taking care to make implicit assumptions explicitly available is one way of being careful. Often there will be a fallacious inference that has been made without being noticed, and reconstructing the argument will reveal the error.

STUDY SETS 4

Place these arguments in standard form. If they are enthymemes, then make the argument explicit by adding the missing premise(s).

1. Bill will be late for dinner; he stopped for a pint with the guys after work.

2. Mary didn't study for the test tomorrow; I guess she is going to fail.

3. Death cannot be the final end; it wouldn't be fair.

4. I'm sorry, I cannot sell you any beer. I am not permitted to sell to underage kids.

5. Mary went to Burger King so she was hungry.

6. Boxing should be banned in Canada because it is dangerous.

7. If today is Tuesday, either Eric is in class or he is sick. It is Tuesday so he must be sick.

8. Don't ever buy a Taurus. It's a Ford!

BELIEF, CRITICAL THINKING, AND FALLACIES

SO FAR IN THIS BOOK WE HAVE INTRODUCED THE IDEA OF *ARGUMENT* AND HAVE SEEN THAT it is a way of regimenting and making explicit what happens in the mind in a process of reasoning. We introduced the ideas of *validity* and of *soundness* and the idea that good arguments are good because they are examples of good *patterns of argumentation*—the idea that good valid arguments are good in virtue of their form.

We also introduced the idea of *relevance*. We saw that relevance is a broad notion and that it applies to critical thinking in a number of ways. Firstly, it figures in the relation that premises have to the conclusion they support: The truth or plausibility of premises must be relevant to the truth or plausibility of the conclusion of an argument. But premises also need to be relevant in the sense of making some appeal to the beliefs and interests of the hearer. An argument will not be successful if it does not make some kind of connection with the hearer's tendencies to believe. The truth of premises should, if possible, be uncontroversial, or at least worth taking seriously.

We also looked at the ideas of *classification* and *definition*, both of which rest on the fact that the words in a language have meanings that connect them to the meanings of other words. Good definitions will connect the meaning of a word with a set of necessary and sufficient conditions, which produces a kind of web of meanings in language. We also saw that the meanings of words reflect the way things are in the world; language is not just a web of meanings, it is also a knowledge system revealing truths about the world.

Finally, we saw that because people know about the meanings of words and the meanings of words attach to empirically real patterns in the world, by knowing a language, people implicitly know many facts about the world. If people hear that Bill is Leslie's father, they implicitly come to know that Leslie is the son or daughter of Bill, that Bill is male, and so on. Since they know such things merely from the meanings of the words, these things do not need to be made explicit before you can correctly attribute that knowledge to them. We saw that because there are many facts that everyone (or everyone relevantly placed) can be expected to know, there are many arguments that are good but that rely on information that is only implicitly available. Because an important part of critical thinking is being careful, in order to evaluate arguments with implicit parts we need to reconstruct them so that the implicit information in them is made explicitly visible.

These considerations impose burdens on our conception of what a critical thinker is like. They also help us understand the ways thinkers can fail to be critical. In the remaining chapters of this book, we will focus on a variety of ways that thinking can be more critical and ways in which it can fail. Before we turn to the specifics of this task, let us start by collecting together some facts about what an *ideal critical thinker* will be like, a thinker who is completely guided by canons of good reasoning and responsible argument.

Ideally, a critical thinker will have a *good mastery of the language* with a large vocabulary and very clear and explicit understanding of what each word in his or her vocabulary means. A critical thinker's response to lacking a word with precisely the right meaning or failing to know exactly what a word means will be to turn to a good dictionary. A good vocabulary provides a critical thinker with a great deal of knowledge about what the world is like, so the ideal critical thinker will also be well-informed about what can be taken to be common knowledge. Because what is commonly believed is not always true, a critical thinker will have resources for *evaluating the testimony* of others and distinguishing reasonable claims from unreasonable ones. These recourses will include skills for evaluating claims on the basis of argument, but also skills for evaluating the reliability and knowledgeableness of other speakers. A critical thinker will be good at reconstructing arguments, filling in the implicit premises, identifying the patterns of reasoning to which the arguments appeal, and paying attention to factors that are being left out. People have finite abilities to pay attention to all of the relevant features of arguments, and a critical thinker will therefore attempt to guard against the possibility that attending to one consideration might blind one to another equally relevant consideration. The best way to guard against such possibilities is to be methodological and thorough. The question of how reasonable it is to accept a claim as true or credible will partly depend on how clear a conception a critical thinker is capable of forming about what is being claimed, so a critical thinker should have skills in analyzing the clarity and plausibility of the speech of others.

Over the next three chapters in Part II, we will expand on these ideas by looking at a variety of *informal patterns of reasoning* and looking both at the strengths of those patterns and the ways they can be misused. Many aspects of critical thinking follow directly from the nature of belief and our double nature as believers and language users. So before we move on to Part II, it will be useful to have a brief discussion of the way language shapes thought.

When we look at inference from the side of argument we are led quickly to considerations of relations between premises and conclusion and from there we are led to questions about formalizing or regimenting rules of inference. In the last chapter we saw some reasons for this pressure. In argument, we attempt to support claims by reference to other claims to which it is reasonable for others to assent, and the clearer and more explicit we can make evidential relations the stronger our arguments are likely to be. But when we look at inference from the side of belief and the demands it imposes on us, another set of considerations becomes salient, having to do with truth and reliability. Most of these considerations are what philosophers call **epistemic** considerations, from the word "epistemology," which means the study of belief and knowledge and the relations that truth, reliability, and justification have to one another.

To believe a statement—for example, that it is raining—is to take it to be true. So to believe that it is raining is just to take it to be true that it is raining. The natural expression of belief is thus just the assertion of what is believed, so we typically express the belief that it is raining by saying, "It is raining." Normally, if I tell you it is raining, then you take me to believe it. In addition, if you have no prior reason to think that I am mistaken or a liar, if I tell you that it is raining then I have given *you* a reason to believe it, too. Of course, the mere fact that I believe something isn't by itself a reason for me to continue to believe it; it is instead a *sign* that I probably have reasons to believe it (since, after all, I *do* believe it). So when you come to believe that it is raining because I tell you it is, the reasons you have are grounded in *trust*: You take me to have reasons and in the absence of counterevidence that is good enough for you. That gives you a reason (a different reason than I have) to believe it, too. Despite the occasional liars, con artists, and spies among us, for the most part when we speak frankly *we say what we believe*, and so human conversation is from the very beginning the business of offering reasons to each other.

The fundamental question for method is "What should I believe?" Answering that question directs us to two fundamental rules. First, *I should believe what is true*. Since belief is taking something to be true, a belief gets things right—it is materially correct—if what I believe is true. On the other hand, my belief is not made true by magic; rather, it is made true by the way the world is. For example, my belief that it is raining is made true, if it is true, by the fact that it is raining. Since our beliefs can be wrong, merely having a belief is not good enough. I need reasons for thinking that I have the belief that I do *because* what I believe is true. So the second rule that the fundamental question for method directs us to can be put like this: *I should believe what I have reason to believe*. Because truth is the target at which belief aims, I need to aim at the truth, but my aim also needs to be guided by skill if I am to hit the target reliably. The very nature of belief demands that it be guided by *good* reasons, by *evidence*. A critical thinker will be moved to form beliefs by evidence, or epistemic reasons, and not merely by desires or fears or wishes.

Belief aims at the truth about the world and so our beliefs must defer to the way the world is. These facts make goodness in inference more complicated than the formal goodness of arguments narrowly taken. Earlier in the chapter we saw that the criteria of relevance and dialectical acceptability make appeal to the relationship that premises in an argument have to other arguments and stories that establish them as acceptable premises, and this appeal takes us beyond the question of the formal goodness of the argument itself to the larger question of goodness of inference. To evaluate the formal goodness of an argument, it is merely necessary to analyze the relationship between the premises and conclusion; if the argument is valid it is formally good; if it is invalid it is not. But when we attempt to evaluate goodness in inference, many more things need to be taken into account. For one thing, inference is something that happens inside a particular person's belief set.

This means that only an agent's own beliefs and belief-forming processes are available as resources for reasoning.

The main difficulty is this: Because the inferences we make are situated in the midst of the rest of the things we believe, the question of whether they make sense or not to us depends upon what we already believe. When we think about what to believe, we attempt to increase the overall *coherence* and *explanatory power* of our beliefs, but part of what makes our beliefs appear more coherent to us depends on what we believe already. When we make inferences we also aim to increase the overall likelihood that our beliefs are true, and that attempt will also depend in part on what we believe already. Among the things we believe already, there will be views about what is true, there will be views about what makes things more coherent, there will be methodological principles, and there will be models of how the world hangs together. All of these things will affect what makes for overall coherence of belief for us.

Of course, our beliefs have not been formed in isolation from the influence of others. While inference, being a mental process, is private, the beliefs we form are deeply influenced by the beliefs of others. As a general rule, another person's beliefs are just as likely to be as well considered or true as your own, and on many topics they will be much more likely than your own. As a result, the stories we tell each other in conversation and the arguments we give each other deeply influence the inferences we make. The testimony of others together with our direct experience and our memory are the three great sources of reasons for belief.

The capacity of human beings to take instruction from each other through speech may be the most important thing that sets human beings apart from other creatures in the world. Like us, other animals have sense organs, so they can perceive the world around them in immediate experience; they have memories, so that they can profit from past perception and learn more about what the world is like. What they do not have is language. To have language requires both a specific kind of intellectual capacity—the power to process and thus understand grammar—and a kind of social nature that makes the members of a community care about each other in a way that allows them to take and give instruction to each other. Humans alone in the animal world have *culture*—a great repository of shared belief and practices. I want to spend a minute talking about both of these capacities.

Human beings begin the journey into language as infants by imitating the sounds their elders make and by connecting these sounds with meanings that have currency. Learning how to use a word like "table," for example, is not simply learning how to make a certain sound; it is learning *what a table is* and *how to tell tables from non-tables*. Children learn words together with the correct conditions of their use. To be able to do this requires a very sophisticated set of skills. Children need implicitly to realize that what they can respond to depends on the things they can directly experience in the present—a fact that depends on where they are and when they are there. They also learn that other people know things about where they are that are specific to their environment. The child can talk to them about what was happening where they were. This may seem like a simple thing, but to be able to do this, the child needs a sense of time and space and to possess a "theory of mind"; to understand that everyone has one and that different people know different things. By the age of three, children develop the capacity to attribute minds to others—they come to realize that others have beliefs about the world that may be either true or false and more importantly they come to see others as possessing *a point of view* on the world that is guided by reasons and that they can take up in imagination. They come to be able to put themselves in the place of someone else and understand what it is like to be where that other person is and thus to have the beliefs that the other person has— beliefs different from one's own. If they take Mommy's purse and hide it under the pillow while she is out of the room, Mommy will not know where the purse is even though they do. Being able to put yourself in the shoes of another also makes it possible to develop a moral sense, to grasp what is fair, how to do things right, and many other necessary social skills, but my focus here is on *belief*. The point is that children come into a capacity for understanding what a belief is, which involves its connection with correctness and the giving and taking—sharing—of reasons for belief, and they do this very early in their journey into mastery of language. These developmental powers are not simply grounded in raw intelligence but in the fact that humans take a deep interest in each other's minds, give each other instruction, and defer to each other's knowledge. Human beings live in a world of right and wrong even simply with regard to belief.

How do human beings communicate and understand information by speaking a language? Because the words in a language are only accidentally or conventionally correlated with the things to which they refer, the cognitive content of statements must be largely conveyed by the compositional structure of the sentences used to express them. This structure is *grammar*. Although we live immersed in a sea of language, most of us have only the haziest conception of what this structure is. This is not particularly surprising, since we grow up inside of our language and learn how to speak before we gain explicit conceptual skills. There is an air of paradox about this. Language is essentially a rule-governed activity and it is hard to understand how we can follow rules without knowing what they are. Yet it seems that we do exactly that. In speaking a language, we obey a vast system of rules that allows us to distinguish grammatical from ungrammatical utterances, to correct both ourselves and others in both grammar and pronunciation, and to know what is meant by what is said. This *system of rules* is grammar. Thus grammar is far more than a set of maxims of correct usage; it is an enabling condition of our understanding of language.

Grammar consists in the structural features that distinguish sentences that can be understood from those that cannot. A large part of what makes a statement intelligible to a hearer is the *context* in which it is made, and that context consists in *knowledge*: knowledge about the topic or situation being discussed and a vast store of background knowledge that is shared by the speaker and hearer. In short, language is a *knowledge-based* process of communication, in which grammar is a crucial enabling feature. Speakers and hearers rely on their joint possession of grammatical rules, which make the context of their speech to the other intelligible; they rely on broadly shared systems of classification and shared definitions of terms. They rely on being members of a community that consists primarily of a shared mastery of language.

I have discussed these facts because they impose important constraints on the critical thinker. Beyond the obvious ones like *speaking the truth, not exaggerating,* and *answering requests for clarification,* critical thinkers should always attempt to provide those with whom they speak enough information so that what they are saying can be clearly understood.

Finally, we need to introduce the notion of fallacies: the various ways critical thinkers can go wrong. So what makes something a fallacy? The term "fallacy" is often used rather broadly to indicate any kind of error in inference or belief, but we will use the term somewhat more narrowly. We will not use the term to refer to mistaken beliefs but only to refer to some kind of mistake in reasoning or inference. A **fallacy**, in the strict sense, is a form of argument that is invalid or violates a relevance condition. Fallacy is thus different from simple falsity. A statement or set of statements may be false, but an argument is the *transition from a set of premises to a conclusion.* What is fallacious in a fallacious argument is that one or more of the criteria of good arguments are violated. Let us remember how we defined *cogent argument* in Chapter 1. There we defined it as an argument that meets the following conditions:

1. A cogent argument must be *grounded in premises that are accepted or are rationally acceptable to a reasonable audience.* The arguer's assertion of the premises cannot therefore be silly or arbitrary.

2. *The premises must be relevant to the conclusion.* They need to make a rationally grounded connection to the conclusion, so that the truth or reasonableness of the premises genuinely bears on the truth or reasonableness of the conclusion.

3. The premises *must provide sufficient or strong rational grounds for asserting the conclusion.* The bearing that the premises have on the conclusion needs to be sufficiently strong to permit the mind to move from asserting the premises to asserting the conclusion.

A *fallacious argument* is one that is *not cogent.* This means that there are three fundamental ways in which fallacies can occur and there are a number of ways that each condition can fail. Formal fallacies, like *affirming the consequent,* which we saw in Chapter 1, are argument patterns whose form is logically invalid. But arguments can go wrong in many informal ways—for example, by violating criteria of relevance or clarity—so there are many kinds of informal fallacies. Some are used deliberately to mislead or influence others, but most are simply the result of an incautious use of language or sloppy thinking. They are exceedingly common. In the next three chapters we will examine and analyze a number of common informal fallacies and discuss ways critical thinkers can avoid them. Fallacies usually have a deceptive appearance and pass for good arguments. In large part this is because they are usually distortions or failed versions of argument forms that *are* good. So we will not look at fallacies in isolation, but will also examine the good patterns of reasoning that fallacies distort.

As a matter of fact, we all use fallacious forms of argument many times every day. These fallacies frequently cause no damage, because we could, if we were more careful, reformulate our arguments in cogent terms. However, often the very thinking behind our arguments is at fault, and the fallaciousness of our arguments can only be removed by rethinking our opinions and correcting our tendencies for sloppy and irrelevant thinking. So the study of fallacies and informal patterns of reasoning is valuable not simply by showing us what to avoid but because it provides us with tools for thinking more coherently and increasing our ability to discover the truth.

ADDITIONAL STUDY SETS FOR PART I

YOU SHOULD KNOW WHAT THE **PREMISES** AND **CONCLUSION** OF AN **ARGUMENT** ARE AND grasp what **argument** and **validity** and **soundness** mean. These are central concepts for the whole book and you should remember that they are technical terms and so have special meanings. The ordinary meaning of these terms is likely to be unhelpful or misleading. Understanding the concept of **validity** in particular gives students great difficulty; you will see it discussed in every chapter of the book.

Part A. Here is a set of assertions involving these terms. Use a **T** or **F** to indicate whether these statements are true or false.

1. _____ No sound argument has false premises.

2. _____ If an argument has true premises and a false conclusion, then it is invalid.

3. _____ Every valid argument has a true conclusion.

4. _____ If an argument has a counter-example, it is invalid.

5. _____ Some unsound arguments have true premises.

6. _____ No valid argument has false conclusions.

7. _____ Some invalid arguments have true premises.

8. _____ Every sound argument has a true conclusion.

9. _____ No sound argument has a counter-example.

10. _____ All valid arguments have true premises.

11. _____ If an argument has false premises, it cannot be sound.

12. _____ If an argument has true premises and a true conclusion, then it is valid.

13. _____ No valid argument has a counter-example.

14. _____ All unsound arguments have false premises.

Part B. Circle a, b, c, or d to indicate which is the <u>best</u> choice for completing these sentences.

1. A fallacy is an argument that

   a. leads to a false conclusion

   b. is a bad argument that appears good

   c. will persuade you to believe what is false

   d. all of the above

2. An argument that is valid may have

   a. false premises and a false conclusion

   b. false premises and a true conclusion

   c. true premises and a true conclusion

   d. all of the above

3. The argument "If Toronto is in Ontario then Toronto is in Canada; and Toronto is in Ontario, so Toronto is in Canada" is

   a. valid

   b. sound

   c. an example of *Modus Ponens*

   d. all of the above

4. An argument is sound if and only if

   a. it does not lead to a false conclusion

   b. it makes sense on reflection

   c. it is a valid argument with a true conclusion

   d. it is a valid argument with true premises

5. To show that an argument is invalid, show that

   a. the conclusion is false

   b. the premises are false

   c. both premises and conclusion are false

   d. none of the above

6. An argument with true premises and a true conclusion may be

   a. valid

   b. sound

   c. neither valid nor sound

   d. all of the above

<u>Part C.</u> Following is a list of one-liner definitions; imagine they are in a small pocket dictionary. Trying to be charitable, answer whether these definitions are *too broad, too narrow, slanted, circular, vague, negative,* or *acceptable*.

1. "No-fly zone" means an area off-limits to aircraft.

2. "Cat" means a small long-haired feline animal.

3. Lasagna is a delicious Italian dish with lots of cheese.

4. "Psychologist" means a person who practises the art of psychology.

5. Sex is a disgusting and sinful animalistic activity unless consecrated by marriage.

6. "Dusk" means twilight as the evening darkens.

7. "Merchant" means a person engaged in the purchase and sale of commodities.

8. A circus is a show with clowns, happening in a tent.

9. "Cheese" means any kind of solid food made out of cheese.

10. "Soldier" means a person who serves in the army.

11. A horse is an animal used for riding and pulling carts.

12. "Sexy" means causing men to find one very attractive.

13. An oboe is a wooden wind instrument.

14. "Poodle" means a very small curly-haired show dog.

15. A salad is a dish made of lettuce, onion, and tomatoes and a dressing.

16. "Politician" means a person who nobly serves his country as a lawmaker.

17. A virtue is a state of character exhibiting a particular moral excellence.

18. "Guard" means one of the players stationed in the back court.

19. A philosopher is a deluded dreamer bent on answering meaningless questions.

20. "Mac and cheese" is a delicious dish containing cheese.

21. "Dawn" means the time of day when the sun rises.

22. "Tennis" means a game played with racquets and a net.

23. A novel is a piece of literature that isn't a poem.

24. A shovel is a long-handled tool for moving snow.

Part D. Below a number of informally stated arguments. Identify the conclusion and add any missing premises needed to make the argument explicit and then put these arguments in standard form.

1. "Many that live deserve death. And some that die deserve life. Can you give it to them? Then do not be so eager to deal out death in judgement. For even the wise cannot see all ends." (Gandalf, *The Lord of the Rings*, 1954)

2. The kids said they were hungry so Stella took them to Burger King.

3. Mary isn't answering the phone and she always answers if she can. So either she isn't home or something is wrong.

4. A square circle must be logically impossible. God can do anything that is logically possible but God can't make a square circle.

5. The Conservatives won't win the election because they won't have enough support in Ontario and so they won't get enough seats to form the government.

6. Shanghai is the size of New York so it is much bigger than Saskatoon.

7. If Dr. Shipley elected president of our club, we will have the first woman president in our history.

8. People don't trust the Liberals. This means that Stéphane Dion will probably lose the election because people just won't vote for a leader they don't trust.

9. Bob is bound to be late for dinner; he had hockey practice this afternoon.

10. Mary didn't study for the final exam. So, of course, she will fail the class.

11. Danny's farm is a ways southwest of here because to get there you have to drive two miles south to Deergrove Road and turn west and then drive about a mile and a half to the farm.

12. Never hit your child. Health professionals have shown that hitting children fosters rage and self-loathing in them.

Part E. These arguments are all examples of the patterns of valid and fallacious arguments seen in Chapter 1. Identify the pattern of each argument.

1. If God exists, then all the evil that exists is necessary. If all existing evil is necessary, then this is the best of all possible worlds. Thus, if God exists, this is the best of all possible worlds.

2. If the banks are still open, then I'd better hurry downtown. But the banks are closed, so I guess there's no need to hurry.

3. Either evolution is true or creationism is true. But creationism is not true. So evolution must be true.

4. We'll need to go for groceries either Thursday or Saturday. If we go Saturday, we'll be late for the opera. If we go Thursday, we'll have to miss *Star Trek*. So it looks like we will either be late for the opera or we'll miss *Star Trek*.

5. If you are a super-genius, then you don't need to study. But you do need to study, so you are not a super-genius.

6. The Saskatchewan Roughriders are better than the Argonauts and the Blue Bombers stink compared to the Argonauts so the Roughriders are better than the Blue Bombers.

7. No birds are lions but all ducks are birds so no ducks are lions.

Part II
Informal Reasoning and Fallacies

INTRODUCTION

In the three chapters making up this section of the book, we will look at informal reasoning and its fallacies. There are many ways in which an argument can be fallacious and we will not look at them all. The fallacies we will examine are all well-known and, for convenience, will be divided into three types.

In **Chapter 3** we will look at the fallacies of ambiguity and circularity. Ambiguity and circularity violate fundamental features that any argument, formal or informal, must possess: An argument must not be ambiguous because if the meaning of terms change the argument will fail to have a stable subject matter, and an argument must not be circular because an argument that assumes as a premise what it attempts to show in the conclusion cannot discharge the fundamental burden of demonstrating, or offering support for, the conclusion.

In **Chapter 4** we will look at inductive reasoning and its associated fallacies. We will examine reasoning by analogy and causal reasoning as well as appeals to authority and common knowledge. The distinctive feature of inductive forms of reasoning is that they are made good not by their form but also by their content. A successful inductive argument picks out a genuine regularity in nature. As a result, the fallacies in this section typically fail to respect relevant constraints on evidence or constraints of precision.

In **Chapter 5** we will examine the need for objectivity in critical reasoning and examine forms of reasoning that are fallacious because of considerations that are irrelevant due to bias. In these fallacies, considerations that are irrelevant to the truth of the conclusion are introduced in order to sway us to accept the conclusion. Usually the fallacies of relevance use inappropriate appeals to emotion or to commitments that the hearer holds dear to produce their effect.

Chapter 3
Ambiguity and Circularity

AMBIGUITY AND ITS FALLACIES

AMBIGUITY IS THE CONDITION OF HAVING MORE THAN ONE INTERPRETATION OR MEANING. When an expression or set of words is ambiguous, it can be used to convey more than one meaning and it can be unclear which meaning is intended. One resolves ambiguity either by adding additional background information that rules out all meanings except the intended one, or by using a different phrase that lacks the ambiguity in question.

Fallacies of ambiguity are unsound because they contain words or phrases that can be understood in more than one way. There are two basic ways in which ambiguity can arise. The first is *lexical* ambiguity or **equivocation**, in which a word or phrase has more than one lexical definition and so can be understood in more than one way. Alternatively, two different words that look or sound the same may become confused and lead to fallacious inference. The second basic way ambiguity can arise is *structural* ambiguity or **amphiboly**, in which a string of words in a sentence have more than one legitimate grammatical interpretation and so can be understood in more than one way. We will examine five fallacies of ambiguity: the fallacies of *equivocation, amphiboly, accent, composition and division,* and *hypostatization.*

Equivocation

The fallacy of *equivocation* is due to *lexical ambiguity*. This fallacy occurs when a key word or phrase is used in two or more senses in the same argument and the apparent success of the argument depends on the shift in meaning. One way to understand a simple form of equivocation is by way of the syllogism pattern we introduced in Chapter 1. You will remember that the syllogism pattern involves two premises and a conclusion, and three terms that are arranged so that each premise relates two terms, of which one is in the other premise and one is in the conclusion. The validity of the pattern depends on the transitivity of the relation:

A bears relation R to B		Fred is older than Joe
B bears relation R to C	for example	Joe is older than Peter
∴ A bears relation R to C		∴ Fred is older than Peter

The term "Joe" is what is called the middle term, the term that links the two premises in a way that orders the three terms with respect to each other. The point of this brief excursion into the question of how syllogistic arguments depend on transitivity is to introduce a very typical kind of syllogistic fallacy of ambiguity called the *fallacy of four terms*. Consider an argument in which the two premises have no term in common, such as: "Fred is older than Joe" and "Mary is older than Peter." Because they have no term in common, the two premises are not connected by the ordering relation in any way so no conclusion can be drawn from them. We don't know whether Fred is older than Mary or Peter, and neither do we know whether Joe is older than Mary or Peter. If it is commonly known by the people hearing the argument that Joe is older than Mary, then we can resolve the difficulty. We now know that Fred is older than Joe, who is older than Mary, who in turn is older than Peter; the transitivity of the "is older than" relation allows us to infer that Fred is older than Mary and then that he is therefore older than Peter.

Now, if a syllogism uses a term equivocally—that is, in two different senses—it can look like a valid syllogism but upon analysis it will be seen to be a fallacy of four terms. Here is an example:

The argument	looks like this	but is really like this
Only man is rational	Only **A**s are **B**s	Only **A**s are **B**s
No woman is a man	No **C** is an **A**	No **C** is a **D**
∴ No woman is rational	∴ No **C** is a **B**	∴ No **C** is a **B**

If we are to take the premises seriously in this argument, the word "man" must mean *human being* in the first premise and *male* in the second. In short, although the two uses of "man" *look the same* they are really different terms with different meanings. But the conclusion of the argument would only follow from the premises if "man," the middle term, is a single term having the same meaning in both premises so that it can tie them together. The first premise says that only As are Bs (which is the same as saying that *if something is a B then it is an A*), the second premise says that no C is an A (which is the same as saying that *if something is a C then it is not an A*); from these premises it *does* follow logically that no C is a B. But since the two **instances** of "man" represent different terms in the two premises, we really have four terms—A, B, C, and D—and thus no middle term to tie the two premises together in a way that could support the conclusion. And if you tried to add as a missing premise the claim that only males are human beings, you would see right away that the claim is false.

Of course, no one would take such an argument seriously because the equivocation on the word "man" is so obvious. Similarly, no one would be deceived by an equivocation on the word "bank" (as, for example, in the phrases "bank of commerce" and "river bank"), or an equivocation on the word "nothing" in the argument

"Nothing is better than world peace, but a crust of bread is better than nothing, so a crust of bread is better than world peace."

In these cases, the two meanings are obviously completely different. However, most words in the English language have more than one meaning and in many cases the meanings are closely enough related that it is easy to use them equivocally. Equivocation is especially likely when a key term in an argument is a *figure of speech*, a *theoretical term*, or a *metaphor*, and since many terms in our language are dead or dying metaphors, equivocation is a fairly common fallacy.

Consider, for example, the phrase "public interest." It often means something like *public welfare* or what is good for the public; it also often means *what the public desires*, and even *what the public takes an interest in*. Clearly something could be in the public interest in one of these senses without being in the public interest in either of the others. Indeed the questions "What are the various senses of 'public interest'?" and "How are they related?" are complex, subtle, and require study. Such questions constitute an important part of the subject matter of political theory. Here is another example: Consider the phrases "power corrupts" and "knowledge is power." While it is hard to say how the meaning of the word "power" shifts across these two phrases, it is pretty obvious that there is something wrong with the argument "Knowledge is power and power corrupts therefore knowledge corrupts."

Here is yet another example: *The end of a thing is its purpose; death is the end of a thing therefore death is the purpose of life*. Here the two meanings of "end" are related, although only loosely. We can see this by noting that things undergo change and many things undergo a process of change that culminates (or "ends") in an intended result, the function of that process being to bring about the result. Accordingly, calling that result its *end* makes sense. But, of course, death is not the end of life in *that* sense of "end"—it is in fact not at all clear that life has an end, or purpose, in that sense.

Another kind of equivocation comes from the misuse of *relative terms*, which have different meanings in different contexts. The word "tall" is a relative term in the sense that a tall man and a tall building are tall relative to different tallness measures. A tall man is a man who is *tall for a man*, whereas a tall building is a building that is *tall for a building*. Forms of argument that are valid for non-relative terms may be invalid for relative terms. Thus, "An elephant is an animal, therefore a grey elephant is a grey animal" is valid, but "An elephant is an animal, therefore a small elephant is a small animal" is invalid. This is because as we use the word "grey" for animals it picks out pretty much the same range of tones (indeed colour terms are typically like this); size terms, however, pick out different ranges of size for different animals since the normal size of an animal depends on what kind of animal it is. Actually, it is not always easy to tell when a term has a relative use (for example, we use the term "red" for a range of natural hair colours that lies completely outside of the usual range of "red"); we have to think about whether we are using the word in the same way across different cases. No one would be taken in by the argument about small elephants as everyone knows that an elephant is not a small animal, but there are relative terms that can be used equivocally without obvious error. Words like "good," "fun," or "hot" (as advertisers use it) are especially easy to misuse because they are used in so many different but contextually relative ways that it is often easy to use them equivocally without noticing that one is doing so.

There is another reason to take equivocation seriously. When we write or speak at any length we are likely to describe the thing we are writing or talking about in slightly different ways. Partly this is due to the fact that we have a reservoir of common knowledge that usually links the various things we say together in a reasonable way, but it is also partly due to lack of care or sloppiness. Suppose you see a man crash into the broad side of another car at a busy intersection and you tell me, "He crashed right into him in the middle of the intersection; people responsible for bad accidents like that should go to jail." Here we have the makings of two premises in a syllogism, but from what has been said, I don't yet know whether the man is responsible for the accident. Maybe the other person ran a red light. If I make a judgment without knowing more information, I have jumped to a conclusion that the information doesn't support. On the other hand, as the speaker you have a conversational obligation to tell me what I need to know to make the right inference, so if you say nothing more I get to *assume* that *no additional information was needed to draw the inference.* And of course I can ask you for more information. But in writing the situation is different. If I am reading an essay you wrote and what you say is potentially ambiguous, I cannot ask you what you meant. You have to be clear enough from the start or I won't know what you meant.

Amphiboly

The fallacy of *amphiboly* is due to *structural ambiguity* in the grammar of a sentence. Structural ambiguity is usually caused by poor grammatical construction. The rules of grammar typically determine a single meaning from a well-formed linguistic string, but the rules of grammar are fairly weak, so they can be overruled by background information. A statement is amphibolous when its meaning is unclear because of the loose or awkward way in which its words are combined, or because insufficient contextual information is supplied to decide on which meaning is intended. Amphiboly is especially common in advertisements and news writing, where it is sometimes even done intentionally in order to produce a kind of joke. Consider the following three sentences:

1. We offer clean and decent dancing, every night except Sunday. (Pub sign)
2. We guarantee to dispense with accuracy. (Druggist's sign)
3. Killer says dead man was chasing him with machete. (Headline)

In these three sentences it is possible to find an unintended meaning as well as the intended meaning because of sloppy sentence construction. The rules of grammar weakly suggest that the unintended meaning is the correct one. Thus in sentence 1, the pub sign suggests that the dancing on Sunday is indecent rather than that there is no dancing, which it obviously actually means. In sentence 2, the druggist's sign can be read to mean either that accuracy is dispensed with (or done without) or that drugs are dispensed accurately; no druggist would advertise lack of accuracy, so clearly the second meaning is the intended one. In sentence 3, there is a conflict between what the rules of grammar require and what we all know—dead men cannot chase people—but this is what the rules of grammar suggest.

These three cases are examples where the rules of grammar and background knowledge suggest different meanings. Sentence 2 is a case where grammar offers two interpretations that, from a grammatical point of view, are equally good, but background knowledge (the knowledge that no druggist would advertise being sloppy) guides us to pick one. The World War Two slogan "Save soap and waste paper" is also of this type. The word "waste" could be a verb with paper as its object, or part of a compound "waste paper" referring to a kind of paper: The interpretation involving wasting paper (treating "waste" as a verb) is ruled out by the seriousness of shortages during a war. Sentences 1 and 3 have a different structure. In these two cases grammar offers you only one interpretation, but background knowledge overrules grammar because the result is absurd. The laundromat sign that says, "Customers are required to remove their clothes when the machine stops," is also of this type; unless it is in a nudist colony, no laundromat would require customers to undress. But in both kinds of cases the sentences can easily be rephrased so that the unintended meaning is explicitly ruled out.

Now consider these sentences:

4. I heard about her at the bar.

5. The children were eating good cake and candy.

6. Mary and Frieda are visiting doctors.

Unlike the first three examples where there is a *conflict* between what grammar requires and what background knowledge does, here the problem is that there is *insufficient* background information available for us to determine the meaning. We need more information even to know how the parts of the sentence fit together properly. Thus in sentence 4, we don't know whether "*at the bar*" refers to the place where the speaker was when the speaker heard about *her* or where *she* was: Was *I* at the bar when I heard about her or did I hear about what she did while *she* was at the bar?

In sentence 5, we don't know whether it was it candy and *good* cake that the children were eating, or whether *both* the cake and candy were good. The explanation for this is quite straightforward. There is a word deletion rule in grammar that one can delete unnecessary words: Sentence 5 can be produced by that rule from

5'. The children were eating good cake and eating good candy,
by first deleting the second instance of "eating" to get

5'a. The children were eating good cake and good candy,
and then by deleting the second instance of "good" to get

5. The children were eating good cake and candy.
But sentence 5 can also be produced by that rule from

5". The children were eating good cake and eating candy,
by deleting the second instance of "eating." Notice that 5' tells us that the candy is good and 5" does not, so the sentence is grammatically ambiguous.

In sentence 6, the sentence tells us either that Mary and Frieda are doctors who are visiting or that they have gone to visit doctors. To know which, we simply need more information about the world (for example, that "Mary and Frieda were not at the party that night. They were visiting doctors.") Merely knowing the meaning of words is not enough; we typically need knowledge of the world (knowledge about what is being talked about) in order to process a sentence grammatically to understand what is said. In fact, the two versions of "Mary and Frieda are visiting doctors" are really two different sentences with different grammatical structures that have the same surface appearance; in one "visiting" is a verbal adjective modifying "doctors" (telling us that they are doctors who are visiting") and in the other "visiting" functions as the main verb in the verb phrase "were visiting" (telling us that in the past moment we are talking about, Mary and Frieda visited doctors and were continuing the visit throughout the time to which we are referring). Figure 3.1 illustrates these different grammatical structures.

Another common kind of structural ambiguity is called *ambiguity of cross-reference*. This occurs when a referring phrase refers back to something mentioned the sentence, but it isn't clear to what. Consider the sentence:

7. Bill became disgusted with Fred at Mary's party, so *he* went home in a funk.

To see that sentence 7 is ambiguous, it is only necessary to see that the statement could be an answer either to the question "Why did Fred leave?" or to the question "Why did Bill leave?" Unless we know who went home, the sentence is ambiguous.

Here is another case of ambiguity of cross-reference, even though here we know what is intended.

8. Launching the ship with impressive ceremony, the admiral's daughter smashed a bottle of champagne over her stern as she slid gracefully down the slipway.

While we know perfectly well what the speaker *intends* to say, the rules of grammar we intuitively apply to the sentence suggest another reading; normally the word "her" in a sentence refers back to the *nearest* linguistically female object (in sentence 8, that would

Figure 3.1

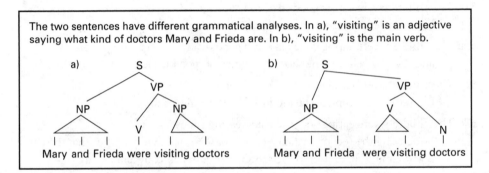

The two sentences have different grammatical analyses. In a), "visiting" is an adjective saying what kind of doctors Mary and Frieda are. In b), "visiting" is the main verb.

be the *admiral's daughter*, not the ship). In this case, there is a mismatch between what the speaker intends to say and what grammar dictates.

Simple arguments that are amphibolous usually fool no one; they are simply funny or confusing. In a context where two people are talking, the speaker can wave her hands, point to things, and fix meaning in various non-linguistic ways; and in any case the hearer can always ask the speaker what she means. But in writing, these opportunities to clarify meaning are not available and so ambiguity in writing is a genuine and continuing danger. Amphiboly is most dangerous to understanding in extended passages of exposition or argument. Five or six sentences taken together may contain so much structural ambiguity that even a sympathetic reader cannot figure out what the writer means. A reader is only rarely in a position to know in advance either what the writer knows or what the writer is intending to convey. This is, unfortunately, a common failing in student essays. It is also difficult for an unskilled author to avoid, because after all, the author does know what the intended meaning is and it may not occur to the author that grammar tells the reader—who is unaware of what the author intends—something different. There is only one sure way to avoid this problem. It is to construct each sentence with care and attention and to make sure that enough background information is provided as context to rule out all possible, or at least all likely, unintended interpretations.

The Fallacy of Accent

In addition to these two kinds of ambiguity, there are several other fallacies that depend on words or phrases shifting their meaning. The first we will look at is the *fallacy of accent*. The fallacy of accent arises when it is unclear where the stress should fall in a statement, or what tone of voice is intended. A speaker's tone of voice often conveys important information about background assumptions the speaker makes and thus against which the meaning of an utterance is to be understood. Since tone of voice cannot be conveyed directly in writing, we need to find other ways to convey what the underlying assumptions are. Consider, for example, the difference accent makes in the following statements:

1. Did *you* steal the butter? (assumption: someone stole the butter)
2. Did you *steal* the butter? (assumption: you acquired it somehow)
3. Did you steal the *butter*? (assumption: you stole something)

In sentence 1, the accent on "*you*" in the question being asked suggests that the speaker believes that *someone* stole the butter and is asking you whether that someone is you. In sentence 2, the speaker presumably believes you have acquired the butter by some means and is asking you whether you stole it as opposed to, say, being given it or having bought it. In sentence 3, it appears that the speaker believes or presumes that you have stolen something and wants to know whether it was butter that you stole (perhaps with the implied expression of astonishment that if you were going to steal something, you could have stolen something valuable, say, a stereo system instead).

These examples reveal some important facts about communication. Remember that a statement is the use of a sentence to make *a claim that can be true or false*. So a statement is a public vehicle for expressing beliefs and making claims. But communication, whether it takes the form of argument or merely conversation, is more than just the making of claims that express beliefs. It is a social process in which persons engage in a give and take of asking or answering questions, or making assertions or responses to assertions. There are two quite different ways in which conversations are more complicated than just claim-making. *First*, people can (and often do) discuss topics and situations that they don't think are actually real; they can discuss imaginary situations or situations that could have been real had some event in the past been different; they can discuss future events which have not and may never come to pass. In short, human beings can think and talk about a vastly larger *range of possibilities* than those that are believed to be actual. They can also disagree deeply about what the actual facts are, and so a conversation may often have the form of asking which of several possible situations the actual one is. Human beings live in a *sea of possibilities* that extend, beyond the actual, partly because they can imagine things being different than they are and partly because, being ignorant of the truth, they must attempt to determine which possibilities are more likely to be true.

The *second* important way in which communication is more complicated than simple claim-making rests on the fact that, to a very large degree, people understand the world by way of stories, narratives, scenarios, and scripts. A story organizes a set of claims, real or hypothetical, into a structure that makes sense in terms of normal human interests and concerns. We live largely in a human-centred world in which our beliefs and indeed the very words we know refer us to ways of living with which we are familiar. Let me give you an example. I tell you that Joe went to Wendy's and had a burger. You have no trouble understanding that Wendy's is the name of a restaurant, that Joe is someone I (perhaps we) know, and that people typically go to restaurants to purchase and eat food. And so given your background knowledge of "what one does at a restaurant," you interpret my statement to tell you that a person named Joe went to a particular restaurant because he was hungry and ordered and ate and paid for a burger. And, of course, you know what a burger is, and so on. If you knew in addition that Joe had a friend named Wendy with whom he sometimes ate, you might be unsure of whether Joe went to Wendy's the restaurant or to his friend Wendy's home to eat. Part of the reason that you make these background assumptions is that human beings are creatures who periodically need food; we live in a culture in which food can be purchased at restaurants; people often go to restaurants; and so on. All this background knowledge gives you the resources to understand the point and significance of a great variety of human stories. If I told you instead that Joe went to Wendy's and had a baby, you would bring different knowledge structures or scripts to bear. "Had a baby" means "*gave birth to* a baby." People do not give birth to babies at restaurants, except by accident in very unusual circumstances. You would take "Joe" to refer to a woman, and so on. As a result of this, the meaning that a sentence has in an argument or conversation is *more finely grained* than the fact or proposition to which it refers. The factual meaning of a statement plays a *certain role in the story* or narrative that is being told.

Because you have a general sense of how narratives unfold, you will know what questions to ask regarding a situation under discussion and how to interpret the answers.

Although these two dimensions of conversation are quite different, in practice we understand the meanings of utterances made in conversation in the same ways. We recognize certain cues as imposing constraints on what sort of information is relevant to the conversation, and we can make these constraints explicit by laying out certain statements as relevant background information or presuppositions of the conversation. If our knowledge of the presuppositions is not adequate to determine what is meant, we ask questions. The questions we ask will themselves presuppose some background assumptions, and the answers we receive will fill out the background assumptions we need to know to see how the person with whom we are talking envisions the situation under discussion. We can put the point simply by saying that facts by themselves are mute and that they only speak or provide information *as answers to questions*. To return to the three sentences we began with, the claim "I stole the butter" provides quite different information depending on which question was asked. In response to question 1, it provides the information that it was *I* who stole the butter; in response to question 2, it provides the information that it was *by theft* that I acquired the butter, and in response to question 3, it says *what it was* that I stole: butter.

The misuse of accent can often deceive, as is the case when someone tells a woman that her husband wasn't out with *Betty* last night (in the attempt to lead her to believe that her husband was out with some other woman), or when a child tells his father that he only ate *some* of the cookies in the package when he ate all but one. A fallacy of accent consists in first mistaking the intended accent of a premise and consequently deriving a conclusion incompatible with the intent of the premise. Fallacies of accent are often used by newspaper writers who deliberately take quotations out of context to distort their meaning or write in large headlines REVOLUTION IN FRANCE and then, in smaller type, " . . . feared by authorities if inflation continues to rise." Movie magazines and supermarket tabloids are common places to find examples of abuse of accent. Here are two examples:

> **Who was Frankie Lasagna seen with at the Gilded Nickel while wife Lona cries at home?** (Facts: Wife Lona asked Frankie to pick up their friend Lola at the Gilded Nickel as Lola's car broke down and she could not otherwise come to dinner at Frankie and Lona's house. Frankie is seen with Lola. Lona is cutting onions while making the dinner and is crying as a result.)
>
> The commandment says, "Thou shalt not covet thy neighbour's wife," so men should only covet wives of those living outside the neighbourhood.

Although the fallacy of accent is connected with distortion, it reveals something important about the way language works. Language comprehension is deeply dependent on background information. The background information is necessary to fill our understanding of the story that is being told. So the facts making up the background story are selected to answer questions appropriate to the story. Our cognitive attitudes are not passive in the face of information. We seek out information that will confirm or disconfirm our hypotheses. To understand what people say, we need to see their sentences as part of structured conversations that presuppose both shared information between speaker and hearer and shared interpretations of that information. Writing is more anonymous than speaking and the author loses control of the context. People who write for a living are very familiar with the need to set a context for the reader and they know that the reader cannot figure out what is being talked about without this help. The lesson for critical thinking is this: When you write about a subject you need to give the reader clear cues about the assumptions you are making.

The Fallacies of Composition and Division

The fallacies of *composition* and *division* are closely related to each other, fallacies of division being the reverse of those of composition. We will look at fallacies of composition first. The term "fallacy of composition" is applied to two related types of invalid argument that involve confusing the meaning of terms so that they are fallacies involving a kind ambiguity. In the *first*, one reasons fallaciously from the *properties* of the **parts of a whole** to the *properties of the whole itself*. For example, from the fact that every part of a machine is light, it does not follow that the machine is light. Of course such a machine will be lighter than a similar one made of heavy parts, but the machine may be composed of a great many parts and so be very heavy. Similarly, from the fact that every sentence in a book is well written it does not follow that the book is well written. Such patterns are not always fallacious; some properties have what is called *compositional heredity*[1]. A property F is *compositionally hereditary* with regard to a whole if and only if when every part of the whole has property F, then the whole does as well.

Thus if *all* the parts of a machine are made of iron then the whole machine is also made of iron. But whether a property has compositional heredity depends on what kind of property it is. The property of being iron is, so to speak, an absolute property of a thing; its attribution to a thing is context independent—if all its parts have that property the whole does as well. By contrast, the property of being heavy is a relative property. When we judge that something is heavy, we take that thing to be heavy for an object of that kind. We saw in the discussion of relative terms that a light elephant (which is light for an elephant) is not light for an animal, as even a very light elephant is heavy compared to a very heavy mouse. The class of comparison for a relative term typically varies from part to whole so a relative term will not generally have compositional heredity. Consider the following fallacious inference regarding a hockey team: "Every player on the team is a superstar and a great player, so the team is a great team." The term "great" is a relative term and so its application is dependent on the context given by the comparison class. Consider the features making a player great (relative to other players) and compare that with the features that make a team great—there is no need to think that if a set of players have great-making characteristics for an individual player they will form a team that has

---

[1] John Woods and Douglas Walton introduce this term, I believe, in *Argument: The Logic of the Fallacies*, McGraw-Hill Ryerson, 1982.

great-making characteristics for a team. A team must, for example, have players whose skills complement and balance those of other players; a team composed entirely of terrific goaltenders will not be a good team.

In the second type of fallacy of composition, one reasons incorrectly from the *properties possessed by the individual* **members** *of a class or collection* to the *properties possessed by the* **class** *or* **collection** *itself*. When we talk about the properties of collections or groups, we do so in two quite different ways, which are not marked by a difference in grammar. There is no grammatical difference between "Dogs are mammals" and "Dogs are variable in size," but the properties of being a mammal and being variable in size are attributed to the class of dogs in quite different ways. In the first case it is true of each and every dog that it is a mammal, but it is not true of each and every dog that it is variable in size, but rather some dogs are large and some dogs are small so there is variation in size between individual dogs. This difference rests in a grammatical difference in the subject terms of the two sentences. In "Dogs are mammals," the subject term "dogs" is functioning as a *general term* referring to the *class of dogs*; it is equivalent to the statement "The class of dogs is a subclass of the class of mammals." In the second sentence, "dogs" is functioning as a singular term referring to *individual dogs*; it is equivalent to the statement "Individual members of the class of dogs differ in size." General terms often look exactly like singular terms. When we say, "The unicorn is a mythical beast," we usually mean to be talking about the class or species of unicorns (of course, since there are no unicorns this class is empty of actual individual unicorns). But consider "The lion has a magnificent mane"; this sentence could be used in one context to make a statement about the class of lions or lion-kind (roughly equivalent to "The class of lions is characterized by the adult male members of the class having a large mane"), and it could also be used in a different context to be a description of a particular lion (roughly equivalent to "This lion has a (particularly) magnificent mane"). When the subject of a sentence is a general term, the predicate of the sentence can apply to it either distributively or collectively.

- The members of a class can, as a class, have properties *distributively* (so that each member of the class has that property—every dog is a mammal), or

- The members of a class can, as a class, have properties *collectively* (so that the class as a whole has that property but not its members—dogs do not individually have the property of being variable in size).

Again, in "Rodents have four feet" we predicate the property of having four feet to rodents distributively (each rodent has four feet), but in "Rodents are widely distributed over the earth" we predicate the property of being widely distributed over the earth to rodents collectively; that is to say, as a class. We certainly do not intend to say that each and every rodent is widely distributed over the earth. This gives us a kind of test for distinguishing the two uses. Can I preserve the truth and sense of the sentence if I replace the general term (applying to the whole class) by a phrase referring to each and every member of that class? For example, in "Cows are mammals" I can say, "Each and every cow is a mammal" and say the same thing so the property of being a mammal is predicated of the class of cows distributively. But in "Cows are found in many countries" I cannot say, "Each and every cow is found in many countries" and say the same thing because the predicate applies to the class of cows collectively only. The fallacies of composition and division involve ambiguity in the way predicates apply to general terms.

Let us consider an example:

Atoms are so small they are invisible
My arm is composed of atoms
∴ my arm (is so small it) is invisible

This foolish argument commits the fallacy of composition. It assumes that a predicate that applies to a subject distributively applies collectively. It is true of the atoms of my arm that each and every atom is so small that it is invisible (the predicate applies to the atoms of my arm distributively but not collectively).

The term *"fallacy of division"* is also applied to two related types of invalid argument that are the reverse of the two above. The first kind consists of reasoning invalidly from the *properties of a* **whole** to the *properties of its parts*. "Exxon is a very important company and Marsha Speed is an official of Exxon, therefore Marsha Speed is very important" is an instance of the fallacy of division. As we saw in the case of composition, relative terms do not in general permit reasoning from properties of the whole to the properties of the parts, but many context independent terms do.

■ A property F is divisionally hereditary with respect to some whole if and only if whenever the whole has property F, then its parts do as well.

(We should note that there are special self-referential properties that are context independent but are not compositionally or divisionally hereditary. For example, every part of some whole X has the property of being a part of X, but X doesn't have this property, and similarly every whole X has the property of being the whole of X and no part of X has that property.)

The second kind of fallacy of division occurs in reasoning from the *properties of a* **class** *or* **collection** *of things* to the *properties the* **members** *of that class or collection*. Reasoning from "This vase is part of a very valuable collection of antiques" to "This vase is very valuable" is an example of that fallacy. Obviously a collection can be made valuable having a few very valuable members together with a large number of members of moderate value. Reasoning from "Dogs are common and Japanese Spaniels are dogs" to "Japanese Spaniels are common" is equally fallacious, as the property of *being common* is true of dogs only as a class, or collectively, and does not imply that every (kind of) dog is common. The old riddle, "Why do white sheep eat more than black sheep?" turns on a fallacy of division. The answer "Because there are more of them" treats collectively what seemed to be referred to distributively in the question. The fallacy of division occurs in assuming (wrongly) that a predicate that applies collectively must also apply distributively. Here is a last example:

The people in this class are half female
Jack is in this class
∴ Jack is half female

Here the predicate "is half female" is predicated of the members of the class collectively, not distributively (it is not true that each and every member of the class is half female!).

The Fallacy of Hypostatization

This fallacy consists of regarding an abstract word or a metaphor as if it were a concrete one. An abstract word designates a general quality, such as *virtue* or *roundness*. While roundness exists only in the particular objects that are round, we can talk about it without reference to the individual objects that possess roundness. The fact that we can talk about general qualities adds greatly to the power of our language and enables us to talk about such things as truth, goodness, and beauty; it also creates potential dangers. We may make the mistake of assuming that because we can refer to general qualities, they name specific individual entities. We may be misled, for example, into thinking that in addition to individual red balls and such, there are also separate entities such as redness and roundness. We are not likely to commit many intellectual errors talking about redness, but many general terms that are easy to misuse get their meaning by a similar kind of abstraction.

Think of the terms "science" and "the state." We are likely to use these terms without any sense of ambiguity or lack of clarity and yet it would be a mistake to think that these terms refer to discrete objects in the world. When we say things like "Science is on the march" or "The state opposes anarchy," it sounds as though we are saying something with determinate truth conditions. But these statements are *metaphors* and have no clear truth conditions. However, we often forget this and thus talk, and think, as though there really are concrete entities like *Science* or *The State* or *Nature* that act and think. Often hypostatization takes the form of personification, as in the case of "Nature favours the survival of the fittest." Here the statement invites us to think that nature is a person or at least person-like (in terms of having mental attitudes and the power to reason and act) and that she guides or directs the process of evolution. Hypostatization is a danger to clear thinking because it blurs the distinction between metaphor and literal truth. Fortunately, the dangers can be circumvented. Ask what cognitive claims are being made by a sentence and whether they are adequately supported by evidence. In short, attempt to replace the metaphorical associations of the claim with literal commitments. When you come to a sentence that resists replacement, like "The state is the march of God through history," avoid it like the plague.

FALLACIES OF CIRCULARITY

WE HAVE JUST SEEN A NUMBER OF WAYS THAT AMBIGUITY IS DESTRUCTIVE OF A FUNDAMENTAL feature that any argument must possess; if it is unclear what the terms in an argument mean, it will fail to have a stable subject matter and will fail to make a claim. Circularity violates another fundamental feature of argument. An argument cannot legitimately assume as a premise what it attempts to show in the conclusion. When one attempts to show or demonstrate the truth of a claim, one is justifying that claim by offering reasons that support it. The fallacies of circularity involve the failure of support by offering as support for the conclusion the conclusion itself. We will look at three kinds of fallacies involving circularity: the fallacies of *begging the question*, *question-begging epithets*, and *complex question*.

The Fallacy of Begging the Question

This fallacy is often called the fallacy of *petitio principii* or simply the fallacy of *circularity*. This fallacy consists of assuming as a premise the very thing one shows in the conclusion. This is fallacious because it is circular. For example,

1. Belief in God is universal because we all believe in God.
2. Joe is the rightful possessor of that bike because he owns it.

   A circular argument is not necessarily unsound. For example,

3. Rome is the capital of Italy, therefore Rome is the capital of Italy.

The argument in example 3, like all circular arguments, is *logically valid* because its conclusion is entailed by its premise (if the premise is true then the conclusion must be true too; after all, it is the same thing!), and it is *sound* because the premise and conclusion are both true (Rome *is* the capital of Italy). The problem is that even though it is valid, it fails to give the person who does not know that Rome is the capital of Italy any *independent reason* for asserting its conclusion. It provides no reason for belief and therefore it ought not to persuade anyone.

Justification is a *dependence relation* of support. The premises in a good argument must provide genuine support for the conclusion, but a circular argument cannot offer support for its conclusion since it offers the hearer nothing beyond what is already in the conclusion in support of it. To avoid fallacy, an argument must be dialectically acceptable. Since every proposition implies itself, what is needed for an argument to be dialectically acceptable is that the conclusion be in some sense *independent of the premises*. Consider, for example, a traditional categorical syllogism that does offer support for its conclusion.

Premise 1	All A are B
Premise 2	All B are C
Conclusion	∴ All A are C

The conclusion is not identical to either premise nor does it follow from either premise alone; it requires the truth of *both* premises for the conclusion to follow. The truth of either premise by itself is independent of the truth of the conclusion, but they jointly necessitate it.

The examples of begging the question given in sentences 1 to 3 above do not deceive anyone because they are easy to see. But in a long argument it is often easy to miss the fact that it is circular; this is especially likely if different versions of the offending statement are used in premise and conclusion. This example is slightly more difficult to spot than those above:

4. Free trade is obviously good for the country. It is quite clear that allowing unrestricted commercial relations will yield great benefits for all sectors of this country's economy due to the free flow of goods between countries.

The only reason that example 4 is more difficult to spot is that each part of the conclusion is replaced by an extended phrase with approximately the same meaning in the premise, thus "free trade" becomes "unrestricted commercial relations" and then "unrestricted commercial relations with other countries," and "great benefits for all sectors of this country's economy" becomes "bestow great benefits on all sections of this country." Here is another example that is only implicitly circular:

5. A: God exists.
B: How do you know?
A: The Bible says so.
B: But how do you know that what the Bible says is true?
A: I know because the Bible is the word of God.

If you add the implicit premise that God *must exist for the Bible to be the word of God* then this argument becomes explicitly circular.

Another common form of the fallacy of begging the question is to use an unfounded (or at least controversial) **generalization** to support a conclusion that would fall under that generalization if that generalization were true.

6. Government ownership of public utilities is dangerous because it is socialistic.

In example 6, if the larger generalization (that socialism is dangerous) were true then it would imply that the conclusion were true. But since it is the larger generalization that is really at issue in the argument and the argument offers no support for the larger generalization, the argument is indirectly circular.

The Fallacy of Question-Begging Epithets

An epithet is a descriptive word or phrase used to characterize something. So this fallacy lies in the use of slanted language, which is question-begging because it implies what we wish to prove but have not yet proved. This fallacy has a number of names: *loaded words, mud slinging, verbal suggestion*, and others. It is easy to spot because of the implicit circularity.

Here are some examples:

1. This criminal has been charged with a terrible crime.

To refer to someone as "a criminal" before they have been convicted begs the question of the person's guilt by implying that they are guilty, so it is circular.

2. You shouldn't listen to this dangerous radical's ideas.

In example 2, the assumption is that the ideas are dangerous to listen to and so the speaker is a dangerous radical, but the only evidence given is that the person is a dangerous radical, which is what is in question.

3. Of course the husband ought to support his wife and family as it is the duty of the breadwinner.

In example 3, by calling the husband "the breadwinner," we impute to him the duty of supporting his wife and family implicitly, but that is in fact what needs to be proved, and it is merely implied rather than shown.. So we can see that in all these cases the fallacy is one of circularity but the circularity is not directly asserted, it is instead implicitly presupposed.

The Fallacy of Complex Question

This fallacy is the interrogative, or question-asking, form of the fallacy of *begging the question*. It begs the question by asking a question that presupposes the truth of the question at issue. It goes by many names, a few of which are *trick question*, *leading question*, and *false question*. The classic version is "Have you stopped beating your dog?" which assumes that you beat your dog, the very thing in question. Others are

1. What is the explanation for mental telepathy?
2. Where did you hide the murder weapon?
3. When should you buy your first Cadillac?

When you are asked, "Have you stopped beating your dog?" there are only two direct answers to the question, "yes" or "no." If you answer yes, you admit to beating your dog, but if you answer no you *also* admit to beating your dog. So whether you answer in the affirmative or the negative you are guilty; this is because the question *presupposes* that you beat your dog. Of course one can answer other things, but other answers in some important sense change the subject. We can see this by thinking in general terms about what we may call *the logic of interrogative inquiry* (or the logic of question and answer).

Interrogative inquiry is a form of structured argumentation that hangs on the asking and answering of questions. A familiar form is legal examination, in which lawyers question a witness. Since the aim of legal examination is to reveal the truth, it is central to this form of inquiry both that the *answers be given truthfully* (witnesses are asked to swear to tell the whole truth and nothing but the truth) and that *the questions are relevant* (questions can be ruled out of order by a judge). Scientific inquiry can be seen as in part constituted by a structured exercise consisting of a series of questions the experimenter puts to nature, which need to be put carefully so that nature's "reply" will lead to the truth. We can think of genuine interrogative inquiry as a kind of game in which it is a rule that questions must be answered truthfully; lying or refusing to answer will be considered a breakdown of the game. Questions are asked one after the other, later questions depending upon the answers to earlier questions, so that the whole process builds a case, revealing the truth about some matter.

As we saw in the fallacy of accent, when one asks a question one presupposes background assumptions both about what is true and what the point of the question is. Even an open-ended question like "What do you know about teen fashion?" presupposes that you can offer an answer, even if that answer is "Nothing" (in which case no further questions could be asked on that topic). Typically a question asks the respondent in effect to choose from a number of alternative *direct* answers. For example, the question "Is it time for dinner yet?" invites the respondent to answer, "Yes, it is time for dinner," or "No, it is not time for dinner (yet)," and the question "Are you still angry with me?" invites the respondent to answer, "Yes, I am (still) angry with you," or "No, I am not (still) angry with you." The alternative direct answers to the first question presuppose that dinner *will be soon* and the alternative direct answers to the second question presuppose that I *was angry* with you. Both the yes and no responses imply that the presupposition is true. We can expand the direct answers to make the presupposition explicit, as in "I *was* angry with you and, yes, I *am still* angry with you," or "I *was* angry with you and, no, I *am not still* angry with you."

Appearing by itself, the question "Are you still angry with me?" is an example of the fallacy complex question, because the only allowable direct answers to it imply that I was angry with you, which may not be true and in any case has not been established. But if the question, "Are you still angry with me?" is only one of a series of questions and follows a prior question, the answer to which has already established that I *was* angry with you, then it is a *legitimate* question that is part of a course of interrogative inquiry. It is not an accident that a complex question is called a "trick question"; the trick is that the question violates the rules of interrogative inquiry.

STUDY SETS 1

Identify these fallacies of ambiguity or circularity and explain briefly what makes them fallacious.

1. Russian threats are no news. So Russian threats are good news, since no news is good news.

2. Our X-ray unit will give you an examination for tuberculosis and other diseases, which you will receive free of charge. (Public service announcement)

3. I am surprised at you. A person of your culture and background defending these hoodlums.

4. The owners of this laundromat should be arrested for indecency. Look at the sign over the washers: "People using washers must remove their clothes when the machines stop."

5. Why isn't a nice girl like you married?

6. The font so generously presented by Mrs. Smith will be placed in the east end of the church. Babies may now be baptized at both ends.

7. Very improbable events happen all the time. Whatever happens all the time is a very probable event. Therefore very improbable events are very probable events.

8. I will not do this act because it is not right. I know it isn't right because my conscience advises me against it, and my conscience tells me so because the act is wrong.

9. The bald eagle is disappearing. This bird is a bald eagle. So it must be disappearing.

10. Since every third child born in New York is a Catholic, Protestant families living there should have no more than two children.

11. The belief in God is universal because everyone believes in God.

12. The Bible tells us to return good for evil. But Fred has never done me any evil, so it will be all right to play a dirty trick or two on him.

13. Our MPs from Saskatchewan must have done a fine job this past year, for in the last session Parliament accomplished a great deal.

14. Richard Hudson is the most successful mayor the town has ever had because he's the best mayor of our history.

15. He who is hungriest eats most, but he who eats least is hungriest; consequently he who eats least eats most.

16. (From *Alice in Wonderland*) 'In that direction,' the Cat said, 'lives a Hatter and in that direction lives a March Hare. . . . They're both mad.' 'But I don't want to go among mad people,' Alice remarked. 'Oh, you can't help that,' said the Cat: 'we're all mad here. I'm mad. You're mad.' 'How do you know I'm mad?' said Alice. 'You must be,' said the Cat, 'or you wouldn't have come here.' (. . . Alice didn't think that proved it at all.)

17. Whenever the state butts into private enterprise, it makes a mess of things.

18. I like chocolate the best since it's my favourite kind of ice cream.

19. Race is the natural basis of the people. As a political people, the natural community becomes conscious of its solidarity and strives to form itself, to develop itself, to defend itself, to realize itself. Nationalism is essentially this striving of a people that has become conscious of itself toward self-direction and self-realization, toward a deepening and renewing of its natural qualities. This consciousness of self, springing from the consciousness of an historical idea, awakens in a people its will to historical formation: The Will to Action.

20. Good steaks are rare these days, so don't order yours well done.

21. Belief in God is universal. After all, everyone believes in God.

22. You should support the God-given right of parents to raise their children according to their own beliefs.

23. Anything obtuse is dull-witted. Some triangles are obtuse, so they are dull-witted.

24. Of course things like bribery are illegal; if such actions were not illegal, then they would not be prohibited by law.

25. All right, Jimmy, fess up! Where did you hide the cookies you stole?

Chapter 4
Inductive Reasoning and Its Fallacies

INTRODUCTION

IN CHAPTER 1 WE SAW THAT DEDUCTIVE ARGUMENTS ARE *VALID* IN VIRTUE OF THEIR FORM OR pattern. The truth or falsity of the premises in an argument that fits the *modus ponens* pattern ("'X' and 'If X then Y,' therefore 'Y'" for example), is not relevant to its validity—you could substitute *any* two sentences for "X" and "Y" and the argument would be valid. Of course, it takes true premises to make the argument *sound*, so a good or cogent deductive argument is one in which the truth of the premises *conclusively verifies* the conclusion; if the premises are true it is impossible for the conclusion to be false. *Inductive arguments*, on the other hand, provide reason to think a conclusion probable or likely, and a *strong* inductive argument is one in which, given the assumption that the premises are true, the truth of the conclusion is very probable or highly likely. Like coffee, inductive arguments come in different strengths, and depending on the context an inductive argument can be a good argument even if it is rather weak. Inductive reasoning is harder to study than deductive reasoning because it is messier, but the vast majority of our ordinary inferences are inductive and most of our knowledge of the world, whether scientific or common sense, is merely probable rather than demonstratively certain.

The fact that most knowledge is merely probable rather than certain is pretty obvious; most of our predictions are based on estimates or fallible signs of things to come; for example, we rely on the weather report knowing well that it may be wrong. It would be a mistake to suppose that the problems associated with inductive reasoning can be dissolved by gathering more information. They are not temporary defects that will remediated by education and more knowledge. Human beings have intellectual limits and live in the present; much of what we care about lies in the future and has not yet, and may not ever, occur. The human condition is permanently a situation of incomplete knowledge in a world full of risks and opportunities. Rather than thinking of the human intellect as a single faculty of reason, it is in many ways more appropriate to see the human mind as made up of a variety of fast, automatic modules for solving particular problems reasonably well. And it makes evolutionary sense to think of these modules as variations on inferential powers that other animals have as well. If your cat comes running whenever you open a can, she has clearly learned to recognize the reoccurrence of the sound of the can opener as a sign of probable food. Even if only one in four cans you open contains cat food, your cat likely thinks that it is worthwhile to check and see what is in the can. Your cat has come to recognize a low probability sign of future food and she adjusts her behaviour to be in the right place at the right time. Many of the inferences we make are of just this sort: They are fast, very fallible intuitive judgments that rely on *typical* features, *probable* signs, and *reasonable* assumptions and allow us to avoid risk and pursue goods. While they are individually more like guesses than knowledge, they cohere with each other—some being ruled out by the joint testimony of others—to give us, overall, a reasonably reliable sense of what is going on around us. The assumptions we make are collectively very powerful. If we decide to go to the store to buy milk or cheese, we make a very large number of assumptions that are reinforced by other assumptions. We assume that the store will have what we want and that the store will sell it to us for a price we can afford. More generally, we assume the existence of money, we know what a store is, the fact that we want milk involves us in beliefs about the existence of cows, that milk is a food, that we need and benefit from food, and so on, and when we buy the milk many of these beliefs are implicitly confirmed. Our "merely probable" beliefs are enmeshed in a network of support relations with other beliefs. The fact that your beliefs are merely probable doesn't mean that you can just believe whatever you like. Try it and see. Pick a statement that you take to be false and try to believe it (that you have a Ferrari or that your parents live in Argentina or that you are eight feet tall), and think of all the consequences the truth of such a statement would have for your actual day-to-day life, which are shown to be false by all the other things you know. Of course you may be able to *imagine* that the statement is true, but you cannot actually believe it at will. Our "merely probable" beliefs are not only enmeshed in a network of support relations with other beliefs; they fit together into patterns of meaningfulness that make them psychologically accessible. Our general knowledge base is not simply a large list of beliefs to which we give assent. Instead our general knowledge is organized into various kinds of patterns that make our beliefs relevant and accessible. Here are some examples: stories, plots, goal-oriented plans, schemas, and scripts, or stereotypical and casually regular situations. These function as organizing structures that package our judgments into useful patterns for our lives—plans and activities we pursue. Think about these patterns: going to a restaurant, playing a game, going on a holiday, getting married, solving a problem. Imagine that you are playing a game of improvisational theatre at a party and you are told to act out "going to a restaurant." Whether you would be good at acting or not you know what to do—after all, you know what to do when you actually do go to a restaurant. It is also useful to reflect on how we understand the behaviours of pets or of small children and how their knowledge is organized, since they show simpler forms of our own patterns.

The point is that we make many kinds of implicit inferences that do not involve definitional truth but rather typical features that "everyone knows" or probable consequences based on function or a likely purpose or goal. Most human stories are plan-based stories; information is organized around *people* in particular *situations* who perform understandable *actions* for *reasons* that are available to anybody. The inferences that depend on these structures may be called *material* inferences, since they depend not on a formal pattern but on an informal pattern, which, while neither universal nor necessary, is useful and productive. It is a general characteristic of material inferences that they can be *defeated* by additional information; they are "defeasible" or fallible. A formally valid pattern of inference is quite different in this regard. A formally valid pattern of inference *cannot be defeated by additional information*. If its premises are true, its conclusion is also true and you cannot change this by adding additional premises; this property is called *monotonicity*.

Material inferences are *non-monotonic*. They are always potentially vulnerable to more information; it rains and so plans for a picnic get changed, you get offered a job and your summer plans shift to accommodate it. The non-monotonicity of material inferences is both a strength and a weakness. The strength is that it permits you to form a conclusion that you can act on with the information you have at hand; it allows you to assume that things are normal and will go as you expect. Here is an example: If I tell you I am going to the store you may conclude (in the absence of further information) that I want to buy something. But if I now tell you that I have promised Fred a ride home and that Fred is at the store, then you would probably no longer conclude that I want to buy something. But if you heard me tell Fred that I would give him a ride because I need to pick up some things at the store anyway, then you can after all conclude that I want to buy something. Of course, if you know that I acquire goods by shoplifting, you will not be able to conclude that I want to buy something . . . and so on. Each additional bit of information can potentially change what you may infer. Deductive inferences are quite unlike this: A cogent deductive inference *cannot* be overturned by the addition of new information. By contrast, the conclusions of material inferences are fallible or *defeasible* (they can be defeated by new information). Here are some examples of different types of ordinary material inferences.

A *motivational* inference is the inference to a "reasonable" motivation for an action you know about. People have motives for their actions and their actions are organized into plans, which are guided by purposes. We understand a person's behaviour by recognizing both what kind of action it is and what kind of motive would explain why the person did it. Since people can have many motives, our inferences are easy to overturn. However, when we speak to each other we tend to give people salient information, that is, relevant information that will make it easy for them to infer what we wish to convey. So if all we

Monotonicity

An inference or argument is *monotonic* if the addition of information cannot overturn an established conclusion. In a non-monotonic argument, additional information can change the reasonableness of the conclusion. A *defeasible* argument is one whose conclusion can be *defeated* by additional information; non-monotonic arguments are defeasible.

are told is that someone performed a stereotypical action (Bill went to the store), we will infer that they were moved by the likely motive (he wanted to buy something). Motivational assumptions are potentially risky. People may have unusual motivations that you don't know about; they may lie to you or attempt to swindle you and so mislead you about their motives. On the other hand, they are unavoidable and we make them constantly because they make other people and their actions intelligible to us.

A *feature* inference is an inference grounded in the knowledge that someone or something has a property that is typical of individuals of a certain kind but is otherwise rare. So it is an inference from a stereotypical property to the bearer of that property. Babies typically wear diapers (but, of course, so do incontinent adults and some invalids). If I tell you that I need diapers for Andy *and I don't tell you anything else*, you assume reasonably that Andy is a baby because diapers are stereotypically used by babies and most diapers that are used are used by babies. Additional information can block the inference; if you know that I have a sick and aged poodle named Andy then you will not infer that Andy is a baby.

A *resultative inference* is an inference to a result or consequence of a typical kind of action or event. If you ask why Fred didn't come to the movie and I tell you Fred hit his head, you will infer that Fred was injured and that his injury *explains* his absence. Obviously, such an inference can be defeated by additional information. Resultative inferences are required in ordinary prediction: I step on the gas because I believe that this will make my car move, for example.

A *functional inference* is an inference grounded in the fact that many objects and events have typical purposes or do recognizable jobs. Hammers are for hammering, chairs are for sitting on, food is for eating, and so on. If I ask for a hammer you justly infer I wish to hammer something, or at least to obtain a hammer for someone who wishes to hammer something.

You will probably be able to think of other stereotypical forms of inferences that are reasonable to make. Here are some examples of the types of inference mentioned above:

motivational	Bill ate a burger . . . he must have been hungry
	Martha got into her car . . . she wanted to drive somewhere
feature	Andy's diapers are wet . . . Andy is a baby (it is a feature of babies that they wear diapers)
	Liam has a child . . . Liam is married (this is less likely than it once was)
resultative	Fred hit his head . . . his head hurts
	Joe gave Mary the book . . . Mary has the book
	Bill ties his shoes . . . his shoes are tied.
functional	Bill got the saw . . . he wanted to cut something
	Stan opened the fridge . . . he wanted some food

Material inferences of this sort are central to language use and successful communication; after all, they are based on patterns we all use and take for granted. Material inferences are a kind of enthymeme, and their pervasiveness leads some logicians to argue that material inferences are fundamental to human reasoning. We saw in the last chapter how understanding ordinary sentences is a function of both weak grammatical rules and background information that can overrule one interpretation in light of something one knows. Because information is always limited, I normally expect you to organize the information you communicate to me so that it is easy for me to understand. Furthermore, you will normally give me the information I need to understand what you are saying, and because you do this, you have a right to expect me to understand your point. The misuse of material inferences, whether deliberately or by accident, is a common cause of fallacious informal reasoning.

Material inferences are *inductive* inferences because they draw defeasible conclusions from limited information, and they are central to both ordinary and scientific reasoning because we are almost always forced to act on limited information. In inductive arguments we are interested in two central features of conclusion: their likelihood or *probability* and their *reliability*. These two features are usually run together, but they sometimes come apart in important ways. Probability concerns the likelihood of an occurrence, whereas reliability concerns causal structure, and we may have useful, inductively fruitful knowledge of either without the other. In this section we will look at approaches to the study of induction by way of probabilities and in the next section by way of models and causal reasoning.

Inductive arguments are typically based on probabilities in this sense: We support an inductive argument by gathering empirical evidence. Gathering evidence often takes the form of collecting data points, counting the frequency of outcomes of differing types, or polling individuals. The evidence acquired is often expressed in a set of numbers that measures objective likelihoods and is processed by statistical methods to generate an outcome expressed as a probability. An inductive argument is *inductively strong* just in case: If the premises are true, the conclusion has a *high* probability of being true, unlike deductive arguments, which conclusively verify their conclusions. Deductive arguments support their conclusions to a greater or lesser degree—the arguments are inductively stronger or weaker—depending on the probability that the conclusion is true given the truth of the premises.

Such arguments are typically aimed at calculating risk factors or giving evidence for causal hypotheses. The statistical methods used in the sciences are powerful and sufficiently counterintuitive that, like differential calculus (the other principal language of empirical investigation), they will be passed over here. Our discussion of probability will be limited to conceptual matters needed to answer the question "What features of a statistical method make arguments inductively strong?" As we will see, inductive reasoning gets its strength from the fact that the relation, probabilistic or causal, of evidence to conclusion can be made explicit and precise.

ENUMERATIVE INDUCTION AND PROBABILITY

THE SIMPLEST FORM OF INDUCTIVE INFERENCE IS CALLED *ENUMERATIVE INDUCTION*. IT ARGUES from a set of premises about members of a group to a generalization about the entire group or generalization. The claim is that information about members of the group supports a generalization about the whole group, or, put another way, that a generalization is confirmed by its positive instances. Almost all our beliefs about the world are about the unobserved. We assume that the unobserved will be largely like the observed, and that our past experiences will give us guidance in the future. Enumerative induction is a simple reflection of that assumption. A brief look at enumerative induction is useful when considering what makes an argument inductively strong. Following is traditional example of enumerative induction.

The swan example:

P1   swan # 1 is white
P2   swan # 2 is white
P3   swan # 3 is white
       . . . . .
Pn   swan # n is white
C   all swans are white

The intuition is that as n gets larger, the truth of the conclusion becomes more likely and thus more reasonable to believe. The irony of this example is that when Australia was colonized by the British, a species of black swan was discovered, and finding a single black swan *conclusively falsified* the universal generalization in the conclusion. Because an inductivist conclusion yields a universal claim (covering all the swans that have ever lived or ever will live), no number of observations of white swans could verify it; however, a single observation of a non-white swan did falsify it. The universality of the conclusion posed another difficulty as well. Since there are an indefinitely large number of swans living at different times and in different environments, no finite set of observations could provide the basis for a particular likelihood of truth. This means one cannot assign any particular support value to any finite set of observations. This tells us something important about the use of induction and its limits.

Karl Popper, an Austrian philosopher of science, argued that science should not pursue an inductivist account of scientific method aimed at showing which theories are true, but instead should concentrate on crucial experiments aimed at falsifying hypotheses. On Popper's account we should only accept (and then only provisionally) theories that survive our best

Sir Karl Popper

Sir Karl Popper (1902–1994), a professor at the London School of Economics, was one of the most influential philosophers of science and social critics of the 20th century. Popper is best known for repudiating the classical inductivist/observational account of scientific method and replacing it with an evolutionary account he called critical rationalism, based on the idea of empirical falsification through crucial experiments.

attempts to refute them. His reasoning was rather simple: Because, in the swan example, the conclusion is a universal statement rather than a claim about a finite number of swans, no particular observation can make the hypothesis measurably more likely, but a single black swan falsifies it completely. So we are better off designing experiments aimed at falsifying a universal law hypothesis that seems plausible to us than designing experiments attempting to confirm it. Rigorously practised, this will leave us with universal hypotheses that survive a harsh environment of attempts to refute them.

But the situation is quite different when we are thinking of a *finite population* of things. To see this, let us compare the swan example with an example of an opaque box partly filled with marbles. Let us suppose that you can reach in and pull marbles out one at a time but you cannot look at the marbles until you take them out. Feeling the marbles, you get some rough sense of how many there are—maybe a hundred, give or take a few. You reach in and pull out a black marble, and then another black marble. You stir the marbles a bit with your hand and pull out another black marble. You stir them some more and reach toward the bottom and out comes another black marble. You wonder, "Are all the marbles black? Are a majority of them black?" You formulate an argument:

The marble example:

P1 marble # 1 is black
P2 marble # 2 is black
P3 marble # 3 is black
        . . . . .
Pn marble # *n* is black
C   all the (approximately 100) marbles are black

Unlike the situation in the swan example, your intuitions have something to work with—in fact, several things. First of all, you know that you *could* take out all of the approximately 100 marbles and if every marble were black your conclusion would not only be strong, it would be *deductively certain*. Secondly, by stirring the marbles and reaching toward the bottom, you have made it more likely that you get a randomly selected *representative* sample. (For example, if the marbles were in layers of different colours, you have increased the chance of getting a marble from a different layer.) And the more marbles you take the greater likelihood there is that your sample is *sufficiently large* to give you representative information. Finally, you have probably made some assumptions about how the marbles got into the box and whether the colours of the marbles should exhibit a regular pattern.

These assumptions may or may not be well supported, but in any case their support will come from other beliefs you have—background beliefs that you bring to the problem. Here is an example. The box you are testing might look just like three other boxes on a shelf that have the labels "100 black marbles," "50 red and 50 black marbles," and "50 red and 50 blue marbles," except that this box has the label torn off. In this case, you have reason to think that probably all the marbles are one colour or that there are two colours half and half, and at least *that there will be a regular proportion of marbles of different colours*.

If you make such an assumption, then you will be testing for the relative probability of a small number of alternative hypotheses given your evidence. This is important because if there were 99 black marbles and only one red one in the box, you could pull out a very large number of marbles before picking the red one—you couldn't easily rule out that hypothesis on inductive grounds alone; after all, if the box is from your grandfather's toy chest in the attic, it might well contain his favourite red agate shooter and 99 black marbles. If you think about this case for a moment you will see that probability of the conclusion of an inductive argument *doesn't depend on* the evidence alone, but upon the alternative possible conclusions that are compatible with the evidence. Part of what made the swan example weak was that we have no difficulty envisioning different breeds of swan that have different colours (since this is so common among other species), and so even testing *all* the swans in England does nothing to rule out a differently coloured kind of swan in Australia.

Suppose we settle on testing for one of two conclusions—C = *All the marbles are black* and C = *Half the marbles are black*—and we assume that there are exactly 100 marbles. Our intuitions about probabilities can now (perhaps with a little training) give us *very exact* conclusions. Suppose we have taken out four marbles randomly selected. If all the marbles in the box are black, the probability that the four will be black is, of course, 1 or 100 percent; if half the marbles in the box are red and half are black, we can calculate exactly what the probability of four black marbles should be. The chance of one black marble is $50/100 = 1/2$ or 50 percent; the chance of a second black marble, given that there are now only 49 black marbles and 50 red ones, is $49/99$. The chance of the first being black and the second being black is accordingly $1/2$ times $49/99 = 49/198$ (or less than $1/4$). (See Box 4.1 for an explanation of how to calculate probability.)

The chance of pulling four representative black marbles in a row, if the marbles are half another colour and half black, is slightly less then 6 percent.[1] Six percent is a very small number, so on the assumption that the box has *either* 100 black marbles or 50 black marbles and 50 of another colour, the argument that it contains only black marbles is *very strong* after even four (representative) draws.

This example has utilized two related probabilistic notions. The first is the notion of *conditional probability*. For two events p and q, the conditional probability of p given q is written $\Pr(p|q)$ and is defined as $\Pr(p|q) = \Pr(p \text{ and } q)/\Pr(q)$, as long as $\Pr(q) \neq 0$. The second is the difference between *probabilistic independence* and *probabilistic dependence*. If I throw a fair die, the chance of any side coming up is $1/6$, because a cube has six sides. So the probability of throwing a two is $1/6$. If I throw the die a second time, the probabilities are the same because the two events are *probabilistically independent*. To determine the probability of two independent events you multiply the probabilities of each, so the odds

---

[1] The number is $1/2$ times $49/98$ times $48/98$ times $47/97 = .0587$; as you take more black marbles the proportion of red to black marbles increases and so the likelihood drops more rapidly than if the draws were independent of each other.

Box 4.1

Probability Theory

According to probability theory, every statement is assigned a number on the interval between 0 and 1 representing the likelihood of its truth as a fraction. Impossible statements have a probability of 0 and necessary statements have a probability of 1; contingent statements have a probability between 0 and 1. The utility of simple probability theory rests on the fact that the likelihood of discrete events depends on the likelihood of other events. Consider a single six-sided die. Once thrown, what is the chance of any of its sides coming up on top? Of course this will depend on whether it is a fair die, on the presence of gravity, the kind of surface it is thrown onto, and the like, but if *normal* conditions are met, then each side is equally likely to come up; there are six sides and one will be on top. On the condition that it is thrown, then the probability that one side or another comes up is 1 and the probability that, say, a 2 is on top is 1/6.

We say "the probability of p is x," written as

$Pr(p) = x$,

and the "the **conditional probability** of q given p is x," written as

$Pr(q/p) = x$.

So if p is "the die is thrown" and is q is "the 2 is on top,"

$Pr(q/p) = 1/6$.

Since for any statement the probability of its negation is 1 minus the probability that it is true, the probability that 2 doesn't come up on the condition that the die is thrown will be 1 minus 1/6 or 5/6, so

$Pr(\neg q/p) = 5/6$.

To calculate the probability of the disjunction of two events, we need to know whether the statements are *mutually exclusive* as they are—for example, in "a 2 or a 5 comes up—or whether they are *not mutually exclusive,* as in "a 2 or an even number comes up."

If p and q are mutually exclusive, then.

$P(p \text{ or } q) = Pr(p)$ plus $Pr(q)$.

But if they are not mutually exclusive, then

$P(p \text{ or } q) = Pr(p)$ plus $Pr(q)$ minus $Pr(p \text{ and } q)$.

Similarly, to calculate the probability of the conjunction of two events, if p and q are mutually exclusive, then

$P(p \text{ and } q) = Pr(p) \times Pr(q)$.

But if they are not mutually exclusive, then

$P(p \text{ and } q) = Pr(p) \times Pr(q)$ minus $Pr(p/q)$.

---

of throwing two successive twos is 1/6 times 1/6, which is 1/36. But suppose I have three nickels and three quarters in my pocket and I pull one out randomly. The chance of a nickel is 3/6 or 50 percent. If I pull a second coin out of my pocket at random the chance of pulling a nickel is 2/5 (since there are two nickels and three quarters in my pocket, which makes five coins) or 40 percent, and the probability of two nickels is thus 1/2 times 2/5 or 20 percent. The probability of the second nickel is dependent on the fact that the first has already been drawn, so the two draws are *not probabilistically independent*. Two events are *probabilistically independent* if the probability of one does not affect the probability of the other (that is, if $Pr(p|q) = Pr(p)$).

Let us review what we have learned in attempting to answer "What features of a statistical method make arguments inductively strong?"

First we say that enumerative induction is not *by itself* a good answer to the question, because it relies on a *vague* intuition about probability, that the mere accumulation of positive instances makes a generalization probable. Furthermore, the intuition depends on the presence of background assumptions that may not be true. As we saw, universal generalizations—which can be refuted by a single negative instance together with an arbitrarily larger number of positive instances—are not made stronger by additional positive instances. And not every hypothesis about even a small population can be made probable by positive instances. Here are two examples that show this.

Example
Bill's Five Siblings

Fred knows the following: Bill has five siblings. He has a brother named Shane. He has a brother named Peter. Fred infers that probably all Bill's siblings are brothers.

You can see immediately that this hypothesis is not made probable by the two observations. This is because the probability of any sibling being male is only 1/2, and given the fact that two are known to be male, the probability that the rest are male is still only 1/8 (that is, $1/2 \times 1/2 \times 1/2$).

Example
High Grades in Intro to Psych 110

Alva knows the following: Sandeep and Carl each got 90 percent in Psych 110, and Fred was in the same class, so probably Fred got 90 percent too.

Once again, given that Psych 110 is an introductory course and is presumably graded fairly, the grades of any one student will be independent of the grades of the other students in the class. (Compare the case where three people eat the casserole at a dinner party and we know that two of them got food poisoning.) The only information that would make it probable that Fred got 90 percent would be either a) information about Fred's ability or b) information about abnormal grading patterns in the class in question. Information about Carl and Sandeep is just not relevant.

We have also seen that before we can treat evidence as relevant to a generalization, we need to know two things about the relation of the evidence to the population. We saw that samples of evidence need to be *representative of the sample*. (This implies that the samples be randomly selected from within whatever constraints on representativeness we already possess.) The number of samples needs to be of *sufficient size* relative to the population being measured and the kind of generalization being investigated. Finally, we saw that non-probabilistic background hypotheses are often necessary. Earlier in the chapter we distinguished two central features of inductive conclusions: their *probability* and their *reliability*, and indicated that reliability concerns causal structure. We will take up the discussion of the non-probabilistic features of inductive argument in the next section. In the natural sciences, these background hypotheses will usually involve hypotheses about causal laws or the interactions of processes known to be regular; in the social sciences, these are likely to involve persistent social attitudes.

Fallacies involving generalizations are very pervasive and require special vigilance. There are a number of reasons for this, some of which we will deal with as we go through the section on individual fallacies. But there are some very general reasons that inductive fallacies are so deeply entrenched. One reason is that human beings often have epistemically inappropriate attractions to certain beliefs: Human beings are social conservatives when it comes to belief and we often believe what others do simply because they do. We want to believe that certain ideas are true and tend to protect them from rational scrutiny by systematic inattention to relevant facts and by isolating them from counter-argument. Prejudice and bigotry function very largely through subtle processes of protection and defence against clear reasoning. We are also likely to believe what our parents and peers do, and not always for very good reasons. So we have various non-rational motives to engage in subtly fallacious forms of reasoning, which prevent us from being clear-minded and critical. We will see numerous examples of critical thinking failures in the sections on fallacies.

There is another reason that the inductive fallacies are pervasive: Human beings have limits on their ability to pay attention and focus. The human reasoning capacity is not a single unified process but a hodgepodge of special-purpose mental powers and mechanisms, each having a natural history and origin that may be quite remote from its present functions. When one focuses on one kind of evidence one is likely to lose sight of other relevant evidential considerations. Being a critical thinker involves harnessing the uses of our separate capacities and minimizing the problems they pose for each other. We have seen that a way to clarify and correct reasoning is to bring implicit processes of reasoning into our awareness by *making them explicit*; by doing this we can ameliorate their deficiencies and perfect them. But we cannot make everything explicit because we cannot give focal attention to everything at once. Most of the basic mechanisms of belief production work, so to speak, on automatic, and unless we have reason to distrust their reliability in a particular case we pay very little attention to them and their presuppositions. I have already suggested that when we regiment our belief-forming processes it allows us to better monitor how well they are working. For example, by becoming skilled at seeing argument patterns like *Modus Ponens*, we become more certain that our reasoning proceeds correctly, leaving us energy and attention for other aspects of our reasoning. Later in this chapter we will see several examples of common reasoning failures that depend largely on blindness to relevant information. But let me give an especially clear example now, generally known as the *conjunction problem*, where our intuitive skills at determining likelihood come into conflict with regimented skills in probabilistic reasoning.

The *conjunction problem* was first presented by Tversky and Kahneman in 1982[2] and is often presented as follows. Subjects were given the following paragraph.

> Linda is 31 years old, single, outspoken, and very bright. She majored in philosophy. As a student, she was deeply concerned with issues of discrimination and social justice, and also participated in anti-nuclear demonstrations.

They were then asked to rank the following statements by their probability, using 1 for the most probable and 8 for the least probable:

a. Linda is a teacher in elementary school.

b. Linda works in a bookstore and takes Yoga classes.

c. Linda is active in the feminist movement.

d. Linda is a psychiatric social worker.

e. Linda is a member of the League of Women Voters.

f. Linda is a bank teller.

g. Linda is an insurance sales person.

h. Linda is a bank teller and is active in the feminist movement.

When a group of ordinary subjects with no background in probability and statistics was given this task, 89 percent judged that statement (h) was more probable than statement (f), despite the obvious fact that one cannot be a *feminist bank teller* without being a *bank teller*. Surprisingly, when the same task was given to a group of graduate students in the decision science program of the Stanford Business School (highly selected students who were well acquainted with statistics), 85 percent made the same judgment! This conclusion is striking because, as I just said, to be both a bank teller and a feminist one must be a bank teller, so the choice that Linda is a bank teller *cannot* be less probable than the choice that she is both a bank teller and a feminist. Results of this sort of error are very robust and have been repeatedly confirmed by other researchers. It is referred to as the *conjunction* problem because subjects attribute higher probability to the truth of a conjunctive sentence of form *p-and-q* than to the sentence *p*, even though it is logically impossible for this to be true.

Subjects conclude that option (h), that Linda is a bank teller who is a feminist, is more likely than option (f), that she is a bank teller, because the biographical sketch they are given fits a *stereotype* of being a feminist more closely than that of being a bank teller. In ordinary situations, when subjects compare the likelihood of two scenarios, they typically use *stereotypical likeness or fit* as a measure. This is a fast and usually reliable intuitive process where one assumes to be likely facts that fit a story or narrative.

---

[2]Tversky, A. and Kahneman, D. (1982) "Judgments of and by representativeness." In D. Kahneman, P. Slovic, & A. Tversky (Eds.), *Judgment under uncertainty: Heuristics and biases.* Cambridge, UK: Cambridge University Press.

Some researchers have seen the conjunction problem as evidence that *people are not good at measuring probabilities*, but this conclusion does not fit the facts; the graduate students at Stanford Business School did badly and they may be presumed to be very good indeed at measuring probabilities. What seems more likely is this: The subjects in the experiment implicitly make the reasonable assumption that the eight choices they are given form a *coherent classification* of the possibilities. You will remember from Chapter 2 that a good classification system will be *exhaustive* and *exclusive* so that every member of the set of alternatives is put into a group and only one group, making the members of the set genuine alternatives to each other. On this reasonable assumption, choice (f) "is a bank teller" is *implicitly* taken to mean "is *just* a bank teller" (that is, is a bank teller who *is not* a feminist). But the eight choices the subjects have been given are *not* genuine alternatives; the researchers have rigged the choices so that they do not form a coherent set of alternatives—the set violates the conditions of being both exclusive and exhaustive. As a result, by implicitly making what is normally a reasonable assumption, that they have been given a genuine set of alternatives, the subjects *don't even notice* that the two alternatives (h) and (f) stand in the relation of *p-and-q* and *p*. They are just *blind* to that feature of the set; it is invisible. They make an entirely reasonable inference and they are wrong!

We can draw *two* lessons from this study. The *first* is that it is very important when one is considering a set of alternatives for comparison that they be genuine alternatives for purposes of comparison. This is why classification is important for critical thinking. One cannot notice everything when thinking about a problem, so one should begin by setting the problem up as clearly as possible. *Secondly*, when one engages in argument with others it is important to be as charitable and clear as possible. In a psychological experiment it may be acceptable to ask a trick question of the subjects to see whether they catch on, but in ordinary decision making where you are trying to find out the truth, to use trick questions would be to commit a fallacy and would simply cause others to reason badly.

STUDY SETS 2

Part A. In a game with a pair of dice, you throw two fours.

1. What is the probability that you throw two fours on your next throw?

2. What is the probability that the two dice have a combined total of eight on your next throw?

3. If you do throw two fours on the next throw, what was the probability that you would throw two successive pairs of fours before you threw any dice?

Part B. There are five books on your desk and you are talking on the phone across the room. You ask your roommate to bring you your psychology text (which is one of the five) from your desk and he picks one of the books at random.

1. What is the probability that the book is your psych text?

2. If he brings you the wrong book and then gets you another (also randomly picked), what is the probability that the second book is your psych text?

3. If the first two weren't your psych text and if he brings you a third, what is the probability that it is your psych text?

4. If in the beginning he had brought you three books, what is the chance that one of them would have been your psych text?

Part C. You have a well-shuffled standard deck of cards (52 cards containing four suits, hearts and diamonds red and spades and clubs black, each with 13 cards: 2–10, three face cards, and an ace).

1. What is the probability of selecting a black king?

2. What is the probability of selecting a red card or a black ace?

3. What is the probability of selecting a spade or any face card?

4. (Without replacing the first card) what is the probability of selecting first a spade and then a red face card?

5. (Without replacing the first card) what is the probability of selecting first the queen of hearts and then another red face card?

6. (Without replacing any cards) what is the probability of selecting first a spade and then a diamond and then another spade?

7. What is the probability of selecting a spade, and after returning it to the deck, selecting another spade?

8. What is the probability of selecting an ace, and after returning it to the deck, selecting a second ace?

Part D. In each of the following questions, estimate whether the conclusion is inductively strong or weak. Is the evidence of sufficient size or representativeness? Is a specific causal hypothesis required to make the conclusion plausible? How could the argument be made more precise?

1. Japanese high school students work harder than Canadian students. They spend more time in school and they have more homework. So they will be better at mathematics than Canadians when they enter university.

2. Japanese high school students work harder than Canadian students. They spend more time in school and they have more homework. So they will be better at Canadian history than Canadians when they enter university.

3. I found a 10-dollar bill on the street yesterday. Likely I will find one on the street tomorrow.

4. In a study of anabolic steroid use among male university students, 27 (about 3 percent) of males reported using steroids. Of these, 13 were competitive athletes at their

schools, 10 were bodybuilders, and 4 reported wanting to improve their personal appearance. We concluded that students in athletic programs were more likely to take steroids than other students.

5. Most Canadians do not speak French; therefore, the leaders of the major political parties are unlikely to speak French.

6. It snowed on Halloween last year in Edmonton, and the year before, and two years before that. It is likely to snow on Halloween in Edmonton this year.

7. Carol Shields's novel *The Stone Diaries* is over 300 pages long, Margaret Atwood's novel *The Edible Woman* is over 300 pages long, and so too are the novels *The Love of a Good Woman* by Alice Munro and *The Underpainter* by Jane Urquhart; probably all novels are over 300 pages long.

8. My friend Bill votes NDP. So does my friend Mary. In fact almost all my friends vote NDP. The NDP are sure to win the next election

9. Carol Shields's novel *The Stone Diaries* is over 300 pages long, Margaret Atwood's novel *The Edible Woman* is over 300 pages long, and so too are the novels *The Love of a Good Woman* by Alice Munro and *The Underpainter* by Jane Urquhart. These are all novels written by Canadian women; probably all novels by Canadian women are over 300 pages long. (Is this conclusion significantly stronger than the conclusion of question 7?)

10. On four different occasions in the last month, dead animals were found in parks in Winnipeg. All were dogs, and all had been suffocated and had their tails cut off. The police think all were committed by one person.

11. (Compare with 10.) On four different occasions in the last month, paper cups were found on the street in Toronto. All were coffee cups, all were labelled "Tim Hortons," and the rims were rolled up. The police think all were committed by one person.

ANALOGY, MODELS, AND CAUSAL REASONING

IN AN ANALOGICAL EXPLANATION ONE ATTEMPTS TO EXPLAIN HOW SOMETHING WORKS, OR what something is like, by comparing it to something else and claiming that it is like that other thing in an explanatorily relevant sense. The aim of the explanation is to *transfer* the understanding we have of the explaining thing (the *explanans*) to an understanding of the thing to be explained (the *explanandum*). Analogy is a powerful tool because it allows us to understand an unfamiliar or difficult thing or set of facts by comparing it to something that is better known or understood. In fact, we can hardly help doing this when we are in an unfamiliar situation; our first step toward orienting ourselves is to try to discover something that *seems* to be similar, in important or relevant ways, to something with which we are already familiar. A productive way to think about analogies is to see them as relying implicitly on explanatory models. If one thing or process is analogous to another in a way that is genuinely explanatorily relevant, then the two share a set of features that constitute an explanatory model of a set of phenomena of which they are both examples. By contrast, a *false* analogy offers such an analogical explanation when the purported similarity is *not relevant* and there is no explanatory model that fits both cases. Analogy is a powerful tool of human reasoning, but it is also easily abused. The fallacy of false analogy is the comparison of two things that are only *superficially similar*, or that even if they are very similar are *not similar in the relevant respect*.

Unlike a deductive argument, which, when it is valid, actually pays its way by *proving* what is at issue, analogies can only offer the promissory note that there is an underlying account that explains what the analogy points to; it offers the mind a model or interpretation that makes something initially strange seem more familiar. Analogies operate on all kinds of levels and do different kinds of intellectual work, but because they always depend on a relevant likeness to have explanatory power, they are theory-dependent and posit some hidden sameness as a conjectural account about how things might be. This is not in itself a bad thing; it merely shows that analogies are incomplete by themselves. Analogies point to explanations that they do not themselves provide. Let me give a couple of examples of famous analogies that pointed ways to different kinds of explanations.

The Water Closet Model of Instinct

Konrad Lorenz, a famous ethologist who received the Nobel Prize in 1973 (together with Karl von Frisch and Nicolass Tinbergen, for discoveries concerning organization and elicitation of individual and social behaviour patterns), posited a psycho-hydraulic model to explain instinctive behaviour in birds. He called this the "water closet (*aka* toilet) model" of instinctual behaviour. The model pointed to two similarities: Once you flush a toilet by pulling the handle, all the rest follows in a rush and then it takes the tank a while to fill again, so that if you flush it again before the tank is full the flushing response is much weaker. It is a *hydraulic* model because it compares instinctual motivation to the liquid in a water closet, whose accumulation and discharge influences behaviour. The time it takes for the tank to refill corresponds to the time between occasions of instinctually driven behaviours. The longer the time since the behaviour was performed the stronger the response will be. This simple model was very fruitful in organizing a wide range of different

Konrad Lorenz

Konrad Lorenz (1903–1989) was an Austrian zoologist and Nobel Prize winner. Regarded as one of the founders of modern ethology, he studied instinctive behaviour, especially imprinting, in birds. Among his many books, *On Aggression* (1963) was especially influential.

behaviours together and was very fruitful in efforts to explain animal motivation. Of course, it is just a model and does not even pretend to offer a physical account of structures that actually exist within an animal's brain. But what was valuable about it was that it offered *an intuitive way of visualizing* how various unknown systems need to work together to organize an animal's response to its internal and external environment. What made the analogy fruitful in organizing research was that the phenomena under study *really do* stand in a set of relations that, in a very simplified way, is something like how a toilet works. So it was a good analogy because it was fruitful and helped animal behaviourists come to understand instinctual behaviour better. But the world might have turned out differently; instinct might have worked differently, in which case the analogy would have been a bad one. So in this case the analogy was a hunch about a structural hypothesis or model that paid off because the world turned out to fit the hunch.

Archimedes and Heiro's Golden Crown

Here is a quite different example. In the first century BCE, Heiro II, the king of Syracuse, commissioned some goldsmiths to make a golden crown in the form of a wreath of laurel leaves as a religious offering, and gave them a weight of gold. Upon receiving the finished crown, Heiro suspected that they might have replaced some of the gold with an equal weight of silver, a lighter and much less valuable metal. Heiro reputedly asked his friend, the famed mathematician Archimedes, to determine whether the wreath was pure gold or had been adulterated with silver. Because the wreath was dedicated to the gods and was thus a holy object, he could not melt it down or harm it. As the story goes, Archimedes went to the baths, and upon entering the water he noticed that the water level rose as his body displaced some of it. In a flash of analogical insight, he saw that the wreath crown would, like his own body, displace liquid and he had a solution: Take a weight of gold equal to the crown and determine how much water was displaced by each when immersed in water. If the crown had been adulterated with silver it would have a greater volume for the same weight and would displace a greater quantity of water; since the relative densities of gold and silver were known, the precise amount of silver (if any) could be accurately

---

Archimedes

Archimedes of Syracuse (c. 287 BCE–c. 212 BCE) was a Greek mathematician, physicist, engineer, inventor, and astronomer. He is generally regarded as the greatest mathematician and scientist of antiquity and was responsible for the foundations of hydrostatics, statics, and the first explanation of the principle of the lever. He designed many machines to defend Syracuse from attack, reputedly including great claws that lifted attacking ships out of the water and systems of mirrors for setting ships on fire. He was killed by a Roman soldier during the sack of Syracuse.

calculated. Famously, Archimedes was excited by this insight and ran naked through the streets to his home crying, "Eureka!" (I have found it!), and the goldsmith who had indeed adulterated the gold had his head cut off. Now the analogy in this case is quite different. The crown was like Archimedes's body not in its shape or size or weight, but in its capacity to *displace a volume of water equal to its volume*, and in this respect the two are *exactly* alike and so behave in *exactly* the same way. While this didn't by itself give Archimedes his solution to the problem—he needed also to know some mathematics and know (or at least know how to calculate) the relative density of gold and silver—once he had entertained the solution, the rest was just measurement. The analogy did not function merely as a potentially fruitful guide to research or a hypothesis that needed to be tested but as an intuition into geometrical relationships.

Torricelli and the Sea of Air

Let me give one more example from the history of science that falls between the two prior examples, both historically and conceptually: Evangelista Torricelli's *analogy of the sea of air*. Evangelista Torricelli lived in the first half of the 17th century and was a student of Galileo. His important work on the motion of fluids and his invention of the mercury barometer initiated a flurry of scientific research into the nature of gases and atmospheric phenomena. Unlike Galileo, who believed that air was weightless, Torricelli conjectured that air, like water, has weight and that we live "immersed at the bottom of a sea of elemental air." This was his sea of air hypothesis and it led directly to a new conception of the nature of gases, and to his invention of the mercury barometer.

Actually, the discovery came about as a result of a practical problem in mining. The miners in the late Middle Ages developed suction pumps to pump water out of mineshafts, but a suction pump will only lift water about nine metres. Galileo attributed this limit to

Torricelli/Galileo

Evangelista Torricelli (1608–1647) was an Italian physicist and mathematician, best known for his invention of the barometer. A student of Galileo, he contributed to the beginnings of atmospheric science and the study of gases.

Galileo Galilei (1564–1642) was the most important physicist, mathematician, and astronomer of his day and played a major role in the scientific revolution. His improvements to the telescope, astronomical observations supporting the hypothesis that the Earth revolves around the sun, and his imprisonment by papal authorities made him a world-famous martyr to the beginnings of modern science. His contributions to the study of uniformly accelerated bodies, discovery of the phases of Venus, and discovery of the four largest satellites of Jupiter (named the Galilean moons in his honour) led to his reputation as the father of modern science.

the cohesive strength of water. But Torricelli was able to show that the limit of nine metres of water in the suction pump was due to atmospheric pressure—the weight of the sea of air above us—which pushed the water up the pipe when air was sucked out of it. By experimenting with heavier liquids, first honey and then mercury, Torricelli showed that the height of the column of liquid in an evacuated tube placed in a bowl of the liquid was proportional to the density of the liquid. By using mercury, which has a density of 13.6, Torricelli could observe the effect of a vacuum in reasonably short tubes sealed at one end. Torricelli could fill a tube about a metre long with mercury, put his finger on the open end, and then invert the tube in an open bowl of mercury. The column of mercury would drop part way down the tube, leaving an empty space at the top. By measuring the height of the column (about 76 cm), Torricelli showed it to be proportional by weight to the nine-metre column of water at its limit in a suction pump. This in effect settled an important scientific debate of the time about the nature of the vacuum: The vacuum does not pull mercury up the tube; instead the weight of air pushing down on the dish of mercury prevents the mercury column in the tube from falling out of the tube.

Later the French mathematician Blaise Pascal, with the help of his brother-in-law Périer, designed an experiment taking a tube of mercury to the top of a local mountain to determine whether the height of the column would drop as one went up the mountain. This is what one would suspect if Torricelli's explanation were correct, since the "sea of air" would be shallower at the top of a mountain, and indeed it was what happened. This experiment confirmed Torricelli's account (and showed at the same time that a barometer and an altimeter are really the same instrument calibrated and used for different purposes). The analogy of the sea of air proposed that gases are like fluids in relevant respects and thus opened up a number of important questions for empirical study. In addition to suggesting an explanation of air pressure and the problem of understanding the vacuum, it also made the analysis of weather amenable to empirical study, treating it as the result of differences in air pressure due to changes in atmospheric temperature. This analogy is unlike the water closet model because it proposes an *actual identity* of explanatorily relevant properties in gases and fluids, whereas Lorenz's analogy proposes nothing about the causal structure of the mechanisms of instinct but merely a certain formal structure. It also differs from the Archimedes example in two important ways. First, it both proposed and required *empirical confirmation* in very precise ways. For all Torricelli and Galileo, and everyone else of the time, knew, the world might have been as Galileo believed—air might have had no weight and the problem of the limits on suction might have been explained by limits of the cohesive force of water. Had that explanation been correct, then the height of columns of different fluids in suction pipes could not have been expected to vary with the density of the fluid, but instead with some other property having to do with cohesive force. As it turned out, Torricelli was right and Galileo was wrong, so the sea of air hypothesis was a *genuine bet with empirical consequences* which further research would confirm or refute. The second way it differed from the Archimedes example was that the analogy is *explicitly* partial. Gases are not literally fluids and Torricelli knew this. In particular, gases are highly compressible and liquids are not, and although Boyle's law was not discovered until

20 years after Torricelli's death (and probably could not have been without Torricelli's work as a backdrop), Torricelli was well-acquainted with the fact that gases expanded when heated and made use of that fact in his study of weather.

Let me summarize some of the properties of good analogies. Firstly, when I attempt to explain or understand one thing by saying that it is like another in certain ways, those ways must be *relevant* ones. To say that they must be relevant is to require of them that those respects give *some insight* into the issue to be explained or understood. Analogies are always partial and that means that there are always dis-analogies. If two things are different, there will be ways in which they are not alike. Relevant dis-analogies undermine relevant analogies, because they suggest that although the two things may be like each other in relevant ways, they are at the same time unlike each other in ways that are also relevant. Analogical reasoning is therefore non-monotonic—additional information can undermine the conclusion one draws—and so analogical reasoning is always provisional. Secondly, in the examples we have seen the analogies were *fruitful*. They suggested that there were explanations to be found in a certain direction of study, which, when found, could stand on their own. Analogical reasoning is therefore like writing a cheque on the bank of empirical explanations: If the explanation is in the bank you can cash the cheque but otherwise it bounces. Analogies are members of a large family of suggestive concepts: metaphor, analogy, hypothesis, model, proposal, and so on. Their utility is partly a function of whether they can be cashed. Of course, I have just used the metaphor of a cheque to explain analogies. I am not suggesting that we can or should always attempt to cash the analogical and metaphorical structures in our thinking by turning ourselves into unrelenting scientists. Life is too complicated and fleeting to make quantifying everything a remotely attractive epistemic policy. But at the same time we want the feelings of explanatory success we experience when we use a good analogy or metaphor to be grounded in some promise of genuineness. We will return to analogies when we discuss the fallacy of false analogy, but let us first turn to a fuller discussion of *empirical confirmation of a model*.

Scientific theories can be seen as precise theoretical models, where certain phenomena—the ones captured by the model—stand in exact mathematical relationships to one another. We saw that Torricelli's sea of air hypothesis had precisely confirmable predictions. Two columns of fluids of different densities will have heights exactly proportional to their densities. By showing that the height of the column of mercury stood in that relation to the height of a column of water—the water was 13.6 times as high—Torricelli effectively settled the issue of what mathematical model (or more properly, what class of models) governed the behaviour of gases. The design of an experiment offering empirical confirmation of a model will of course depend on facts about the model and may be very complicated, but usually the epistemic character is rather simple. The debate between Torricelli and Galileo about the vacuum can be expressed as a bet between two models: Galileo predicted that the height of a column of liquid in the appropriate experimental setup would be a precise function of its cohesive force; Torricelli predicted that it would be a precise function of its density. The known difference in density between water and mercury, 1 to 13.6, led to a corresponding difference in height of column.

MILL'S METHODS

In 1843, British philosopher John Stuart Mill published A System of Logic, in which he proposed a set of five inductive laws for discovering causal relationships between natural phenomena. While all of these methods appear in the work of other philosophers and scientists before him, they are called Mill's methods because he was the first to formulate them explicitly. These methods are, respectively, the method of agreement, the method of difference, the joint method of agreement and difference, the method of residue, and the method of concomitant variation. They rest on the following background assumptions: A causal condition of an effect is *necessary* if it is present in all cases of the effect; a causal condition of an effect is sufficient if its presence guarantees the effect; laws are deterministic in the sense that the same causes produce the same effects.

The Method of Agreement

If two or more instances of the phenomenon under investigation have only one circumstance in common, the circumstance in which alone all the instances agree, is the cause (or effect) of the given phenomenon.[3]

Suppose Ali, Joseph, Kara, and Stephen all get food poisoning after eating at the cafeteria. The student health nurse asks them what they had to eat. Suppose this table represents what they each had:

Person / Food	Salad	Noodles	Pizza	Ice Cream	Food Poisoning
Ali	No	Yes	No	Yes	Yes
Joseph	Yes	Yes	No	Yes	Yes
Kara	No	Yes	Yes	No	Yes
Stephen	Yes	Yes	Yes	No	Yes

---

[3] Mill, John Stuart, A System of Logic, New York: Harper and Brothers C., 1874, p. 280.

The student health nurse applies Mill's method of agreement and infers that eating noodles was the cause of the food poisoning because it is the only common element in what they ate.

The Method of Difference

> If an instance in which the phenomenon under investigation occurs, and an instance in which it does not occur, have every circumstance in common save one, that one occurring only in the former; the circumstance in which alone the two instances differ, is the effect, or the cause, or an indispensable part of the cause, of the phenomenon.[4]

Suppose that the table of foods above had looked like this instead:

Person / Food	Salad	Noodles	Pizza	Ice Cream	Food Poisoning
Ali	Yes	Yes	Yes	Yes	Yes
Joseph	Yes	Yes	Yes	Yes	Yes
Kara	Yes	Yes	Yes	Yes	Yes
Stephen	Yes	No	Yes	Yes	No

In this case, eating noodles is the only difference between what Stephen, who did not get sick, ate and what the others, who did get sick, ate. So the student health nurse applies the method of difference and again infers that eating noodles was the cause of the food poisoning.

The Joint Method of Agreement and Difference

> If two or more instances in which the phenomenon occurs have only one circumstance in common, while two or more instances in which it does not occur have nothing in common save the absence of that circumstance: the circumstance in which alone the two sets of instances differ, is the effect, or cause, or a necessary part of the cause, of the phenomenon.[5]

We can use the same example again to illustrate this method, which combines the first two:

Person / Food	Salad	Noodles	Pizza	Ice Cream	Food Poisoning
Ali	No	Yes	Yes	Yes	Yes
Joseph	Yes	Yes	No	Yes	Yes
Kara	Yes	No	Yes	Yes	Yes
Stephen	Yes	No	Yes	No	No

---

[4] Ibid
[5] Ibid, page 284.

Although Ali, Joseph, and Kara, who all got sick, ate different things, the only thing they all ate was ice cream. Stephen, who did not get sick, did not eat ice cream. This time the student health nurse infers that ice cream was the cause of the food poisoning.

The Method of Residue

> Deduct from any phenomenon such part as is known by previous inductions to be the effect of certain antecedents, and the residue of the phenomenon is the effect of the remaining antecedents.[6]

What this comes to is that if we identify a range of factors as the probable causes of a range of phenomena, and we have identified all the factors except one as the causes of all the phenomena, except one, then the remaining phenomenon may be attributed to the remaining factor.

Here is an example:

I want to measure the weight of the potatoes I have just dug. I pick up the pail of potatoes and step on the scale—it reads 88 kilos. I know that I weigh 76 kilos and that the pail weighs one kilo. The potatoes are responsible for the residual weight, which is 11 kilos, so the potatoes weigh 11 kilos.

The Method of Concomitant Variation

> Whatever phenomenon varies in any manner whenever another phenomenon varies in some particular manner, is either a cause or an effect of that phenomenon, or is connected with it through some fact of causation.[7]

The method of concomitant variation rests on the reasonable supposition that when effects can vary in intensity, that variation is typically proportional to a variation in their causes. If we think back to the example of the method of agreement, where the student health nurse infers that Ali, Joseph, Kara, and Stephen—who all get food poisoning after eating at the cafeteria—were poisoned by noodles, we can imagine that Ali ate two helpings of noodles and got very sick whereas Joseph and Kara had one helping and got moderately sick, while Stephen didn't like the noodles and barely ate any and hardly got sick at all. In such a case, the nurse has a second reason to infer that the culprit was the noodles, as the severity of the symptoms is proportional to the amount of noodles eaten. Another example would be that while driving you notice a ticking sound that varies with the speed of the car. Since the speed of the car varies both with the pressure on the accelerator and the speed of rotation of the tires, there are several possibilities to check. If you speed up and then cut the engine, you eliminate the engine from the list of locations to check—if the ticking continues and slows as the car slows down, then the problem will likely be in the axle or the tire.

---

[6] Ibid, page 285.
[7] Ibid, p. 287.

All of Mill's methods provide procedures for eliminating irrelevant candidates and narrowing in on what remains. As Sherlock Homes famously says to Watson, in his brilliant story on the science of deduction, "The Sign of the Four," "How often have I said to you that when you have eliminated the impossible, whatever remains, however improbable, must be the truth?"[8] The trick, of course, is to eliminate the impossible, so Mill's methods have important limitations. The methods are guaranteed to succeed only if very relevant antecedent circumstances are taken into account, and that is impossible to guarantee in advance. As inductive procedures, they are non-monotonic, and the addition of new information can always throw their results into uncertainty. On the other hand, used together they form part of a tool box of procedures for good experimental design. Each of Mill's methods assumes that we are already part of the way to a causal explanation. First, they assume that we have already identified a number of possibilities and have tentative hypotheses about which possibilities represent possible causes. If we have already developed several specific hypotheses about what may be the cause of an observed event, then using the methods will be helpful, since we may be able to eliminate some or all of the possible causes we have identified. Second, they depend on a central relationship between causes and true beliefs: Causes are *truth makers*. What makes your belief that putting your finger in the fire will cause you to burn your finger true is that putting your finger in the fire will cause you to burn your finger. You can harness this fact by designing an experimental situation in which all the other reasonable possibilities for causing your finger to burn are eliminated, and then you put your finger in the fire. You adopt low intensity versions of this method every time you look at your watch to see what time it is: You look at your watch and see that the watch says 10:45 a.m. and you are caused to believe that it is 10:45. This is an application of the method of concomitant variation: Watches are designed to co-vary with the time; when they work properly, as they usually do, you can use them to tell the time. In fact, just about any measuring instrument is like this. We have designed it to co-vary with something we care about so that we can use the instrument to have true beliefs about that thing. Empirical beliefs, especially those precise, well-designed ones we know as scientific theories, embody commitments or gambles that the world is a certain way and not another. A well-designed experimental confirmation is a structure that will cause you to have the relevant belief if it turns out to be true and only if it turns out to be true. It will do that by ruling out as impossible all the outcomes except the desired one *if the hypothesis is true*. In doing so it will rely on the truth of many other claims that function as background. Not every empirical proposition can be experimentally confirmed—there just are truths that cannot be known by human beings. Here is an example: The number of stars in the galaxy is exactly divisible by three. Surely that statement is either true or false and its truth (if it is true) depends on whether the number of stars in the galaxy *is* exactly divisible by three. But no one could design an experiment that could confirm that fact.

---

[8] Doyle, Arthur Conan, "The Sign of the Four," (Chapter 6, "Sherlock Holmes Gives a Demonstration"), p. 111, *The Penguin Complete Sherlock Holmes*, 1981.

STUDY SETS 3

Part A. For each of the descriptions below, pick which of Mill's methods (1. The method of agreement; 2. The method of difference; 3. Joint method of agreement and difference; 4. The method of residue; or 5. The method of concomitant variation) applies best.

1. Bill ate beans, rice, corn, and cantaloupe; Mary ate beans, rice, corn and cantaloupe; Phil ate beans, corn, and cantaloupe; Tom ate beans, rice, corn, and cantaloupe. Everyone got sick except Phil.

2. Bill ate beans, rice, and cantaloupe; Mary ate beans, rice, corn, and ham; Phil ate beans, corn, cantaloupe, and cheese; Tom ate rice, cantaloupe, and cherries. Everyone got sick except Phil.

3. As the day got sunnier and warmer, at a certain point the radio conked out; as the darkness and cool of evening came it came back on. Turning on the lights didn't affect the radio, but when Mary baked a pie in the evening the house warmed and the radio conked out again. It must be a temperature problem.

4. Sandy drank a beer, ate two pickles, and had chips and ice cream. Kieran ate three pickles, ate chips, and drank a beer. Howard drank a beer and ate chips and ice cream. Lois drank a beer, ate two pickles, and had ice cream. Kieran got really sick, Lois and Sandy felt queasy and ill, and Howard was fine.

5. Mary had an annoying rash. She thought it might be the sun, so she covered up outside, but the rash persisted. She had started drinking a lot of beer before the rash appeared, had moved into a new apartment, and had started taking new multi-vitamins. She spent a week at her parents', she spent a week not drinking beer, and she spent a week not taking the new vitamins. Each time she kept her other activities the same. The rash went away when she stopped taking the new vitamins. She switched back to her old brand and the rash did not recur.

6. Part of the damage in the accident was due to hitting the tree. Another part was clearly caused by the car rolling over before it hit the tree. But some of the damage seems to have been caused by something else. Perhaps we should look for evidence of a bomb.

7. After Fred started smoking marijuana, his life became more fun, so he started smoking more. After a while he started getting depressed, so he quit. He started drinking beer instead and his life became fun again, so he started drinking more and after a while he started getting depressed, so he quit. Then a friend gave him some meth and he took some and started to have fun, so he started to take more. He was beginning to get depressed when he concluded that the problem wasn't what he took but how much. So he quit meth and went back to (moderate use of) marijuana, because it was the cheapest.

8. Many of the kids at St. Albert school would smoke marijuana outside the school. School authorities correlated observed smoking and absenteeism, and discovered that

when Bill Dodd or Ricky Jalapeia missed school for more than a day or two the number of kids smoking marijuana would decline.

9. A B C occur together with x y z, B is known to be the cause of y, C is known to be the cause of z, so likely A is the cause of x.

INDUCTIVE FALLACIES

WE WILL NOW LOOK AT THE INDUCTIVE FALLACIES INVOLVING GENERALIZATION, ANALOGY, and causation. First we will look at three inductive fallacies involving generalizations in which we overlook significant facts or relevant features of a problem entirely. In *sweeping generalization*, the fallacy involves assuming that what is true or likely under certain conditions is universally true or likely. In the fallacy of *hasty generalization*, the problem lies in assuming that the evidence on which the argument is based is sufficient to warrant the conclusion, when the evidence is in fact either unrepresentative or insufficient. And in the *fallacy of bifurcation*, one incorrectly assumes that the alternatives presented exhaust the field, when in fact other alternatives exist.

Sweeping Generalization

The fallacy of *sweeping generalization* is sometimes called the *fallacy of accident*. It is committed when an argument that depends on the application of a generalization or rule to a particular case is improper because a *special circumstance (accident)* makes the rule inapplicable to that particular case. As we have seen, a generalization is a statement made about a property of all or most members of a class. Some generalizations are grounded in or explained by natural processes governed by causal laws of nature, and other generalizations are probabilistic or dependent on local features of a subclass. There are typically exceptions even to strong generalizations, which makes reasoning using generalizations non-monotonic. As a result, adding more information frequently cancels the force of a generalization. Laws and rules, like generalizations, have boundary conditions beyond which the rule does not apply.

For example, expressions of legal or natural rights, while usually stated universally, contain *implicit* limits and exceptions that constrain their application to specific cases. The right of free speech and its public expression is not a warrant to yell, "Fire!" in a crowded theatre. In general, when we express general rules or universal laws, we do not state the boundary conditions of these rules or universal laws. Partly, this is because to do so would be cumbersome and lengthy. But it is also often due to the fact that while we all agree on the general characteristics of the concept, we may disagree about where to draw boundaries or else we are not exactly sure ourselves where the boundaries lie. So to state the boundary conditions would itself be controversial and potentially arbitrary. Consider the right of freedom of speech. Most people in Canada would agree that this right guarantees freedom of religious and political beliefs (at least under ordinary conditions) but that it does not guarantee the freedom to yell, "Fire!" in a crowded theatre. But there is a considerable social disagreement about whether a person has the right to advocate overthrowing the government, or to use obscenities in public. So although we might all agree that everyone has the right of freedom of speech (and all agree that certain things are not covered by the right), there may be no generally agreed upon way to state all the boundary conditions governing that right. Even very widely held generalizations and principles may be vague because there is no general agreement on how to draw the boundary conditions of the concepts involved.

Let us look at some examples of sweeping generalization.

1. Everyone has a right to advance his or her ideas, so judges and other public officials have a right to use their official positions to further their religious views.

   The generalization that everyone has a right to advance his or her ideas cannot be applied to public officials because it is a condition of their holding legitimate office that they refrain from using that office as a platform for their own views. So the fact that you are talking about judges and public officials creates a special circumstance or "accident" that blocks the inference.

2. Everyone has a right to own property, so even though Mary is a violent psychopath we have no right to take away her weapon collection.

   Here the fact that Mary is a violent psychopath blocks the application of the general right to own property to the case of protecting her weapons collection from seizure. Of course, it does not follow from this that we *do* have the right to seize her weapons collection. However, given the special circumstances, a separate argument needs to be given in either direction.

3. Since cross-country skiing is healthful exercise, Mr. Fatbody ought to do more of it because it will help his heart condition.

   What is healthy and safe for someone in normal health is not necessarily healthy or safe for someone with special health problems. We see from these examples that what makes sweeping generalization a fallacy is not that the blocked conclusions are *false* but rather that you cannot correctly draw the inference on the information you have. It might be that cross-country skiing would be good for Mr. Fatbody and even *because* of his heart condition. Still, the argument in example 3 is a fallacy because one cannot infer that what is generally healthful will be healthful for a person with a heart condition. When we make a generalization we often have some information that allows us to make a reasonable inference given that information, but additional information can block that inference. You hear that Pedro is from Mexico, and you might wonder whether he speaks English. When you hear that he is a professor of English literature at the University of Guelph, your prior wonder is no longer reasonable. Or your neighbours ask if you can to look after their child for a while and you agree; had you known that they intended a six-month holiday in France you would have had reason to rethink your agreement.

Hasty Generalization

Hasty generalization is the converse of sweeping generalization. It has a number of other names, including *the converse fallacy of accident, overgeneralization,* and *secundum quid* (which in Latin means "in a certain respect"—to indicate that what is true in a certain respect need not be true in all relevant respects). It occurs in arguing incorrectly from a *special case* or from limited information to a general rule. Often the reason we overgeneralize is that we draw a conclusion from an evidential sample that is either too small or biased and therefore is not representative of the target population.

One common form of hasty generalization occurs when the issue in question is complex and there are arguments on both sides. Although it is fallacious to do so, people often select only the arguments that are favourable to their own opinions and present them as though they were all that there was to say on the matter. Of course, if one's objective is only to convince another person, this strategy may be effective. But as a piece of reasoning that establishes the truth (or even the probable truth) of a conclusion, the method is fallacious.

Here are some examples of hasty generalization:

1. Large-scale polls were taken in Florida, California, and Maine and it was found that an average of 55 percent of those polled spent at least 14 days a year near the ocean. So we can conclude that 55 percent of all Americans spend at least 14 days near the ocean each year.

   Since the states of California, Florida, and Maine are all coastal states and most states are not, they do not represent an unbiased sample of "all Americans" with respect to spending time near the ocean. As a result, they represent a special case of Americans from which the conclusion cannot be legitimately drawn.

2. Mary Olsen crashed her car and because she had her seat belt on she couldn't get out quickly and was badly burned, so wearing seat belts is more dangerous than going without.

   Some accidents are made worse by wearing seat belts, but they are rare and unusual in comparison to the class of cases where seat belts make accidents less harmful. So they are "special" cases (in fact, they are *exceptions* to the general rule) and cannot support the generalization that wearing seat belts is more dangerous than going without.

3. During the war, enemy espionage rings were exposed by tapping the telephone wires of suspects. So the authorities should tap the phones of all suspicious persons.

   This is hasty generalization because wartime is a special circumstance, regarding which it is widely (although not universally) agreed that some peacetime rights can be temporarily ignored. Whatever one's view on the conclusion, this fact blocks the generalization made in the argument.

Students sometimes confuse the fallacies of *hasty generalization* and *sweeping generalization* respectively with the fallacies of *composition* and *division.* They look something alike, but they are actually quite different in their logical structure. *Hasty generalization* improperly generalizes from an unusual specific case, whereas *composition* involves an inference from the possession of a feature by every member of a class (or part of a greater whole) to the possession of that feature by the entire class (or whole). So the difference is between "this X is Y therefore all Xs are Y" and "every X in G is Y therefore G is Y." For the fallacy of composition, the central fact is that even when something can be truly said of each and every individual member, it does not follow that the same can be truly said of the whole class. Similarly, *division* involves an inference from the possession of some feature by an entire class (or whole) to the possession of that feature by each of its individual members (or parts), and this differs from *sweeping generalization*, which mistakenly applies a general rule to an atypical specific case. Here are examples of the difference:

Division	Sweeping Generalization
The elderly have many health problems	Poodles are popular dogs
Martha is old	Ditzy is a poodle who bites people
∴ Martha has many health problems	∴ Ditzy is a popular dog

"The elderly have many health problems" does not mean that each and every elderly person has many health problems, but rather that different elderly people may have different health problems. Martha may have no health problems at all. And even though poodles are generally popular dogs, it does not follow that members of the subclass of poodles *who bite people* are popular.

Composition	Hasty Generalization
Every player on the team is excellent	Lisa, the star centre, is excellent
∴ The team is excellent	∴ The team is excellent

The composition example is fallacious because all the players could individually be excellent but as a group could lack the mix of skills required for an excellent team. The hasty generalization example is fallacious because the fact that Lisa is a "star centre" is a special circumstance that blocks any inference regarding the other players.

The Fallacy of Bifurcation

Sometimes called the *either–or* fallacy, this is the fallacy of treating a distinction or classification as exclusive and exhaustive of the possibilities, when in fact other alternatives exist. This fallacy confuses **contraries** with **contradictories**. Two statements are contradictories just in case the first is false when the second is true and the second is false when the first is true. With two contradictory statements, one is always true and the other false.

Either a man is alive or he is dead; either today is your birthday or it isn't. Because the contradiction of a sentence is true if that sentence is false and false if that sentence is true, we can construct the contradictory of any sentence by adding "it is not the case that" or "it is false that" to the original sentence. Sentences are contraries just in case they cannot both be true. Pairs of contraries can both be false. For example, "today is Wednesday" and "today is Thursday" are contraries because, while they cannot both be true, they can both be false, whereas "today is Wednesday" and "today is not Wednesday" are contradictories.

Because our language is full of opposites, we have a strong tendency to bifurcate and argue *either (the first) . . . or (the second)*. But many situations do not present us with opposites like this. Consider today is your birthday or tomorrow is your birthday. These are not contradictories; they are merely contraries. Since there are 365 days in the year, there are 365 statements of the form "day __ is your birthday"; *all* of them are contraries. Typically then, the fallacy of bifurcation treats a pair of contraries as though they were contradictories.

In fact, most opposites are not genuine contradictories but simply *contrast classifications*. Take "weak" and "strong," for example. Quite apart from the fact that there are different respects in which things can be weak or strong, it is quite possible for something to be neither weak nor strong in whatever respect one considers. Weak and strong represent boundary cases between which there is a normal range. Thus one cup of coffee could be weak, another normal, and a third strong. For example,

1. If you know BMWs—either you own one or you want one.

   Obviously there are other possibilities. (For example, you don't own one and you don't want one).

2. If we were going to buy a car, we would have to buy either a good one or a cheap one. We cannot afford a good one and we don't want a cheap one, so we will just have to do without a car.

   Again, "cheap" and "good" are not contradictories so the argument is fallacious. Sometimes the fallacy of bifurcation makes two terms *appear* to be contradictory when they are not even contraries.

3. We must choose between safety and freedom. And it is in the nature of all good citizens to take the risk of freedom.

   Since safety and freedom are neither contraries nor contradictories, this inference is fallacious.

A good place to look for the fallacy of bifurcation is the editorial page of a newspaper. Letters to the editor are also frequently fallacious in this way. American president Ronald Reagan was famous for making fallacies of this kind, and you may remember President Bush's famous November 2001 claim that "Over time it's going to be important for nations to know they will be held accountable for inactivity. *You're either with us or against us in the fight against terror.*"

The fallacy of bifurcation is easy to identify because an assertion is made that there are only two possibilities when there are three or more (or at least the arguer hasn't provided a *reason* to think otherwise). Student papers often suffer from the fallacy of bifurcation. Often a paper will have the argument form that either A or B and since A is false B must be true. If A and B are only contraries and there are other possibilities (C, D, etc.), the effect is that the paper as a whole fails, even though the individual arguments may be acceptable.

False Analogy

Let us now turn to the topic of *false analogy* and look at some bad analogies to see why they are fallacious.

One way analogies go bad is that they drastically *oversimplify* a complex process by comparing it to something simple. Look for cases of false analogy in the speeches of politicians and cranky letters to the editor. President Reagan, for example, was especially fond of comparing complex international events to homely events that the ordinary person could "figure out" using common sense. The first key to identifying cases of false analogy is to notice when an explanation makes *use of a comparison with something else*. All that is needed is to examine the comparison to see whether the explanation is based on a relevant likeness. Here are a few examples:

1. We must make other people accept the true religion—by force, if necessary—just as it is our duty to prevent a delirious person from leaping off a cliff by any means necessary.

   Here another's disbelief in the religious views of the speaker is inappropriately compared to insanity. The comparison is between delirious people and people who are ordinary except that they do not accept the speaker's version of true religion. Even on the assumption that it is justifiable to use force against the will of a delirious person to save his or her life, this gives no reason to think that one is *ever* justified in using force against the will of an ordinary person, and if it were a case of converting him or her to the true faith. In a religiously dominated society in which people are not allowed to differ in their religious views, this argument might have some superficial plausibility; in a pluralistic society in which there is no unanimity about what the "true" religion is, the argument seems utterly implausible.

2. We should not sentimentalize about the destruction of the culture of Native Americans that occurred when our great civilization was being built. It was unfortunate, of course, but you can't make an omelette without breaking a few eggs.

   This analogy is just *so* simplistic that it couldn't be relevant; there are no relevant comparison classes at all. We may notice, however, that this argument contains a double standard between our great civilization (the delicious omelette) and Native culture (the eggs that need to be broken to make the omelette). False analogy is the friend of bigotry and special privilege.

3. What is taught at university should depend entirely on what students are interested in. After all, they are consumers of knowledge; the teacher is the seller and the student the buyer. No one knows better than the consumer what he or she wishes to consume. The idea that the seller should determine what he or she buys is ridiculous.

Here students are compared to consumers, and there are actually two levels of difficulty. First is the question of whether the situations of students and consumers generally are relevantly similar, and second is the question of whether consumers are accurately portrayed. In response to the first question, one might point out that while a consumer knows what goods he or she is purchasing beforehand, the student does not know the subject before learning it. This suggests at least one relevant difference. In response to the second question, one must ask whether what the consumer buys depends entirely on what the consumer is interested in. When you think about it, it begins to look as though the consumer has to buy more or less what is available, or at least that there are important constraints operating in the background that limit what that consumer can buy. In addition, there are enormous pressures acting on consumers telling them what they want—pressures that are largely absent in university. In fact, when you think about it, the first comment that consumers know what goods they are purchasing beforehand is not completely true. You buy a television set or a computer for the first time and only after you take it home do you really begin to understand the effects your purchase has on your life. It begins to look instead as though consumers are rather more like students than students are like consumers.

Here is another simple false analogy:

4. Why should mine workers complain about working 10 hours a day? Professional people often work as long without any apparent harm.

Here the analogy attempts to make a claim about *fairness*. The two crucial considerations are the difference in the danger and physical difficulty of the two kinds of work and the difference in the rates of pay for the two kinds of work. It is not appropriate to compare physically exhausting, dangerous work for low pay to well-paid, prestigious, physically easy work, at least not without an argument. As one looks at claims like this one begins to see that there are many different considerations that are relevant to the judgment of what is fair and what is not. The claim in 4 looks more like a way of shutting down thinking about fairness rather than furthering it. We saw that good analogies should be fruitful—they should open up our understanding to better and more complete explanations. The bad analogies we have just looked at seem to function most successfully in negative gossip and pseudo-explanations that entrench the speaker in positions by isolating them from scrutiny. Prejudice and bigotry thrive on a rich diet of fallacies that work together to buttress and fortify bad opinions from challenge, and the best diet for prejudice is a wide variety of fallacies, each of which supplies a different form of defence.

False Cause

The fallacy of *false cause* is actually a family of related fallacies that occur when an arguer gives *insufficient evidence* for a claim that one thing is the cause of another. In causal reasoning, one event or event-kind is cited as an *explanation* for the *occurrence* of another event or event-kind. Causes do not occur in isolation: Every event that occurs depends on a set of conditions being satisfied, and a person requesting a causal explanation typically knows some of these conditions and not others. As a result, an appropriate answer will depend on the set of interests and background information that sets the question. Here are four kinds common of false cause.

A. Post hoc ergo propter hoc (Latin for "after this therefore because of this") This fallacy occurs when we assume, without adequate reason, that one event B was caused by another event A because B happened *after* A. Here is an example:

1. "I took echinacea for my cold and a few days later my cold was gone."

   Since colds typically clear up in a couple of days anyway, identifying taking echinacea as the reason it cleared up is fallacious. Maybe it would have cleared up faster without it? A single instance is a usually risky basis for making a causal generalization. Compare the statement above with:

2. "I have a cold because I used Bill's handkerchief to wipe my nose and Bill had a cold."

   It is reasonable to think that I may have caught my cold by using Bill's handkerchief because cold viruses can be transmitted through nasal membranes. In this case the event is *not* cited as a reason to believe that colds are transmitted through contact with the virus with the nasal membrane, but rather *given the implicit* assumption that the causal generalization is true, the event of my cold is explained as an instance of it. Good causal explanations always refer at least implicitly to causal laws or structures, and this can be made *explicit* by expanding the explanation to contain the law or structure supporting it:

2'. "I have a cold because I used Bill's handkerchief to wipe my nose, cold viruses can be transmitted through nasal membranes, and Bill had a cold."

B. Mere correlation Here we assume that B was caused by A *merely* because of a *positive correlation* between A and B. Here are some examples:

3. Variations in the death rate in Hyderabad, India, between 1911 and 1916 match the variations in the membership of the International Association of Machinists in the United States during the same period almost perfectly.

   This is a case of *mere* correlation: It would be a mistake to infer from the correlation that either was the cause of the other. There are two reasons for this. First, no reasonable causal mechanism can be assumed since the events are spatially unconnected and no causal laws have been proposed, and second, an enormously large number of population-related processes occurred between 1911 and 1916 (the number of left-handed people born in Mongolia, the number of widows of cowboys killed in Argentina, the number of children born in Montreal to bilingual parents, and so on endlessly). If one looked hard enough, one could find many near-perfect correlations that are completely accidental, so it is reasonable given the first point to think that this is one of them.

4. As the allowances of teenagers continue to rise, juvenile delinquency has gone up as well. Obviously to reduce delinquency we must reduce teenagers' allowances.

> The positive correlation identified in this example is not indicative of a causal mechanism; there are no doubt many factors that have changed involving teenagers in some way or another and absolutely no reason has been suggested to think that the factor mentioned is a causally relevant one.

C. Reversing cause and effect Here we conclude that A causes B when B causes A, so there is a causal connection but not the connection we believe.

5. The people of New Hebrides have observed, perfectly accurately, over the centuries that people in good health have body lice and that sick people do not. They conclude that lice make a person healthy.

> This is the fallacy of reversing cause and effect: Apparently lice do not like the body they live on to be too warm, so in an example of a person with a fever, his lice would depart to search for cooler bodies to live on. Since lice were common in the New Hebrides, there was a positive correlation, and the correlation was indicative of a causal connection but the conclusion reverses the cause and effect.

6. The spouses of successful executives wear expensive clothing, so to help your spouse become successful buy costly clothing.

7. Twenty-five years after graduation, Yale graduates have an average income five times the national average. So if you want to be wealthy enrol in Yale University.

> Both examples are instances of the fallacy of reversing cause and effect: In the first, the causal connection surely depends on the fact that (financially) successful executives can afford to buy their spouses expensive clothes and that doing so is part of a more opulent lifestyle, which, given that they can afford it, they prefer. In the second, a disproportionate number of people who enrol in Yale are from wealthy families, so Yale graduates tend to be wealthy but wealth is the relevant causal factor in graduating from Yale rather than the other way around. Compare it to the obviously fallacious case:

8. The children of wealthy parents are disproportionately likely to be rich as adults, so if you want to be rich make sure you are be born to wealthy parents.

D. Spurious correlation Here we conclude that A is the cause of C when in fact both A and C are the effects of some event cause B. Compare these two cases:

9. A survey on factory absenteeism found that married women had a higher rate of absenteeism than single women.

> On investigation, it turned out that the rate of absenteeism depended entirely on the fact that married women had more housework in the home due to gender inequality in housework. Because husbands did less housework than wives, getting married caused women to do more housework, which in turn caused more absenteeism among

married women, so the proposed causal connection, while mediated by a fact about housework, was correct: Being married *did* cause more absenteeism.

10. Married people were found to eat less candy than single people.

On examination it was found that the rate of candy consumption was actually strictly a function of age and that married and single people of the same age had the same rates of candy consumption but older people ate less candy than younger people. So getting married was not the cause of a decrease in the consumption of candy—the correlation is *spurious*; the causally relevant factor was age. Aging both increased the likelihood of marriage and decreased the consumption of candy. The difference between these two cases can be visualized in Figure 4.1.

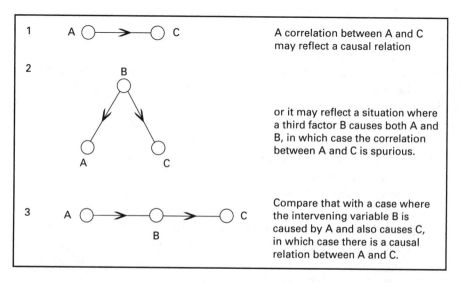

Figure 4.1

Here are two more cases:

11. Since women have entered the workforce, family life has deteriorated, the number of divorces and broken homes has soared, children have become disrespectful, and drug abuse has become commonplace. To cure these ills we must get women back into the home.

12. When people get severe migraine headaches they get nauseous and feel faint, so nausea makes people feel faint.

Both of these are fallacies of spurious correlation. In example 11, the fact of women entering the workforce is not the cause of the other changes in family life, but like them is the effect of broader underlying changes in the structure of society. In example 12, migraine headaches cause both the nausea and the feeling of faintness.

Fallacies of false cause derive from the fact that not every *correlation* between events (and of course there are all sorts of correlations between events) has *explanatory* power in accounting for those facts. Many superstitions depend on the fallacy of false cause. So do many advertisements. The muscular man in the Camaro with beautiful women draped all over it is simply an invitation to thoughtless young men to think that if they bought a Camaro they would suddenly sprout muscles and attract beautiful women. There is an established financial newspaper in Canada that bases its advertising around the idea that the average income of its subscribers is far higher than the average person's. This is probably true, but the reason is likely to be that wealthy people subscribe to the newspaper for tips about how to invest their money, not that people who subscribe to the newspaper become wealthy as a result.

AUTHORITY, EXPERTISE, AND WHAT EVERYONE KNOWS

APPEALS TO AUTHORITY OCCUR WHEN WE SUPPORT (OR TRY TO SUPPORT) A THESIS BY REFERRING to some source of authority. The key mark of an authority is that we accept what the authority says without further demand for proof or justification. Authority does not necessarily require special expertise or skill, although experts are one kind of authority. You take things on authority whenever you accept what another says. For example, you ask a clerk in the store how much something costs, or you ask your roommate what she had for dinner last night. We depend on authority for a great deal of our knowledge. When I ask you what time it is and you look at your watch and tell me the time, your authority is your watch; my authority is you. I take you to have adequate reason for your claim even though I do not have any actual access to it. Testimonial knowledge—the knowledge I have because other people have told me something—is thus based on authority. Some of our memories do not give us access to the reasons we originally had to believe what we remember; all that we now remember is that we think it is true. Much of what we learned as children is like this. We rely on the fact that we once had reason for believing what we now merely remember; we now believe on the authority of our memory and the authority of our past self.

Authority is present whenever reasons are felt to be unnecessary. Authority in a somewhat more official sense is also socially distributed in the form of specialized expertise. We cannot know everything ourselves or on the strength of what we ourselves have adequate evidence for. An appeal to authority is therefore often not only legitimate but completely necessary. We typically are right to take a certain medicine because our doctor has advised it or to use the size of beam over a picture window advised by an engineer. Without our ability to trust the testimony of others on authority, human society in any form would be impossible. In complex societies where much knowledge is socially distributed in positions requiring study and specialized knowledge or skill, our dependence on authority takes on an edge: We need to be able to rely on the specialized knowledge of others—people we don't even know, for the most part. But people are not always knowledgeable, reliable, or honest, and authority is not always legitimate. We need, therefore, to be able to distinguish genuine authority from its mere appearance.

The appeal to authority is *fallacious* when there is no good reason to believe that the authority to whom we appeal has competence in the area under discussion or when there is no relevant connection between the authority cited and the thing at issue. Thus, a doctor who publicly supports a certain medicine because the doctor has been paid to do so (and not because, in the doctor's expert opinion, the medicine is good) cannot be validly cited as an authority. Tobacco advertising is a case in point: The American Tobacco Institute (an industry institute) regularly publishes studies showing that it has not been conclusively proved that smoking leads to lung cancer. Similarly, the nuclear industry (actually, you name the industry) hires scientists who regularly say that radiation doesn't pose a public hazard and then they appeal to the authority of those scientists.

Genuine authority is something that it is *justifiable* for us to rely on in our judgments. If we could not appeal to the knowledge and expertise of others, social life would be impossible, but by the same token, if we are to appeal to an authority, that appeal must *genuinely support reasonable judgment*. As a result, a genuine appeal to authority must meet several conditions. Here are five conditions of genuine authority.

First, the person in question must really have expertise or competence in the area. If you can identify thrushes, then I can rely on you when you tell me that yonder bird is a thrush. Notice that this is not a point about your honesty but an epistemic point about the possibility of my gaining knowledge from your testimony, so the point is that *you* can tell a thrush by looking, which makes it possible for me to make use of your thrush-identifying skill.

Second, the authority's claim must be within the *scope* of his competence. You may be a bird expert, but if you cannot identify this particular kind of bird, then your claim that it is a speckled flycatcher would not have merit. This is because what gives your claim merit is not that you have a diploma or a title, but that you possess a certain skill or theoretical virtue.

Third, the claim of an expert must be free of taint. If you are paid specifically to assert a certain claim—as opposed to being paid to develop expertise in a certain area—then your authority vanishes. This shows us that a person's authority is not the same as a person's knowledge. The issue is the *reliability* of your testimony: You may have expert knowledge in an area but if you are being paid to represent a position, your testimony cannot be relied on to be knowledge because you cannot be relied on to tell the truth.

Fourth, the subject matter must be one in which expertise actually produces agreement in judgment between experts because there is an independent matter of fact to investigate and acquire knowledge about. This can be a difficult matter to determine. It is difficult to determine whether, for example, an oracle is an expert, and this is so precisely because there is no agreement on whether there is an independent way to determine whether the oracle gets things right. Culturally, of course, members of a sect or culture tend to think that their version of religious or spiritual truth is correct, because they do in fact *rely* on the testimony of their appointed experts. But if members of other sects or cultural groups have different views, it is difficult to find independent ways of determining expertise. This leads us to the final condition.

Fifth, disagreement between experts can only be adjudicated *by consensus*—after all, if two experts disagree, to whom can they appeal except other experts like themselves? Since no one has knowledge by magic, the only available basis for taking something to be empirically shown is the unforced convergence on agreement, or consensus, among peers who are knowledgeable in the subject area. One of the most powerful bases for the authority of academic expertise is that the forms of training and the criteria of explanatory success within the academic disciplines does not require prior adherence to doctrine that is unquestioned.

The Fallacious Appeal to Authority

The fallacy of appeal to authority is committed when at least one of the necessary conditions of genuine authority is not met. Determining when an appeal to authority is valid and when it is not is often a tricky business, especially when the authorities disagree, but there are a number of considerations that point to fallacy. Here are nine criteria of the fallacious appeal to authority. The appeal to an authority is likely to be fallacious when

   a. The source cited is not a genuine authority on the subject under consideration.

   b. There is reason to believe that the source is biased; when, for example, the person is paid to express a particular opinion (rather than paid to offer expert opinion).

   c. There is reason to believe that the source's observations are inaccurate.

   d. The source cited (e.g., a media source, reference work, or Internet site) is questionable or publicly recognized to be unreliable.

   e. There is reason to believe the source has been cited inaccurately.

   f. There is reason to believe that the claim has not been interpreted correctly or has been taken out of context.

   g. The source conflicts with expert consensus. Note that if two authorities disagree on a matter, then you, as a non-expert, are not free to pick one and cite the claim of that one as authoritative; not being an authority yourself, you have no reason to cite one of the authorities instead of the other. By the same token, authorities can only resolve their differences of opinion by appeal to consensus.

   h. The claim under consideration cannot be resolved by expert opinion. Some questions cannot be settled by expertise since direct evidence is not even in principle available. Evaluating when this condition is met is potentially difficult. For example, a Catholic may take the Pope to be an authority on the question of God's existence; an atheist is unlikely to believe that the Pope is better placed to have an opinion than anyone else.

   i. The claim is highly improbable on its face.

Here are a few examples:

   1. Brad Pitt thinks the Porsche Turbo is the best car around.

       Whether or not he actually is one, Brad Pitt is not *publicly recognized* as a car expert.

   2. I'm not a doctor, but I play one on the hit series *General Hospital*. You can take it from me that when you need a fast-acting, effective, and safe painkiller, there is nothing better than MorphiDope 2008. That is my considered medical opinion.

The problem here is that the speaker's medical opinion is not credible because the speaker is merely an actor who plays a doctor on TV rather than an actual doctor.

3. Eat corn flakes for breakfast; Tiger Woods does.

Tiger Woods is not an expert on nutrition, and in any case, if he is promoting corn flakes then he is just a paid mouthpiece.

One version of appeal to authority is really snob appeal:

4. Camel Filters. They're not for everyone.

5. We make the most expensive car in the world. You probably can't afford to own it.

The Appeal to Ignorance

One argues from ignorance when one takes the failure to disprove a claim as an adequate reason to take the claim seriously. Here is a simple version.

1. A cure for AIDS hasn't been found, therefore AIDS has no cure.

This is a fallacy because the fact that no cure has (yet) been found is not adequate evidence that there is no cure. Here is a different form of the argument:

2. You cannot prove that AIDS has a cure, therefore AIDS has no cure.

Technically, then, this fallacy is an instance of irrelevant thesis as the inability of a person to prove something is not relevant to the correctness of the thesis.

The fallacy apparently originates with John Locke, who saw the argument in a weaker light as an attempt to establish or shift the burden of proof.[9] The speaker asserts a proposition that the listener must accept as proposed or offer an argument against. This suggests that there can be different grades of the fallacy.

John Locke

John Locke (1632–1704) was an English philosopher, physician, and important supporter of the development of modern science. He was also a political theorist and proponent of the Glorious Revolution of 1688, which brought William of Orange to the British throne. His work on scientific method made him the first of the British Empiricists, and his work on natural rights and the limits of state power and toleration influenced both the American and French revolutions. The phrase in the American *Declaration of Independence* defending the right to "Life, Liberty and the pursuit of Happiness" is a close paraphrase from Locke's writings. In the theory of mind, he proposed that at birth the mind is empty of ideas and that all knowledge derives from experience.

---

[9] See Douglas Walton, "The Appeal to Ignorance, or Argumentum Ad Ignorantiam," *Argumentation*, Vol. 13, 1999. 367–377. (also on his website: www.dougwalton.ca/papers.htm)

Here is a weaker version:

3. You claim that AIDS has a cure but you cannot prove that AIDS has a cure, therefore you must give up your claim that AIDS has a cure.

Or slightly differently:

4. You claim that AIDS has a cure and I claim that it doesn't, but you cannot prove that AIDS has a cure therefore you must give up your claim that it has a cure and acknowledge that I have a right to believe that it doesn't.

One may take the failure to disprove a claim as evidence that it is possibly true, or that it is reasonable to think that it might be true, or that one has a right to believe it without further ado or even as proof of the conclusion's correctness. Because it comes in weak grades, it can form part of a strategy to circumvent the demand that one possess evidence for a favoured hypothesis. Thus I might argue that you have no right to criticize my belief if you cannot show that it is wrong. After all, you think it is wrong and I think it is right and in the absence of evidence either way we are equally authorized to believe what we do. It is important to see that even though this line of reasoning is much weaker than taking the failure to disprove a claim as a proof that it is correct, it is still epistemically irresponsible and a fallacy. To see this, look at version 4 of the fallacy again. The claim here is that you can't prove your point so you have to give up your point and acknowledge that I have a right to mine. But, of course, since there is no proof either way you can offer the very same argument back to me. Version 4 is unstable because we can both offer it and yet the conclusion is that I have a right (the right to believe) that you lack. The correct end point would be to acknowledge that neither party has sufficient evidence for belief and that therefore belief is unjustified for both parties.

The argument from ignorance has a special place in the arsenal of conspiracy theorists and bigots. Consider racist disputes or disputes about the Holocaust—where the racist or the Holocaust denier is *really* quite immune to counting anything as proof against their view—or cases where conclusive evidence is not ever likely to be available, as in the case of disagreement between a theist and an agnostic. The fallacy is best revealed by a consideration of more mundane examples that highlight the comparative craziness of conspiracy theories.

To begin with, consider the question of whether there are exactly 271 Russian wolfhounds in Winnipeg. Wolfhounds are rather uncommon dogs; it is unlikely that you could find out how many there are, but Winnipeg is a pretty big city and there are probably a fair number of wolfhounds in the city. So it is reasonable to believe that that there are some Russian wolfhounds in Winnipeg but not too many, so how about 271? The evidence is so circumstantial and vague that we don't know what to say. There could be, but in the absence of any adequate evidence it is much more likely that it is false than that it is true. Why is this? If it is true there must be *exactly 271* wolfhounds in Winnipeg (so not 272 or 270 or 356 and so on). If there are 272 it is false and if there are 273 it is false; for all we know there are 7,000 in the city. The point is that there are a very large number of ways it can be false and only one that it can be true. So my failure to prove that there are not 271 is *no reason at all* to believe that it is true. Or consider this simpler example. If you were to toss a penny 20 times in a row you might get heads 20 times. It could happen, so there cannot be proof that it won't. Still, you would be crazy to believe it. Since we multiply the odds of the individual tosses (1/2), the odds against it are $1/2^{20}$, which is less than one chance in a million (it is 1/1,048,576)! Many things that *could* be true (and for which there would be a perfectly acceptable explanation if it were true) are nevertheless hugely unlikely and thus not belief worthy at all. So let us bring this lesson to consider conspiracy theories.

Consider a conspiracy theory like the claim that the Apollo moon landing was a hoax or that 9/11 was secretly planned by President Bush or that the Holocaust never happened. There are such conspiracy theories and they are believed by a reasonable number of people, but all of them require a large number of unproved and individually extremely unlikely assertions to be true simultaneously. For example, if the Apollo mission was a hoax, a very large number of people had to be in on the hoax, the video would have been shot somewhere and kept secret then and thereafter, and so on. It is not reasonable to believe that the large number of ways that such hoaxes could be made public if they were true could be effectively and secretly managed by secret agencies. Typically, conspiracy theorists attempt to isolate their views from the reach of counter-argument by concocting elaborate secret conspiracies for which there is no evidence, but are such that *if* those conspiracies *did* exist their views would be reasonable. Arguments from ignorance constitute only one of a variety of strategies that "true" believers use to put their beliefs beyond the reach of criticism. You may remember the movie *The Matrix*. If the hypothesis of that movie were actually true then there would be no way to test or evaluate any belief, but, of course, the hypothesis of the movie is preposterous. There is no reason to believe it to be true at all and it is just one of a very, *very* large number of equally implausible hypotheses, all the others of which would have to be false if that one were true. It is a little like the hypothesis that there are 271 wolfhounds in Winnipeg, in that there are many more ways that it can be wrong than right, but it is unlike the hypothesis about the number of wolfhounds in that there is *no reason to think it might be true at all*, whereas there has to be some exact number of wolfhounds in Winnipeg and so it *just might be*, though it probably isn't, 271.

The important thing about the fallacy of appeal to ignorance is that using the opponent's inability to disprove a conclusion as proof of the conclusion's correctness is a *transparently irresponsible piece of reasoning*. In taking a belief to be true one needs *sufficient* evidence to make the claim belief worthy; it is *not* enough just to have an argument against the claim of one's opponent.

Here are some examples of the fallacy in its strong and more easily identifiable form:

1. There must be life on other planets, since no one has been able to show that there isn't.

2. Chiropractors have failed entirely in their attempts to establish a scientific basis for their theories. The question can therefore be settled: Chiropractic has no basis in science.

3. I have never heard a good argument for price controls; they are obviously a bad idea.

Sometimes an appeal to ignorance will be strengthened by adding *question-begging epithets*, for example:

4. No reputable scientist has proved that the radiation from nuclear fallout causes leukemia. Therefore, we can disregard the alarmists and continue testing nuclear weapons with a clear conscience.

Here the use of "alarmist" and "reputable scientist" renders us virtually unable to respond to the argument without being labelled as alarmist and disreputable.

There are some very well defined situations where an appeal to ignorance is legitimate. In a Canadian court of law, a person is innocent if not proven guilty. Also, there are certain kinds of search in which it is almost impossible to fail to uncover the subject in question and so a negative outcome is a good assurance of the falsity of the statement at issue. These, however, are rare and usually pretty obvious when they occur.

Irrelevant Thesis

In the fallacy of *irrelevant thesis*, an arguer attempts to sidetrack the audience by raising an irrelevant issue and then claims that the original issues have been effectively settled by the diversion. In short, the attempt is made to prove a thesis other than the one at issue. It is often called *ignoratio elenchi*, or *red herring*. The persuasive power of this fallacy derives from the fact that it often does prove something and people simply fail to notice that the thing proved is not the thing at issue. Here are some examples:

1. Advocates of conservation contend that if we adopt ecological principles, we will be better off in the long run. But they are wrong, for it is easy to show that an ecological lifestyle will not produce an Eden on Earth.

Here there is a shift of topic from being better off over the long run to producing an Eden on Earth. Even if it were easy to show that an ecological lifestyle will not produce an Eden on Earth, that isn't the topic. This is *inflationary* irrelevancy. *Being better off* has been inflated to be *an Eden on Earth*—which would be *much harder* to prove than the original conclusion.

2. I fail to see why hunting should be considered cruel when it gives so many people great pleasure and gives employment to others.

Here the issue is whether or not hunting is cruel, but the speaker has shifted the subject to whether hunting is pleasurable and good for the economy, which is a different subject. There is subtle connection: People who profit from hunting and those who enjoy it will not wish to feel that they are engaging in a cruel sport and so they will have an emotional reason to want to reject the conclusion that hunting is cruel. But the question of whether hunting is cruel or not has to do with how the animals suffer (or not) and not with how hunters feel, so it is an irrelevant thesis but also likely to be endorsed by the pro-hunter for emotional but non-rational reasons.

3. Obviously 14-year-olds should be eligible for driver's licences. They are every bit as intelligent as most adults.

The issue here is not whether 14-year-olds are as intelligent as adults but whether they meet sensible conditions of eligibility for having a driver's licence (being responsible, having a need for transportation, etc.). Infants are just as intelligent as adults (in fact, they are much better learners), but they do not meet sensible eligibility requirements for having a driver's licence. The claim is therefore *irrelevant* to the issue in question.

4. Please, Mr. Scrooge, my husband certainly deserves a raise. I can hardly manage to feed the children on what you have been paying him. And Tiny Tim needs an operation if he is ever to walk without crutches.

In this example (from *A Christmas Carol*, by Charles Dickens), the question is whether Mr. Cratchit *merits* a raise for his work, not whether he has *need* of more money. The point here is that these are separate issues and require separate kinds of support. If Mr. Scrooge gives Mr. Cratchit a raise, he could do so for any number of different reasons, and Mr. Cratchit's merit and his need are just two possibilities.

The fallacy of irrelevant thesis is often used intentionally to sway people, sometimes by good arguments, to positions that have nothing directly to do with those arguments. Politicians and advertising designers are usually experts at this sort of thing because their jobs aim them at results rather than offering reasonable arguments. The fallacy of irrelevant thesis has close affinities with appeals to authority and arguments from ignorance, because each is a way of offering the appearance of a reasoned ground for a position. Your doctor, for example, clearly has a domain of specialized competence and thus *is* an authority in that domain. You doctor might well give you an argument of the form "If there were much to the worry you have about your heart, I would see evidence and would know something about it, but I don't, so let go of your worry." This has the appearance of an argument from ignorance but likely isn't. It is likely an expert judgment made by an expert on the subject and thus a legitimate appeal to authority. But if your doctor makes the same argument about your worries about nuclear power or tornados, then these are likely areas outside of the doctor's domain of genuine authority. Then the argument begins to look like an appeal to ignorance. There are similar slides from arguments that are on topic to being cases of irrelevant thesis. In example 2 above, an experienced hunter might have a better sense than you do of just how cruel good hunting practices are and might be seeing the argument in broader terms than you are. For the hunter, the issue might be how to regulate an activity, and the questions of the economy of hunting, how enjoyable it is, and what are unnecessarily cruel practices will all seem equally important. So the question of whether something is or is not irrelevant thesis is sometimes subtle and depends on the background assumptions of the arguing parties as well as their skill at staying on track.

STUDY SETS 4

Identify the fallacies below and explain what makes them fallacious.

1. I am opposed to admitting women into engineering, not because I simply place a value on tradition, even though engineers traditionally have been men. Rather, I take

this fact to be the collective judgment of ages. Over the centuries, people have judged that engineers should be men, and so many people can't be wrong.

2. Most people who smoke marijuana will eventually try cocaine, because in study after study, a majority of cocaine addicts admitted to smoking marijuana before taking cocaine.

3. My last wife treated me terribly. Women are just no good!

4. Doctors don't really know any more than you or I do. This is the third case of faulty diagnosis I have heard of this month.

5. When Komoski had to go to Edmonton with the Huskies to play the Golden Bears, his philosophy professor, Eric, said it was okay for him to miss class. So clearly Eric doesn't care whether we come to class or not.

6. We have just found out that Mary did not get into Harvard or the University of Toronto, so now she must abandon her hopes of going to a truly superior university.

7. It is ridiculous for you to want to be a sculptor. If everyone sat around dabbling in artsy things the world would grind to a halt.

8. A mob is no worse than the individuals who make it up.

9. Rome must have a rotten climate. I was there for a week and it rained almost every day.

10. You seem to have very discriminating tastes! Tell me, do you give top preference to California wines or to Okanagan wines?

11. They just don't care about traffic law enforcement in this town, for they let ambulances go at any speed they like and let them run red lights too.

12. Bill Hotstuff is on the best team in the league so he must be a wonderful hockey player.

13. I do not advocate government action on all irritations faced by the average Canadian. But pornography is an epidemic and just as action is required in other areas of public health to control disease, government action is required here.

14. Jell-O brand pudding pops are the tastiest and most nutritious snack you can get for your child today: Bill Cosby says so.

Chapter 5
Relevance, Bias, and Opinion

The fallacies involving bias might well be called fallacies of irrelevance. In each, a different kind of irrelevancy involving bias is introduced in an attempt to obscure the real issue by stirring up our emotions. We will look at five fallacies, but first offer a brief discussion of bias. It is very common for critical thinking texts to focus on the importance of avoiding bias and the evils of stereotyping, vested interests, prejudice, and conflicts of interest. The danger of this sort of overemphasis is that these failures of reasoning can be overstated and exaggerated so that students come to believe that everyone's opinion is equally valid, that criticizing another's position or argument is a kind of error, and that everyone acts only out of self-interest, none of which are remotely true. So some preventative medicine is called for.

Let me start with the words "stereotype" and "bias." Both words have a neutral origin and meaning but have become used primarily in a negative way. The word "bias" starts life simply as referring to a diagonal line, as when cloth is cut "on the bias" (diagonally across the grid made by the threads) and comes to mean *point of view* or *preference* or *attitude toward*. The idea that bias is bad creeps into usage because these meanings can appear to deviate from, or conflict with, what reason requires. Let us look an example: Parents are typically interested in the welfare of their own children and this does not make them biased, but some parents do treat their own children as exceptions, as though their children deserve special treatment that they do not grant to other children, just because they are *their* children. They might believe that their children shouldn't have to wait their turn, while others should, or excuse the bad behaviour of their own child but not that of their child's friend. In such a case they will *both* care about their children *and* give them unfair preferential treatment. Of course, parents should care about their children; after all, they love them and their children are deeply dependent on them. But to treat their own children in an *unfairly* preferential way is not an acceptable consequence of parental love; it is an intellectual (and moral) failure. It is a failure to universalize a simple moral rule, the failure of being unable, or unwilling, to put themselves into the shoes of others. Any rule that a parent could apply to grant goods to their children could be used by any other parent to grant similar goods to their children. Rules, whether intellectual or moral, apply universally or not at all. This is a *fundamental* datum of critical thinking: Don't distort reasoning by selective procedures.

The fact that people have interests, care about *particular* things or people, and have wants and hopes does not imply that people will reason badly, treat others shabbily, or be "biased" in the bad sense. The point is that having interests or preferences is not by itself bad. What is usually called "bias" in the negative sense is really an intellectual failure to deal properly with one's interests.

A similar story holds for the term "stereotype." The root of the word lies in a process of manufacture where one makes a model of something by means of a mould and the objects produced by the mould share the shape of the original. This is a passive transmission of shape from one thing to another. Applied to reasoning, stereotyping is an important and powerful method of inference we have already discussed; it is the kind of inference where we are led to expect that one thing will be like another because it is superficially like it— basically, it is the application of *analogy*. It provides hypotheses for future evaluation and testing. The word "stereotype" also has a negative use, which emphasizes the passive and superficial sides of the root meaning. After all, things that have the same shape need not otherwise be similar. Chocolate coins, for example, are not genuine currency, and so the word has come to be used to refer to a settled and prejudicial belief and attitude toward those one dislikes. But notice again that the problem with stereotyping in this sense is explicitly *cognitive*. The bigot who "stereotypes" others engages in shoddy reasoning and holds on to dubious and implausible beliefs in the face of counter-evidence by avoiding or discounting available facts. These are failures the critical thinker will avoid because they tend to produce false beliefs through flawed reasoning.

The emotions and interests human beings have provide them with motives for reasoning, and such motives are not *by themselves* sources of rationality or irrationality. And for the critical thinker, the incentives offered by emotion, interests, or hope will not be barriers to critical thinking but only guides for which problems to consider. Rules of clear thought and good cognitive practices have their aim given to them by the task of pursuing the truth; that is, by belief and not by emotion and interest. Selfishness and bigotry, like cheating, lying, and theft, are simply moral failures involving patterns of irrationality; they are not mere products of interest.

In any case, reasoning badly is not likely to aid you in getting what you want—at least, not over the long run. The role of bias in the fallacies to come demonstrates failures to reason correctly because of emotional disturbance.

Having said this much, let us end on a note of caution. The fact that emotions and interests produce persons with motive for reasoning does have consequences for critical thinking. First, because emotions and interests aim you at goals, they highlight some features of a situation, features that you then take into account because they appear relevant. This can make those features appear more important than they really are and can also, by holding your attention, make other important and relevant features invisible. Bias can blind you to important and relevant factors that you should take into account. The appropriate critical response to this fact is care: One steps back, thinks methodically about the whole issue, and attempts to take a more objective view of the facts. If other parties are affected by the issue, one can ask: how the situation would be viewed by each person involved. Other people will have their own interests that will highlight different but equally relevant features of the situation in question. They will thus have a better view of some features than you will and will also be tempted to see those features as the important ones. If there is a purely rational case for intellectual cooperation, it rests in this: Everyone's view of the whole is likely to be partial and real objectivity and requires the contribution of many views. The traditional moral vices of pride, greed, and selfishness are barriers to critical thinking because they distort reasoning, and just because (and to the extent that) each person is vulnerable to these vices, good practices of critical thinking require vigilance against their effects. In short, bias is not intrinsically negative, but it does offer dangers, both in the first person and in others, that the critical thinker must solve in order to reason more clearly and well.

Personal Attack

This fallacy, also known as the *ad hominem* argument, which is Latin for "against the man," indicates that the attack is directed against the speaker rather than his or her argument. This fallacy occurs when we reject someone's claim or argument by attacking the person rather than the person's claim or argument. In short, *ad hominem* arguments are forms of abuse. Here we look at three versions.

A. Simple abuse Here we simply insult our opponent.

1. That view comes from Ms. Bingo, an avowed Marxist. I don't see why we should even listen to it.

2. In reply to that gentleman's argument, I need only point out that last month he was opposed to the very measure he now defends too vigorously.

B. Poisoning the well A closely related form of *ad hominem* is the form called *poisoning the well*. This fallacy occurs when we criticize a person's motivation for offering a particular argument or claim, rather than examining the worth of the argument or claim itself. Our objective is to put our opponents in a position where they are unable to reply by presenting them, for example, as *merely* advocating their own interest or being so biased that we need not listen to them.

3. Those who disagree with me when I say that humanity is corrupt prove that they have already been corrupted.

4. This woman denies being a member of the underground, but you need not pay this any attention. Members of the underground have been trained to lie to conceal the fact.

5. Parliament should not bother to consult with the military leadership about the size of the budget for arms. As members of the military, they will naturally want as much money for the army as they can get and their opinions will be worthless.

C. Tu quoque Another form of the ad hominem is called *tu quoque* (Latin for roughly "Look who's talking"). Here a person is charged with acting in a manner that is incompatible with the position he or she is arguing for. The thrust of the *tu quoque* fallacy is that the opponent fails to follow his or her own advice.

6. You can't tell me not to smoke. You smoke like a chimney.

7. If you think living in a commune is so great, why aren't you living in one?

There is something about the claims in 6 and 7 that touches us. If you think smoking is so bad, why *do* you smoke? But notwithstanding this sympathy we may feel for the argument, it is invalid. Whether someone smokes or not has nothing to do with the quality or the validity of the arguments they can muster against smoking. Smokers are frequently intimately aware of the reasons to quit.

Mob Appeal

Mob appeal, often called *argumentum ad populum* (Latin for "argument of the people"), is simply an appeal to our emotions using theatrical language. This fallacy often incorporates other fallacies as well. The best examples of mob appeal are usually long, but these short examples give some idea of the scope of the fallacy:

1. I'm a working man myself, and I know how hard it is to make ends meet.

2. Since you are a college audience I know that I can speak to you seriously about difficult matters.

3. No one in this room wants to deny any child a decent education. But let us not forget that this school is our school and it belongs to our children, and our first concern must be with the education of our own.

Mob appeal is generally essentially flattery of a group or an appeal to special interests. In effect, it works on people's weaknesses: their desire to think well of themselves, their desire to be happy or safe, their temptations to make an exception of themselves (just this once I will have an extra piece of pie, tell this little lie, make that sucker cry). As a consequence, it is almost always in the service of greed, special interests, and ignorance.

The Appeal to Pity

The *appeal to pity* is really a special form of *mob appeal*. Fundamentally it exploits a single emotion, sympathy. The Scrooge example in the section on the fallacy of *irrelevant thesis* is obviously also an appeal to pity. The argument that Cratchit *deserves* a raise because his family is in need is a case of irrelevant thesis, but the appeal to Scrooge's sympathy is a case of an appeal to pity. Note that if the argument were changed to "Mr. Scrooge, please give my husband a raise. . . ." it would no longer be a case of irrelevant thesis (since the question of Cratchit's merit is no longer at issue) but would remain an appeal to pity. This fallacy occurs when we attempt to evoke feelings of pity or compassion in order to cause you to assent to our claim. It is important to see that the appeal to pity is not a fallacy because pity is somehow wrong or inappropriate. In fact, sympathy (like anger or any emotion) is appropriate in some circumstances and not others. Emotions guide us in living well but they need to be *cultivated* and developed so that they may complement rather than distort rationality; this is, in fact, a central task of critical thinking. Anger, for example, is sometimes directed appropriately at a person or object and sometimes not; it is also sometimes excessive or insufficient even if directed correctly. Similarly sometimes it is appropriate to feel sympathy or pity and to act on it and sometimes not. What makes appeal to pity fallacious *as an argument form* is that it fails by its structure to distinguish between appropriate and inappropriate contexts for having feelings of sympathy; in short, it offers no guidance for understanding whether such feelings ought to guide our action in the case at hand.

1. Please, Professor Dayton, give me an A; I am trying to get into law school.

The Appeal to Force or Fear

This fallacy, known as the *argumentum ad baculum* (literally the argument of the stick), consists in the use of threats of force to cause acceptance of a conclusion. The use of threat can be blatant or subtle; the crucial point is that the person hearing the argument must recognize him- or herself to be threatened. The threat need not be a threat of force on the part of the speaker. An attorney may commit the fallacy of the appeal to force by telling the jury:

1. "If you do not convict this murderer, you may be his next victim."

   Here are some other examples:

2. Don't argue with me, young man. Remember who pays your salary.

3. This university does not need a teachers' union, and any faculty member who thinks it does will discover his error at the next tenure review.

4. Mr. Editor, I hope you will agree that this little escapade by my son has no real news value. I know you will agree that my firm buys thousands of dollars of advertising space in your paper every year.

The fallacy of appeal to force or fear has a particularly ugly ring to it. This is largely due to the fact that the other fallacies we have discussed only work if you don't notice that they are fallacious, but this one only works if you notice its particular fallacious character. So we think of mobsters and thugs and the secret police. It is worth mentioning, however, that there are certain classes of disputes that are not so much disputes about the facts as disputes about who gets what piece of the pie. At the international level at least, these issues are in many cases not solvable any other way than by appeals to force. This is a sad fact, but it is true. Where there are substantially opposed interests and prima facie good claims on either side, a rational resolution of the dispute may be impossible to work out. This, of course, does nothing to make such cases legitimate arguments.

Special Pleading

The fallacy of *special pleading* occurs when we apply a *double standard*, one for ourselves and another for everyone else. Bertrand Russell once illustrated this fallacy by his "conjugation" of the verb to be firm: I am *firm*, you are *stubborn*, he is *pig-headed*. Here is an example:

1. The ruthless tactics of the enemy, his fanatical suicidal attacks, have been foiled by the stern measures of our commanders and the devoted self-sacrifice of our troops.

    The claim in 1, stripped of emotive language, is that our troops and the enemy's troops are doing *exactly the same things*, but somehow when we do them they are great and when the enemy does them they are terrible. But how can it be reasonable to criticize a line of behaviour in others if it is exactly what one is doing oneself? Good examples of special pleading are easy to find in political speeches, news stories, and political commentaries, which are often aimed less at the truth than at persuasion or self-congratulation. We have evidence that a double standard is operating when *literally correct* words are replaced by *emotionally charged* words that are similar in meaning, and then the emotionally charged words are used to move our feelings.

Our language is filled with words that function to give a positive or negative or neutral emotional spin to the very same actions or traits. So the resources for the fallacy of special pleading through the application of a double standard are readily available. For example,

Compare	With
- enterprising plan	- opportunistic scheme
- he smiled engagingly at her	- he leered suggestively at her
- group	- gang
- reserved	- secretive
- boisterous group of young fellows	- rowdy gang of juvenile toughs

When adults of a certain kind are referred to as children, for example when women are referred to as "girls" or when African American men are called "boy" by white men with social standing, it suggests the existence of a double standard. Here is an example of the gender double standard:

2. "Teaching is no longer seen as a woman's job. Teaching is now seen as a tough, exciting place where things are happening."

    In example 2, by contrasting *a tough, exciting place where things are happening* with *a woman's job* the speaker is appealing to a double standard where what *we* (the men) do is exciting and tough whereas what *they* (the women) do is not. (Embarrassingly enough, that claim was made by Albert Shank in 1974, while he was president of the American teachers' union, United Federation of Teachers.)

    Double standards typically reflect differences in prestige or power and they need not be explicitly noticed to operate; indeed, they usually operate covertly. There are often implicit barriers that serve to prevent the explicit public notice of the patterns of inequality that double standards help to enforce (at least by those whose advantage they serve). It is very convenient for those who are advantaged and powerful to not have to notice double standards, since this saves them the embarrassment of having to justify the advantages they have and the inequalities those advantages serve to maintain. Of course, many of our attitudes toward foreign and unfamiliar people and groups, cultures, and religions are grounded in ignorance or at least limited and stereotypical beliefs, perhaps acquired as children. When we think about people or customs about whom we have only a superficial knowledge, it is easy to imagine differences that do not exist and apply double standards without knowing it. A certain level of humility in judgment coupled with a commitment to the truth is probably the best remedy to the danger of applying double standards involuntarily.

All of the fallacies discussed in this section are relatively easy to detect and they all share the feature that they evade the responsibility of supporting the claims they make; it is this evasion of the responsibility to justify what they purport to show that makes them fallacies.

STUDY SETS 5

Identify the fallacies below and explain why they are fallacious.

1. If your idea had any merit, someone would have thought of it already.
2. No, if you don't mind losing a tire, going off the road, and maybe killing yourself, you don't need a new tire.
3. You'd better find the fallacies in these arguments and identify them correctly or you might end up failing this class.
4. A vote for my opponent is a vote for war.
5. Jell-O brand pudding pops are the tastiest and most nutritious snack you can get for your child today; Bill Cosby says so.
6. The Cadillac Eldorado. Life is too short to put it off for long.
7. Of course there is a Santa Claus, but he doesn't bring presents to children who don't believe in him.
8. I'm on probation, Professor. If I don't get a good grade in this course I won't be able to stay in school. Please, could you let me have at least a C?
9. I suppose you think you're going to tell me what to do, you with your boozing and carousing and carrying on.
10. There is no point in listening to Jolene's views about religion; she is an atheist if I ever saw one.
11. Don't listen to what your priest advises you about sexual problems in marriage; what could he know about that subject!
12. Most women think guys who drink espresso are sexy. So, all you guys, get out there and drink espresso.

A REVIEW OF INFORMAL FALLACIES

HERE IS A LIST OF THE MAJOR INFORMAL FALLACIES WE HAVE EXAMINED TOGETHER WITH A brief description. You should review all the fallacies in the chapter. You should be able to *define* each one in a sentence and also be able offer a *brief* (a few words) *explanation* of what goes wrong in the fallacy. You should be able to describe the *difference* between any two fallacies and also be able to explain why using a particular fallacy is *bad epistemic policy.*

Ambiguity and its fallacies

> *Equivocation* - lexical ambiguity
>
> *Amphiboly* - ambiguity of sentence structure
>
> *Accent* - ambiguity of stress on word(s) in a sentence
>
> *Composition* - invalidly going from (1) part to whole or (2) member to class
>
> *Division* - invalidly going from (1) whole to part or (2) class to member
>
> *Hypostatization* - using an abstract word as if it names an individual

Fallacies of circularity

> *Begging the question* - assuming your conclusion as a premise; circular argument
>
> *Question-begging epithets* - using loaded words that assume your conclusion
>
> *Complex question* - asking a question that assumes conclusion

Inductive fallacies

> *Sweeping generalization* - inference from a general rule to a particular case is made invalid by a special circumstance
>
> *Hasty generalization* - inference from a special case to a general rule
>
> *Bifurcation* - illegitimate treatment of two cases as contradictories
>
> *False analogy* - comparing two things that are not relevantly similar
>
> *False cause* - assuming a causal connection between two causally unrelated events; four varieties:
>
>> *Post hoc ergo propter hoc* - assumes B caused by A when B came after A
>>
>> *Mere correlation* - assuming that B was caused by A merely because of a positive correlation between A and B
>>
>> *Reversing cause and effect* - concluding that A causes B when B causes A
>>
>> *Spurious correlation* - concluding that A is the cause of C when in fact both are the effects of B

Fallacies of expertise

> *The fallacious appeal to authority* - inappropriate appeal to an authority
>
> *The appeal to ignorance* - uses inability of opponent to disprove an argument as evidence of its truth, or as proof of its truth
>
> *Irrelevant thesis* - proving something other than what is at issue

Fallacies of emotional bias

    Personal attack (ad hominem); three kinds:

        Abuse - use of abuse to direct attention away from the issue and on to those arguing

        Poisoning the well - attack undercuts opponent's ability to reply

        Tu quoque - "Look who's talking"; opponent doesn't follow own advice

    Mob appeal - flattery or appeal to special interests

    Appeal to pity - exploits a person's sympathy

    Appeal to force or fear - the use of threats of force or the appeal to the fears of audience to make them accept conclusion

    Special pleading - using a double standard

PUTTING FALLACIES TOGETHER

YOU SHOULD BE ABLE TO IDENTIFY EACH OF THESE WAYS ORDINARY REASONING CAN GO wrong. We have seen that these really represent diagnostic categories and there is sometimes more than one way a piece of reasoning can go wrong at once. This is especially true in more extended pieces of reasoning, where there are many opportunities for one kind of error to produce another. Just as a doctor will see certain bodily signs as *symptoms* of disease rather than the disease itself, the careful reasoner will look at fallacies as symptoms of bad reasoning that will guide in both analysis and cure.

In Chapter 2 we defined a fallacious argument as an argument that is not *cogent* and described a cogent argument as one that meets three conditions:

1. *The argument must be grounded in premises that are accepted or are rationally acceptable to a reasonable audience.*

2. *The premises must make a rationally grounded connection to the conclusion*, so that the truth or reasonableness of the premises genuinely bears on the truth or reasonableness of the conclusion.

3. *The premises must provide sufficient or strong rational grounds for asserting the conclusion*, allowing the mind to move from asserting the premises to asserting the conclusion.

These three conditions offer us the beginnings of a diagnostic procedure for evaluating extended arguments. To apply the first condition, we must first of all *identify* all the claims being put forward and *distinguish* the conclusion from the premises. As we have seen in the discussion of the fallacies, what is presented as the conclusion and what is actually being argued for are not always the same. There may be lexical ambiguity or irrelevant thesis or the premises may be designed to move our emotions rather than present reasons. Once we have identified all the claims put forward and identified the conclusion and the premises, we are in a position to ask whether the premises are *dialectically acceptable* (rationally acceptable) to a reasonable audience. To be dialectically acceptable, the premises must not only to be true or likely, they must also be appropriate to support the conclusion. If the argument is circular, then even if the premises are true they cannot offer rational support to the conclusion; if there is ambiguity between premise and conclusion then the appearance of a support relation will be illusory as well. If the argument is neither circular nor ambiguous and the premises are otherwise dialectically acceptable, we can next ask whether the premises make a rationally grounded connection to the conclusion. The fallacies of emotional bias in particular fail this test. To say that there is a rational grounded connection doesn't yet show that the connection is strong enough to allow the mind to move from the acceptability of the premises to endorsing the conclusion. The fallacies of authority and the inductive fallacies can be used as a kind of checklist for determining the strength of the connection. To review, we identify the claims, distinguish premises from conclusion, and ask whether the premises are dialectically acceptable. If they are, we then investigate the kind of connection the premises make to the conclusion. If the connection is not genuinely based on reason, we reject the argument; if it is reason-based, we ask whether the ground of support is rationally sufficient. At each step we can use our fallacy list of "bad argument patterns" as diagnostic tools for identifying symptoms of bad reasoning. Along the way we also bring to bear considerations of good practice, which we have identified in the text. We look at the questions carefully and methodically. If there are implicit premises about what words mean or about what everyone knows, we try to make those assumptions explicit. If appeals are being made to our interests or desires, we step back from them to see whether the appeals are legitimate or whether they are simply attempts to influence our judgment. And so on. Really large extended pieces of reasoning may be too complex to consider all at once, but they will contain parts that can be isolated and evaluated independently. Throughout the evaluation of an argument, we need to recognize that we are not simply following some rules but we are actively exercising our judgment and taking responsibility for the claims and connections being made. In short, we are taking cognitive ownership of the argument as our own, and thus as anyone's. In addition to being careful and seeing all the possible flaws, this also means being charitable. Think for the moment about letters to the editor in a newspaper or a posting on a blog. People who write letters to the editor are often activated by irritation at some public policy or attempting to show others the errors of their ways. So it is understood that it is acceptable, almost a convention, that letters to the editor can be cranky and exaggerative (possibly even abusive) and still make reasonable claims. When you find symptoms of some fallacy or another in an extended passage, you should ask yourself whether it damages the overall argumentation. And this is actually pretty simple to do. Isolate the fallacy and look at the rest. If the fallacy is harmless, the argument will survive intact.

STUDY SETS 6

Here are some fictitious passages based on typical claims made in letters to the editor or short opinion pieces in the newspaper. They are intended for group work in class. In each case, you should attempt to determine whether there are arguments present and if so what the major claim being supported is. Identify the premises and conclusion and determine whether the premises are dialectically reasonable and whether they have bearing on the truth of the conclusion, and, finally, estimate the strength of the support (if any) they offer to the conclusion. Use the fallacies we have learned as methods of diagnosis, and identify any fallacies that are major and damage the argument.

1. "Ontario's graduated licensing system for new drivers is about to get tougher. New young drivers may face more restrictions—a longer wait to get a full licence and more restrictions on the number of passengers—if new legislation is passed this fall. Young and inexperienced drivers are more likely to get in accidents according to Ontario accident statistics, especially at night and when there are other young passengers in the car. While the details on the proposed legislation are sketchy and still under review, Transportation Minister Jim Bradley says that there is broad support for tougher legislation.

    One person arguing for tighter rules for young drivers is Tim Mulcahy, whose 20-year-old son Tyler and two friends were killed in a terrible crash after drinking at a Muskoka restaurant last summer. The three young people died when the car they were in crashed and plunged into Lake Joseph in July. According to police, speed and alcohol were factors in the crash. Mulcahy wants the government to revoke the licences of young drivers caught speeding or drinking for three months or even up to a year.

    Doubtless many young people will feel singled out and resent the proposed restrictions as unjustified constraints on their behaviour as young adults, but parents all over Ontario will breathe a sigh of relief knowing that their children are safer."

2. "Your chamber of commerce brings you this message: 'Say no to panhandling.' Many people believe that panhandlers are poor homeless people victimized by society, but the vast majority of panhandlers are not homeless and some do a lucrative business begging for other people's money. Panhandlers use your money to buy drugs and alcohol, and giving money to panhandlers only makes their self-destructive behaviors worse; it's like giving a gun to someone who is suicidal.

    Many panhandlers are aggressive and can be very intimidating when they demand money from old people who become afraid to shop downtown. When ordinary citizens are afraid to go out in public, it is time for our city and police to take decisive action against these thugs and ruffians.

    We need to change the generosity of ordinary people who think they are helping when they are really just enabling people to live off others and do no useful work. When begging becomes widespread in a city it produces a change in the air—people have a lingering impression that the downtown is unsafe—and this is bad for local businesses. Confronting the panhandling plague is difficult without aggressive police enforcement of anti-panhandling bylaws. It should clearly be illegal to panhandle in the downtown shopping areas so that law-abiding citizens are safe when they go into banks and stores. So support tougher legislation against panhandlers to reduce drug use and fear. Sign our petition, available at most of your downtown merchants, and support a cleaner, safer shopping environment. Just say 'No!' to panhandling in our city."

3. "Most people in Canada agree that marriage is beneficial to society. Marriages offer security, a home for raising children, and long-term companionship. But Canadians are sharply divided over the issue of same-sex marriage.

The Bible states that God created man in His image. Seeing that it was not good for man to be alone, God created a companion—woman. And with the first man and the first woman God created marriage: 'Therefore shall a man leave his father and his mother, and shall cleave unto his wife; and they shall be one flesh' (Genesis 2:24). So in the first book of the Bible, God gives us a standard for marriage. It must be a life-long, monogamous union between one man and one woman. So the term 'same-sex marriage' is a contradiction. A relationship between two persons of the same sex could never be called 'marriage.' It is something else entirely, something God rejects and abhors. Men and women, because of their inherent differences, make the union of mar-riage a unique condition which cannot exist between two persons of the same sex.

Overall, the statistics show that homosexual unions rarely sustain for long peri-ods of time, especially when compared with heterosexual marriages. Gay unions just don't last. This is well known. And the lack of stable same-sex relationships shows that homosexual marriage simply won't work. So it cannot be that stable foundation for family and society that God intended marriage to be. Protecting marriage as exclusively heterosexual does not discriminate against anyone or infringe on anyone's rights; instead it protects the sacred bond of marriage as God intended it.

God does not demand that people hate homosexuals—that would be to be to violate God's commandment that 'Thou shalt love thy neighbour as thyself' (Matthew 22:39). The Bible tells us that all people deserve love and respect, but being tolerant and respectful of homosexuals does not require accepting the idea of same-sex mar-riage. Thirty-eight states of the USA have adopted Defense of Marriage Acts that affirm marriage as a contract between one man and one woman. This wise agreement of so many legislatures should not be ignored but should be accepted as a judgment valid for the ages. Homosexual marriage is a violation of the sacred union which law recog-nizes as essential for a healthy society."

4. "Seven years after 9/11 the United States is still not safe from terrorism. In testimony before the American Senate Committee on Homeland Security and Governmental Affairs, America's top counter-terrorism officials, including the Secretary of Home-land Security and the Director of the FBI, reported that al Qaeda still fully plans a major terrorist attack on the United States soon.

They praised the temporary provisions of the Foreign Intelligence Surveillance Act, FISA, which enables the government to intercept al Qaeda plans, despite criti-cisms of the act being explored by congress.

While some people fear that FISA allows intelligence officers to conduct data-mining operations and other activities which endanger the rights of American citizens, it was pointed out that these allegations are totally unfounded. FISA should not be put in jeopardy because of worries which are totally untrue. Democratic objections to FISA are simply a part of an organized attack on the Bush presidency; losing FISA would cut the government's ability to track terrorism in half. They stressed that while America is safer than it was on 9/11, it is still not safe and will not be for another generation.

According to the administration FISA has not kept up with technology, and the law's requirement for warrants from a special FISA court doesn't permit intelligence authorities to react fast enough to electronically detected threats. Clearly the law needs strengthening rather than weakening, so that America can once again become safe."

ADDITIONAL STUDY SETS FOR PART II

YOU SHOULD REVIEW ALL THE FALLACIES IN CHAPTERS 3, 4, AND 5. YOU SHOULD BE ABLE TO *define* each one in a sentence and also be able offer a *brief* (a few words) *explanation* of what goes wrong in the fallacy. You should be able to describe the *difference* between any two fallacies and also be able to explain why using fallacies is *bad epistemic policy*.

Part A. Here is a set of *fallacies of ambiguity*. Identify each one and in a few words explain why it is an instance of that fallacy.

1. Each oil company is perfectly free to set its own price for gas, so there can be nothing wrong with all the oil companies getting together to fix a common price for gas.

2. Diamonds are rarely found in this country, so be careful not to misplace your wedding ring.

3. Joe: That Lefty is a crook.

   Moe: What makes you think he is?

   Joe: Just look at the crooks he hangs out with.

   Moe: Oh. How do you know that they are crooks?

   Joe: Well, anyone who hangs around a crook like Lefty has just got to be a crook.

4. The NDP was booted out of government in the last provincial election in Saskatchewan, so NDPer Pat Atkinson must have lost her race here in Saskatoon Broadway.

5. Traffic accidents are on the increase. Collisions between Model-T Fords are traffic accidents, therefore collisions between Model-T Fords are on the increase.

6. On a church bulletin: It would be a great help toward keeping the churchyard tidy if we all followed the example of those who clip the grass on their own graves.

7. Alice should get a 95 because she deserves a really high mark.

8. The marriage of Ms. Bianca and Mr. Conrad, which was announced in yesterday's paper, was a mistake and we wish to correct it.

9. Yes, I know Mike had surgery, but that was a month ago and he should have recovered by now. The point is that his term paper ought to have been in by now. That's enough to show me that nobody can ever count on Mike to do his work.

10. Farm folk call the evening meal "supper" and city people "dinner." Therefore we must arrest those farm folk for cannibalism before they eat any more city people.

11. Marcia loves pepperoni and olives and she is crazy about butterscotch swirl ice cream, so she is sure to love the pepperoni and olive butterscotch swirl sundae you made her.

12. Nothing is better than peaches and ice cream! A crust of bread is better than nothing. Obviously, then, a crust of bread is better than peaches and ice cream.

13. Whatever is recognized as a law ought to be obeyed. We all recognize that physics is a body of laws so the laws of physics ought to be obeyed.

<u>Part B.</u> Here is a set of *fallacies of presumption*. Identify each one and in a few words explain why it is an instance of that fallacy.

1. Big tax exemptions for wealthy investors are absolutely justified because people who spend large sums of money in the market should be excused from paying large parts of their income tax.

2. The owners shouldn't negotiate a settlement with the members of the NHL players' association. Those players are the most overprivileged, overpaid collection of prima donnas in sports today.

3. Ladies and gentlemen of the jury. You have heard how the victim was taunted and then tied up, beaten with a metal bar and left to die. This was an incredibly brutal crime! On that basis alone you have no alternative than to find the accused guilty of assault.

4. God must exist, since if everyone believed that there was no God then we would have no reason to obey the law and the world would be in chaos.

5. Prosecutor to defendant on the witness stand: "It seems pretty clear that the accident was your fault. Did you see the red light before or after you ran it?"

6. Consider why you should accept Jesus into your heart as your personal saviour. Do you want to go to hell? You have a choice: salvation or endless suffering. If you accept Jesus and change your life you will be saved. If you don't, you will go to hell. (Notice that this fallacy is, in addition to being a fallacy of presumption, also *force or fear*, which is a fallacy of relevance. The question is, which fallacy of presumption is it?)

7. Every unbiased observer recognizes the importance of the uranium industry to Alberta's future. The industry is doing everything humanly possible to guarantee everyone's safety—every expert agrees. Those anti-nuclear extremists are not fooling anyone with their infantile scare tactics. (Notice that this fallacy is, in addition to being a fallacy of presumption, also *abuse*, which is a fallacy of relevance. The question is, which fallacy of presumption is it?)

8. I'm not hoarding. I am only stocking up on everything before the hoarders get it all.

9. It was 43°C when Albert finished the 18th hole on the golf course. He drank 17 glasses of water in quick succession. Then he drank a beer and immediately passed out. Albert must have trouble with beer.

10. You can argue all you want that democracy in Canada only gives the illusion of popular control over the government, but I don't buy it. I was brought up to believe in our democratic system.

11. Anger is like steam under pressure. Keep it bottled up and let it build, the next thing you know someone might get killed.

12. No genuine religion could ever lead to bigotry, hatred, or conflict. But every so-called religion history has ever seen has done just that. So clearly there has never been a genuine religion, nor is there now.

13. Terminally ill people in hospital are often given morphine drips when they are in pain, so morphine must be a good pain reliever for my headache.

14. When people get severe migraine headaches, they get nauseous and feel faint, so nausea makes you feel faint.

15. Obviously women shouldn't be allowed in engineering. If you let attractive young things into the classrooms the real students won't be able to keep their minds on their work and won't learn the material adequately. The whole engineering profession would suffer.

16. Chelsea told me that I'm her best friend so I must be since Chelsea would never lie to her best friend.

17. Look, after all the hollering and hairsplitting is over on the part of those devious, infant-killing pro-choicers, it is perfectly clear that abortion amounts to the cold-blooded and premeditated murder of babies.

18. When Joe drinks he is no fun to be around. He is unhappy and he hates his job, and Marcia picked up with another guy. Really, Joe should stop drinking. Drinking makes him a real bummer, man.

19. You can be sure that we will give you an honest deal on a used car since we will always deal with you in a forthright and honest way when you purchase a used car from us.

20. A farmer can never make much money from growing wheat. Either he grows a lot of it and the price is too low, or he grows a little and doesn't have much to sell.

21. I met two feminists at the convention who were lesbians and thought that men should be replaced by sperm banks. Feminists are obviously all crazy.

22. Recent studies show that the death rate in Canadian hospitals is considerably higher than the overall Canadian death rate. Obviously Canadian hospitals are not providing proper care.

Part C. Here is a set of *fallacies of relevance*. Identify each one and in a few words explain why it is an instance of that fallacy.

1. Well, I have heard that Michael Stipe of REM has a tattoo of a fish on his butt and if he has a tattoo you should get one too.

2. I am sure you will agree that this is an excellent class and that you are learning a great deal. If you don't, I will have to conclude that you are stupid and give you a bad grade.

3. You should buy this peanut butter. Of course it's good peanut butter: Mariah Carey eats this kind.

4. This theory, as you should know, was introduced by a godless atheist with known communist sympathies. There cannot be much to it.

5. NDP leader Jack Layton is opposed to capital punishment. He talks about cruelty and criminals' rights. That's the sort of corny line we can expect from an impractical, soft-in-the-head socialist.

6. God must have created the universe. Have you noticed that no scientist or evolutionist has been able to explain where the power for the "big bang" came from?

7. Father O'Malley preaches about the dangers and immorality of abortion but we can ignore what he says; after all, he is a Catholic priest and priests are required to hold such views.

8. We should support city council's bid for a nuclear reactor to be built in the city. Surely if there were any economic or safety problems they would know about them and be against the proposal.

Part D. In this group of questions, you are given a choice of five answers for each question. You may find that more than one choice has some merit but you should identify which answer is the *best* one and briefly explain why.

1. Objects with a specific gravity less than that of water will float when you put them in water. The reason is that such objects won't sink in water.

   A Equivocation   B Begging the question   C Force or fear

   D Poisoning the well   E Appeal to authority

2. "There has been a major accident and we have closed this street to regular traffic so we cannot allow you to drive your ambulance down it."

   A Irrelevant thesis   B Appeal to authority   C Sweeping generalization

   D Appeal to ignorance   E Hasty generalization

3. "Why should I take your pro-vegetarian arguments seriously? You wear a leather belt and leather shoes. You are just a hypocrite."

   A Abuse   B *Tu quoque*   C Appeal to ignorance

   D Complex question   E Poisoning the well

4. Students who get help from tutors get lower scores on average than students who don't. This shows that tutors are a waste of time.

    A Hasty generalization   **B** Spurious correlation

    C Mere correlation   **D** *Post hoc*   **E** Sweeping generalization

5. I got a bad mark on my midterm. I can't believe it. The material was so easy that there was no point studying. My prof must just have had it in for me.

    A Mere correlation   **B** Question-begging epithets

    C Appeal to ignorance   **D** Reversing C and E   **E** Hasty generalization

6. It really doesn't cost much for the government to pay for the medicare costs of a sick person. It's just a few thousand dollars a year on average. So medicare can't be a big factor in the national budget.

    A Equivocation   **B** Hasty generalization   **C** Composition

    D Sweeping generalization   **E** Division

7. Prosecuting attorney in court: "When is the defence attorney planning to call that child-molesting rapist Hunk Beedle to the stand? OK, I'll rephrase that. When is the defence attorney planning to call that liar Hunk Beedle to the stand? Sorry, your Honour, I withdraw my remarks."

    A Poisoning the well   **B** Abuse   **C** Special pleading

    D *Tu quoque*   **E** Question-begging epithets

8. "There are two types of people in this world: the rich and the suckers. Do you want to get rich, or are you happy to remain a sucker?"

    A Force or fear   **B** Appeal to authority   **C** Complex question

    D Appeal to ignorance   **E** Bifurcation

9. You must believe that God exists. After all, if you do not accept God into your heart, then you will face the horrors of hell.

    A Appeal to authority   **B** Force or fear   **C** *Tu quoque*

    D Poisoning the well   **E** Begging the question

10. Some people argue that sport fishing is wrong because fish can feel pain and they suffer. But that is nonsense. Fishing is a wonderful sport. It's relaxing and fun for the whole family and you get to eat what you catch!

    A Appeal to authority   **B** Poisoning the well   **C** Irrelevant thesis

    D Appeal to ignorance   **E** Begging the question

11. My boyfriend just dumped me for another woman. Men are such jerks!

    A Hasty generalization   **B** Abuse   **C** Irrelevant thesis

    D Appeal to ignorance   **E** Appeal to authority

12. At a certain point a car gets old enough and breaks down so frequently that it is no longer reasonable to fix it and we junk it. In the same way, when a person gets old and decrepit enough he or she should be mercifully put to death.

A Abuse   **B** Appeal to authority   **C** Hasty generalization

D False analogy   **E** Force or fear

13. Don't even bother to watch the Toronto Maple Leafs this spring. What a bunch of overpaid, under-talented losers!

A Abuse   **B** Question-begging epithets   **C** Appeal to ignorance

D Poisoning the well   **E** Force or fear

14. You don't need to ask Joseph what he thinks about the Holocaust. You know what he will say—he's Jewish.

A Hasty generalization   **B** Special pleading   **C** *Tu quoque*

D Abuse   **E** Poisoning the well

15. Every open-minded historian agrees that the Bible is relatively historically accurate and that Jesus actually existed.

A Appeal to ignorance   **B** Abuse   **C** Special pleading

D Authority   **E** Hasty generalization

<u>Part E.</u> Here is another group of questions where you have a choice of five answers for each question. Identify which answer is the best one and briefly explain why.

1. We need to give the criminals who use violence in committing their crimes especially long sentences because it is the violent criminals who must be incarcerated the longest.

A Equivocation   **B** Begging the question   **C** Force or fear

D Poisoning the well   **E** Appeal to authority

2. It doesn't seem that there is any room for debate here. Either we start selling cigarettes to boost our profit margin or we drift into bankruptcy when we can't pay our bills. So which would you prefer?

A Irrelevant thesis   **B** Force or fear   **C** False analogy

D Bifurcation   **E** Hasty generalization

3. You wonder which of us to vote for, me or my opponent. It is, of course, a weighty question of public morality, but I ask you to consider that at least I have remained faithful to my spouse.

A Force or fear   **B** Bifurcation   **C** Appeal to ignorance

D Accent   **E** Poisoning the well

4. Buses use much more gasoline than automobiles, so the proposal that we all take the bus to work instead of driving a car is completely irresponsible. We would use so much more gas if we did that.

A Hasty generalization **B** Appeal to ignorance **C** Division

D Composition **E** Sweeping generalization

5. Is Psychology still teaching that outdated nonsense about the effectiveness of electroshock therapy?

A *Tu quoque* **B** Question-begging epithets **C** Appeal to ignorance

D Complex question **E** Hasty generalization

6. Look, you don't need to take Father Bob's remarks about gay marriage seriously. He's a priest. He has to be against it or he gets in trouble with the Church.

A *Tu quoque* **B** Begging the question **C** Poisoning the well

D Force or fear **E** Personal attack

7. Yes, my client was drunk when he crashed into the telephone pole, but his car was totalled and he was severely injured. He's been in the hospital for months, and will be injured for life. Surely he deserves something for his pain and suffering. I'm asking you of the jury to help him with a judgment against the power company for putting that pole so close to the street.

A Hasty generalization **B** Weak analogy **C** Spurious correlation

D Sweeping generalization **E** Mob appeal

8. An intelligent and well-read person like you shouldn't have any difficulty understanding how reasonable and important it is to support our town's school budget in the referendum.

A Appeal to ignorance **B** Appeal to authority **C** Poisoning the well

D Mob appeal **E** Accent

9. Silken Laumann eats Wheaties. Catriona Le May Doan eats Wheaties. Myriam Bédard eats Wheaties. These women are major athletes! You should eat Wheaties too.

A Appeal to authority **B** Hasty generalization **C** *Tu quoque*

D Hasty generalization **E** Begging the question

10. In Toronto it has been found that there is a significant correlation between the number of fire trucks spraying water on a fire and the financial losses due to the fire. The extra trucks clearly make the damage worse.

A Spurious correlation **B** Mere correlation

C Sweeping generalization **D** Hasty generalization

E Reversing C and E

11. The University of Saskatchewan is a great university. So if you want to study philosophy, this university is a great place to study.

    A Hasty generalization　　**B** Division　　**C** Irrelevant thesis

    D Appeal to ignorance　　**E** Appeal to authority

12. Don't let worry kill you off—let the Church help.

    A Abuse　　**B** Appeal to authority　　**C** Appeal to ignorance

    D Amphiboly　　**E** Special pleading

13. Now that hockey is back on television, we will once again have to watch those pathetic pretenders, Nik Antropov and Mats Sundin, and the rest of the Toronto Maple Leafs losers.

    A Abuse　　**B** Question-begging epithets　　**C** Appeal to ignorance

    D Poisoning the well　　**E** Force or fear

14. My professor Eric Dayton is always spouting off about superstition and obviously is an atheist. I had better keep quiet about my religious beliefs so he won't be tempted to fail me.

    A Hasty generalization　　**B** Appeal to ignorance　　**C** Force or fear

    D Abuse　　**E** Poisoning the well

15. The *Globe and Mail* says that Toronto is a much more expensive place to live than Thunder Bay. But Toronto is a great place to live. It has great restaurants, live music, museums, and of course it has the Blue Jays and the Maple Leafs. The *Globe and Mail* is wrong.

    A Appeal to authority　　**B** Poisoning the well　　**C** Irrelevant thesis

    D Appeal to ignorance　　**E** Begging the question

Part III
Deductive Argument

INTRODUCTION

In the final two chapters, we will explore two formal systems of deductive argument, the traditional logic of terms and the modern sentence logic. From a theoretical point of view, the importance of formal systems is that they allow for the systematic study of consequence relations in symbol systems, but from a practical point of view, the value of simple formal systems is that they empower the mind. For example, elementary arithmetic is a formal system you have all internalized in a practical and empowering way: You are all capable of adding, subtracting, multiplying, and dividing. As a result, you are able to do many things—purchase food, bank, go to a movie, and the like—which would be impossible if you could not see certain mathematical relationships intuitively. Learning how to evaluate formal arguments for validity and how to translate sentences in ordinary language will enable you to see more deeply into the logical relationships among your thoughts and will give you precise purchase on ideas you could otherwise grasp only vaguely. Here is an example. We saw in the last section how inductive arguments gain their *inductive strength* from the likelihood that the conclusion will be true if the premise(s) are.

Mary has a sister example A
Mary has five siblings

∴ Mary has a sister.

You can see right away that this conclusion is inductively strong. You might rehearse a thought like: "If she has one sibling the chance that she has a sister is 50 percent and if she has two sisters it is even more likely so if she has five siblings it is way more likely." Now look at

Mary has a sister example B
Mary has five siblings

∴ Probably Mary has a sister.

The same line of thought makes it clear that even though "probably" is vague, you could easily turn this argument into one that is deductively valid because it rests on probability theory (which is a formal system). For example, we might clarify the argument by giving an exact meaning to "probably" and adding a premise making explicit that the chance of having a sister if one has a sibling is 1/2.

Mary has a sister example B
Mary has five siblings
For each sibling the probability of having a sister is 1/2

∴ The probability that Mary has a sister = is 31/32 (or .96875).[1]

Given the truths of probability theory, this argument is formally valid, and it specifies precisely how probable having a sister is: almost 97 percent! In scientific reasoning it is usually very important to be as precise as possible, because many statements will stand in relation to each other and vagueness ramifies.

In the chapters to come there are *three* skills that will be most important for you to learn (and also most valuable over the long run). The *first* is learning how to *evaluate* an argument for validity. The *second* is learning to *translate* ordinary English sentences into formal terms, and the *third* is learning to *recognize* the common underlying formal structure of different ways of expressing the same thought. These three skills integrated together give you a very powerful and very general intellectual competency for thinking more clearly and cogently, which is on a par with arithmetic for the universality of its application.

---

[1] We ignore here the fact that the chance is not exactly 1/2—though it could be made more precise if necessary—and calculate the probability as $1 - (1/2 \times 1/2 \times 1/2 \times 1/2 \times 1/2) = 1 - 1/32 = 31/32$.

Chapter 6
Categorical Logic

In this chapter we will examine the branch of formal logic known as **categorical logic** or the logic of terms. Developed by Aristotle, it was studied for many centuries as the only formal treatment of validity in inference. We will look at three topics in categorical logic: categorical statements, the theory of immediate inference, and the theory of the syllogism.

CATEGORICAL STATEMENTS

A CATEGORICAL STATEMENT (OR CATEGORICAL, FOR SHORT) MAKES A CLAIM ABOUT THE relationship between some or all of the members of two classes of things. There are four kinds of categorical statements, represented by the following *standard forms*.

The four standard forms of categorical statements			
Name	Type	Standard Form	Example
A	Universal Affirmative	*All S are P*	All Canadians are farmers
E	Universal Negative	*No S are P*	No Canadians are farmers
I	Particular Affirmative	*Some S are P*	Some Canadians are farmers
O	Particular Negative	*Some S are not P*	Some Canadians are not farmers

Aristotle

Aristotle (384–322 BCE) was the most influential philosopher in the history of Western Philosophy. A student of Plato's at the Academy, and the tutor to Alexander the Great, he was the first to have produced a comprehensive system of all the branches of knowledge into a single body. His influence in all branches of knowledge extended for over 2,000 years and his logic remained the standard of formal method until the development of modern formal logic in the 19th century.

Every categorical statement in standard form has four parts:

- a *quantifier* – the beginning words "All," "Some," or "No"
- a *subject term* – a word or phrase denoting a *class* of things serving as the subject of the sentence
- a *copula* – the linking verb "are," which is a form of the verb *to be*, that connects the subject term with predicate term
- a *predicate term* – a word or phrase denoting a *class* of things serving as the subject complement (which is a noun phrase, linked to the subject by the copula, together with which it forms the verb phrase of the sentence)

Example

	quantifier	subject term	copula	predicate term
	↓	↓	↓	↓
A	All	ducks	are	birds (universal affirmative)
E	No	humans	are	gods (universal negative)
I	Some	humans	are	engineers (particular affirmative)
O	Some	reptiles	are not	snakes (particular negative)

Two forms are *affirmative* (the **A** and **I** forms) and two are *negative* (the **E** and **O** forms), while two forms are *universal* (the **A** and **E** forms) and two are *particular* (the **I** and **O** forms). The names come from the Medieval Latin words "*affirmo*" (I affirm) and "*nego*" (I deny) and are mnemonics that were intended to help monks remember the forms. The names of the two affirmative categorical statements, **A** and **I**, are the first two vowels in "*affirmo*," and the names of the two negative categorical statements, **E** and **O**, are the vowels in "*nego*."

The *quality* of a categorical statement is the character (affirmative or negative) of the relationship it affirms between its subject and predicate terms: It is an *affirmative* statement if it states that the class designated by its subject term is included, either as a whole or only in part, within the class designated by its predicate term, and it is a *negative* statement if it wholly or partially excludes members of the subject class from the predicate class. The *quantity* of a categorical statement, on the other hand, is a measure of the degree (universal or particular) to which the relationship between its subject and predicate terms holds: It is a *universal* statement if the asserted claim holds for every member of the class designated by its subject term, and it is a *particular* statement if it the claim is asserted to hold only for one or more members of the subject class.

John Venn

John Venn (1834–1923), British mathematician and logician at Cambridge, is principally known for his contributions to mathematical logic and probability. His book *Symbolic Logic* (1881) extended George Boole's algebra and introduced "Venn" diagrams as a way of representing sets and their properties, and his earlier book *The Logic of Chance* (1866) was important in the development of the theory of statistics.

John Venn (1834–1923), a mathematician at Cambridge University, devised a method of diagramming categorical statements, now called **Venn diagrams**, that makes representing the relationships between the statements very easy.

We represent the classes denoted by the subject and predicate terms by circles labelled S and P in Figure 6.1. The square containing the circles represents everything in the **universe of discourse**.[2] By "universe of discourse," I mean all the things in the world being

Figure 6.1

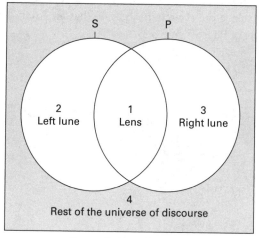

Parts of a Venn Diagram

---

[2] Unless context specifies otherwise, the *universe of discourse* is just reality. But we can narrow the universe of discourse by explicitly giving a context. For example, we might limit discussion to the students in this class, then we could make claims like "All the blonds are sociology majors" (understood to mean "All the blond students in this class are sociology majors.") Or we might, for example, limit discussion to the characters in the novel *Lord of the Rings* (who of course don't really exist at all), then we could make claims like "No hobbits are tall."

discussed. The pair of circles partitions the universe of discourse into four areas. The diagram provides us with a visual model of the two classes. Area 1, called the *lens*, contains everything that is *both S and P*; area 2, the *left lune*, contains only things that are *S but not P*; area 3, the *right lune*, contains only things that are *P but not S*; and area 4 contains only things that are *neither S nor P*. For example, if S stands for the class "Albertans" and P stands for the class "welders," then the lens will represent the class of Albertan welders, the left lune will represent the class of non-welder Albertans, the right lune will represent non-Albertan welders, and the final remaining area will represent the class of non-Albertan non-welders. We call the class formed by the word "non-____", where "____" is some class, the **complement** of that class. For any class—for example, Albertan—everything in the universe of discourse is either a member of that class (is an Albertan) or a member of its complement (is a non-Albertan).

To represent a categorical statement we *black out* any area we know is *empty* (has nothing in it) and put an *x* (or some other letter, say, **y**) in an area to indicate that there is some thing in it. Here is a brief description of the four kinds of categorical statements we described on the first page of this chapter, together with their Venn diagrams.

■ **A. *All S are P*** If all S are P, then if there is any thing that is an S then it is also a P; there are not any things that are S but are not P. For example, if our sentence is "All dogs are mammals," we know that the class of dogs is a sub-class of the class of mammals, so there are not any dogs that are not mammals and we black out the part of the S circle that is outside the P circle to indicate that anything that is a member of S must be a member of P (see Figure 6.2).

Figure 6.2

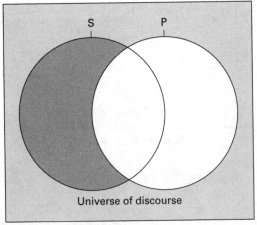

All S are P

■ **E. *No S are P*** If no S are P, then there are no things in the universe of discourse that are both S and P; there is nothing in the overlap area. For example, if our sentence is "No snakes are poodles," we know that there is nothing in the class of snakes that is also in the class of poodles; that is, there is nothing that is both a snake and a poodle, and we indicate this by blacking out the area where S and P overlap (see Figure 6.3). You can see from the symmetry of the diagram that if no snakes are poodles then no poodles are snakes either, so "No S are P" is *equivalent* to (has the same truth conditions as) "No P are S."

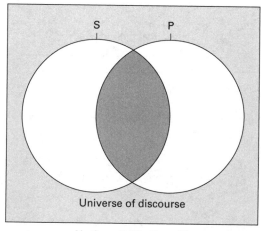

No S are P (No P are S)

Figure 6.3

■ **I. *Some S are P*** The statement "some S are P" tells us *both* that there is at least one thing that is S, and that that thing (and possibly others) is also P. We indicate this by putting an *x* to indicate an individual in the overlap of the S and P circles. For example, there are different sizes of poodle; some are miniatures and some are standards. If our sentence is "Some poodles are standards," we know that at least one poodle in the world is that size. Like **E** categoricals, **I** categoricals are symmetrical (if some poodles are standards then some standards are poodles). You can see this in Figure 6.4.

■ **O. *Some S are not P*** Finally, the statement "Some S are not P" tells us both that there is at least one thing that is S, and that that thing is not P. So we put the *x* in the part of S not overlapping P (see Figure 6.5). For example, there are snakes of many kinds, and some of them are not puff adders, so the statement "Some snakes are not puff adders" is true.

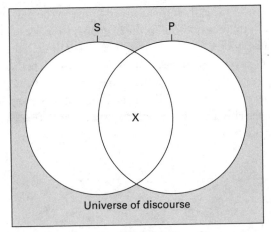

Some S are P (Some P are S)

Figure 6.4

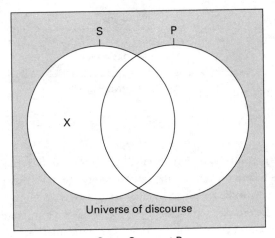

Some S are not P

Figure 6.5

TRANSLATING STATEMENTS INTO STANDARD FORM

WHEN WE TRANSLATE THE PREMISES OF ARGUMENTS EXPRESSED IN ORDINARY LANGUAGE into categorical form, we are regimenting the argument in a way that makes it possible to bring formal procedures to bear on evaluating the argument. We have seen that when we try to express the premises and conclusion in categorical form, we have available quite a bit of contextual knowledge that we can draw on in the task. This task is simplified by having standard ways to translate sentences informally expressed in English. We will now look at a number of them.

Some Standard Translations by Type of Statement

Informal type A categoricals	and replacements
Apples are fruits	All *apples* are *fruits*
You can't lose weight unless you exercise	All *weight losers* are *exercisers*
If it's a fish it lays eggs	All *fish* are *egg layers*
He only likes red smarties	All *smarties liked by him* are *red smarties*
Only engineers will be hired today	All *people to be hired today* are *engineers*

Note: If you have trouble seeing this last case, try to think of it as equivalent to the **conditional statement**, "If anyone is hired today then they will be engineers." This works because if only engineers will be hired today then anyone who is hired will be an engineer and so all the people hired will be engineers.

Informal type E categoricals	replacements
If it's big it isn't pretty	No *big things* are *pretty things*
Cats are never vegetarians	No *cats* are *vegetarians*
Every Baptist is a non-drinker	No *Baptists* are *drinkers*
Pigs can't fly	No *pigs* are *flying animals*

Note that in this set, "Every Baptist is a non-drinker" is *not* to be translated as "All Baptists are non-drinkers" even though that sentence is equivalent to "No Baptists are drinkers" (which, by the way, shows us that **A** and **E** statements are inter-translatable). The term "non-drinker" is called the *complement* of the term "drinker," it refers to everything in the universe of discourse that is *not a drinker.* A term and its complement cover the whole universe of discourse, since everything either falls into the class of things that have a given property or into the complement class of all the things lacking that property. When there is a choice, *you should always use the affirmative form of the predicate* rather than its complement (use "are _____" rather than "are non-_____"), so that the negations are as much as possible expressed by the form of the categorical rather than by the predicates. All of the sentences above *could* be translated as **A** sentences (for example, "All cats are non-vegetarians") but only if we used a complement term as the predicate.

Informal type I statements	replacements
Many men smoke	Some *men* are *smokers*
Engineers are often women	Some *engineers* are *women*
Insects can sometimes fly	Some *insects* are *fliers*
Canadians are friendly	Some *Canadians* are *friendly people*

Note that "most," "many," "some," "a few," and "at least one" all translate the same way as "some." This imposes a burden of care when examining how particular statements fit into arguments. We will discuss this issue more fully in a moment.

Informal type O statements	replacements
Not all animals can fly	Some *animals* are not *fliers*
Most students don't cook	Some *students* are not *cooks*
There are fruits that aren't sweet	Some *fruit* are not *sweet things*
Chemists aren't usually funny	Some *chemists* are not *funny people*

Note that I have treated "Not all animals can fly" as a translational equivalent to "Some animals are not fliers," but this will only be a proper translation if it is known that the subject term "animals" has actual reference. If the subject term is empty or even if it is merely not known whether it has members, such a translation will be illegitimate. "Not all unicorns are white" does not correctly translate as "Some unicorns are not white"—unless we have specifically restricted the universe of discourse to a "world" containing unicorns—since we know that there are no unicorns. I will discuss this issue further in a moment.

Steps in Translations

Reliable translations can usually be made by following these four rules:

1. If necessary, rephrase the *subject* and *predicate* terms so that they are *the names of classes*. Many sentences in English have adjectives as their grammatical predicates. These should be rewritten as *noun phrases*—thus "Some clowns are *funny*" becomes "Some clowns are *funny people*," "All oceans are large" becomes "All oceans are *large bodies of water*," and so on.

2. If the verb in the statement is not the copula ("are" or "are not"), rewrite the *verb* or *verb phrase* so that it takes the *copula noun-phrase form*. Use the copula and a noun phrase that best captures the sense of the verb (in short, use these forms: "are [*noun phrase*]" or "are not [*noun phrase*]")—thus "Fish *swim*" becomes "All fish <u>are *swimmers*</u>," "Some newlyweds *fight with their spouses*" becomes "Some newlyweds <u>are *people who fight with their spouses*</u>," and so on. Do **not** use the complements of classes in your translations of complement non-phrases (so do **not** translate "Fish swim" as "No fish are non-swimmers").

3. Pay close attention to the context and make sure to get the *quantity* of the categorical right. Thus "Dogs are mammals" is clearly a definitional or classificatory claim and so should be written as "*All* dogs are mammals," but "Bankers are conservatives" should be written as "*Some* bankers are conservatives" because it is implicitly a claim about what most (or at least many) bankers are like and is not a universal law or definitional claim about all bankers. When in doubt, look at the argument and ask yourself which translation is best suited to the context of the argument being made.

4. Finally, treat statements about individuals as claims about the unit class (the class that contains only that individual) in question. Usually you should opt for a universal categorical, so "*Prime Minister Harper* is a Conservative" would be written as "All *people identical with Prime Minister Harper* are Conservatives," and "*Ottawa* is the capital of Canada" would be rewritten as "All *places identical with Ottawa* are places identical with the capital of Canada," and "*This beer* doesn't taste good" would become "No *things identical with this beer* are good-tasting things." But sometimes the existence of an entity in the unit class is relevant to the argument and then you may need to opt for a particular categorical. The Prime Minister Harper example above would be written as "Some Conservatives are people identical to Prime Minister Harper." The issues regarding when to do this are discussed more fully in the next section on translation.

STUDY SETS 1

<u>Part A.</u> Identify the form (**A, E, I,** or **O**) of each of the following statements:

1. The gods have no mercy
2. Lead is malleable
3. Squares are always rectangles
4. Rectangles are sometimes squares
5. All co-eds are women students
6. Uranium is radioactive
7. Iron is not radioactive
8. Some dogs bite children
9. Dogs are never reptiles
10. Some students at the University of Manitoba are not Canadians

<u>Part B.</u> Identify the form (**A, E, I** or **O**) of these statements and put them in standard categorical form.

1. Only doctors are surgeons
2. Mustangs are Fords
3. If it moves, shoot it

4. Students often bike to school

5. There are polar bears in Canada

6. Some polar bears do not live in Canada

7. If not you, I'll have no lover

8. Everything worth doing is worth doing well

9. Paris is beautiful

10. Detroit isn't beautiful

THREE ISSUES REGARDING PROPER TRANSLATIONS

FEW STATEMENTS IN ORDINARY ENGLISH LOOK LIKE STANDARD FORM CATEGORICAL statements. But a surprisingly large number of statements can nonetheless be translated into standard form categorical statements in a relatively natural way. We have just seen how to translate a wide variety of ordinary claims. But the quantificational resources of categorical logic are relatively meagre and impose some limitations on the possibility of direct translation. These limitations require discussion if we are to offer translations that preserve the logical structure of certain kinds of arguments. We will look at three issues under the headings: *the problem of empty terms, interpretations of "some,"* and *direct singular reference.*

The Problem of Empty Terms

On the modern interpretation of categorical statements, the universal categoricals "All S are P" and "No S are P" make no claims about whether or not anything actually exists. The statement "All cats have fleas" is understood to be simply about the relation between the property of *being a cat* and the property of *having fleas*; it makes the claim that for *everything* in the universe of discourse, *if* that thing is a cat *then* that thing has fleas. It is not considered part of the job of the statement to say whether or not there are any cats. By contrast, the two particular categoricals, "Some S are P" and "Some S are not P," *are* taken to make claims about the actual existence of *at least one thing* in the universe of discourse that is S. This distinction is observed in the Venn diagrams by the fact that the two universal categoricals are graphed only by blacking out areas known to be empty of anything, whereas the two particular categoricals are graphed by placing an *x* (or some other letter) in an area to show that something exists in the corresponding class.

This feature of the modern interpretation is to some degree at odds with how we normally speak. Usually when we say that something like "All diamonds are hard," we assume that there *are* some things that are diamonds and that all of *them* are hard things. But modern categorical logic treats the universal statements merely as *conditional* claims, so "All diamonds are hard" is understood as "*If* something is a diamond *then* it is hard," or, more accurately, "For all the things that there are, if a thing is a diamond then that thing is a hard thing." And we do speak this way in ordinary language at least some of the time. If I say, "All people cheating on the test will receive a failing grade," you will naturally understand this in a way that does not require that I actually will find anyone cheating on the test. Instead you will understand it as the conditional statement that *if* I find someone cheating on the test *then* they will receive a failing grade. Because this conditional has an antecedent that may not be met, there is no way to show that the conditional has been violated unless you can produce a student I have found to have been cheating who did not fail the test. This has a consequence that can appear very odd. A conditional of the form "If A then B" is only false when the antecedent "A" is true and the consequent "B" is false; when the antecedent "A" turns out to be false then the conditional is *trivially true*. In the case of universal categoricals, this has the unintuitive result that in cases where the subject term is known to be empty in advance, as in the case of the term "unicorn," then "All unicorns are white" will be true in a trivial way— true because there aren't any unicorns. In fact "No unicorns are white" will be true for exactly the same reason.

This way of looking at universal categoricals is still somewhat unsatisfactory. There are a number of problems and I will mention two. *First*, we commonly *do* understand sentences like "Not all Albertans are steelworkers" to mean "Some Albertans are not steelworkers." In fact this is a completely natural proposal for translation of that sentence into categorical form. But for this completely natural equivalence to be correct, we have to assume that there are some Albertans. So much of the time when we make universal conditional claims we do in fact believe that the classes in question have members. But this feature of usage is due to a fact about context: We understand sentences in the context of the beliefs and knowledge we have about the world. So when we assume that there are Albertans, this is not due to the *meaning* of the universal categorical but is an independent piece of knowledge we already have and bring to the task of how best to translate the sentence. The consequence of this fact is that we need to pay attention to context when we are translating ordinary sentences into categorical form (this will have a bearing on fictional contexts, as we will see in a moment).

The *second* problem is that universal claims often make claims to some kind of *necessity* or *conceptual connection* between the terms in question. We can see this by considering a sentence like "If I had a billion dollars I would be rich." We don't want to say that this is trivially true *because* I don't actually have a billion dollars, because knowing what we do about how much money a billion dollars is, we know that if it *were* true then I *would* be rich. (We might express this as "If having a billion dollars doesn't mean being rich, what does?") Compare this to "If I had a billion dollars I would be a duck": Giving me a billion dollars *would* make me rich but it *wouldn't* make me a duck! There is just no meaning relation or any other kind of connection of necessity between the classes. Many of the universal conditionals we use appear to involve *subjunctive* claims as well as merely indicative claims. We know that all diamonds are hard because it is a fact about the *nature* of diamonds, a fact about the kind of thing that they are, so if anything *were* a diamond it *would* be hard. This shows us that the statement "All diamonds are hard" is not only true of all the actual diamonds but of all *possible* diamonds as well. It makes a necessity claim as well as a factual claim and has what we call *modal* force. A modal statement is a statement that makes a claim about necessity or possibility.

The fact that many universal claims have modal force is due to a central feature of our ordinary conception of the world. We have a conception of the possible, of what *could* be true, that is part of our conception of actual things. It is part of our understanding of how things actually are that they could be different than they are in certain ways but not others. It is also part of our ordinary conception of things that if some things *had* turned out a little differently then other things *would be* different as a result. Partly this is a causal matter. Not only are bridges not made of butter, they *couldn't* be—butter doesn't have the tensile strength, or any number of other causal properties it would need to be an adequate bridge-building material. If we had spent the day sunning on the beach we would have been tanned by the sun. Modal relations are very hard to express directly in translation into categorical logic. Since categoricals can only reflect what is true in the universe of discourse, one strategy for expressing modal relations is to restrict the universe of discourse by making some assumptions that are contrary to fact but specify what could have been true or would have been true on the assumptions made. We do this routinely, in fact. We are planning a holiday to Mexico and ask what language the people would be speaking; we have no trouble thinking about what would be true *if* we were in Mexico. The method we use is a simple one. We imagine a change and then we change other things only as much as is required to think about the situation. If we are planning a holiday in Mexico, we imagine ourselves in Mexico in order to plan the details, but we don't imagine that we have a million dollars (that would be daydreaming, not trip planning).

A somewhat similar issue is posed by fictional language. We have no trouble thinking that there are facts about what unicorns are like even though there aren't any unicorns. Properly understood, these may simply be facts about what it is appropriately (or commonly) *said* about unicorns, since there are no unicorns to make those claims true. But this does not mean that we cannot reason about unicorns. When we encounter arguments involving fictional or mythological entities, we have to look at context to see what the implicit universe of discourse is. It is easy to see that the following argument is valid: "All hobbits have hairy feet, and some hobbits are gardeners, so some gardeners have hairy feet." Even though there aren't any hobbits, they appear as characters in stories by J.R.R. Tolkien, and in those stories all hobbits do have hairy feet and some of them are gardeners. The problems of dealing formally with causal and fictional and other sorts of possibility will not be further discussed here. It is a difficult subject and the mathematical and logical resources needed to deal with those difficulties are well beyond the scope of this course.

So to summarize, the problems of empty classes and subjunctive possibilities arise in modern treatments of universal categoricals that do not assume the existence of the members of the classes being described. Technically speaking, logic is mute on what there is and only clarifies the relations between claims in a syllogism, so formal rules concerning things that don't actually exist can sometimes produce strange, or at least counterintuitive, results. As these strange results pose problems for logical formalism that go beyond the scope of this course, we have cursorily responded to them by noting that they give us reasons for careful attention to context when translating ordinary sentences into categorical form. After we have translated our sentences into categorical form, we need to remember that universal categoricals can be true even if the classes they refer to are empty. So you cannot infer as a matter of logic that there are some things in a class from the truth of a universal affirmative or negative term. For example, from the truth of the statement "All unicorns have a horn in their foreheads" you cannot infer that there are some unicorns. Of course, sometimes the context makes it clear that there are members of the classes in question, but then the inference from, say, "All cats are mammals" to "Some mammals are cats" is not grounded in the universal claim alone but in addition our background knowledge that there are cats.

Interpretations of "Some"

Categorical logic, with its meagre stock of quantifiers, cannot do full justice to statements and inferences that depend on distinguishing more from less and thus the differences between exactly one, a few, some, many, and almost all. If there is exactly one member of S that is P, then the categorical "Some S are P" is true, and the same is true if almost all S are P. This means that we need to careful in translation. Compare translating these sentences:

1. Apples are fruit.
2. Men are fools.
3. Economists are conservatives.

The translation of 1 is clear: It makes a claim about *the kind of thing an apple is* and thus says that the class of apples is a subset of the class of fruits and the correct form is clearly "All apples are fruit." The translation of 3 is fairly clear, since while not all economists are conservatives, we reasonably take the sentence to mean "Most (or at least many) economists are conservatives" and thus we will translate it as "Some economists are conservatives."

But how should we translate 2? Should we treat this as the universal claim "All men are fools" or as the particular one "Some men are fools"? The answer will vary and so to see what to do we need to look at the context in which the statement occurs. We need to ask what kind of argument is being made and whether that argument depends on a universal or a particular treatment for that claim. Consider, for example, the argument *Men are fools and fools are rash so men are rash.* Suppose we translated all three of the sentences as particular affirmative categoricals to get:

Some men are fools
<u>Some fools are rash creatures</u>
Some men are rash creatures

The argument would not be valid because although we would know there was at least one man who was a fool and at least one fool who was rash creature, we would have no guarantee that they were the same person. But if one of the premises were translated as a universal claim (for example, if the first premise were "All men are fools"), the conclusion would follow. We will see examples of arguments of these sorts ahead. By giving charitable and careful translations, we can extend the range of arguments that can be successfully translated into categorical form. It is usually clear in a particular context what the best translation is.

Direct Singular Reference

The remaining issue to be discussed before we turn to the practical problem of translating tricky statements in natural language into standard categorical statements is the issue of direct singular reference. English contains many kinds of noun phrases that allow one to make references to individuals and groups of individuals. Proper names ("Bill," "Mary" . . .), determiners ("The," "a" . . .) and demonstratives ("This," "That" . . .) all play roles in fixing reference in noun phrases. If I say, "Bill is tall," you understand me to be referring to a particular person named Bill, even though there are many people named Bill. Similarly, phrases like "that cat," "this old man," "the barking dog," and "my house" all make reference to a specific individual creature or thing, whereas phrases like "a cat," "most old men," and "several apples" typically make indefinite reference, not referring to any particular individual but simply to a member of a class. It is sometimes difficult to know merely from grammatical markers whether specific or indefinite reference is intended. For example, we usually take the indefinite article "a" instead of the definite article "the" or a demonstrative like "that" to imply indefinite reference: If you say, "I want to buy a shirt," the salesperson will not take you to have a particular shirt in mind, but if you say, "I want that shirt" (pointing at a particular shirt), you are making a specific reference. On the other hand, if you say, "I want that shirt in a large," pointing to a small shirt, then you are referring to a *specific type* of shirt (that is to say, a *shirt like that*) but not to a particular instance of that type.

The problem categorical statements pose for translating claims involving specific reference comes to this: The universal categoricals make no referential claim to individuals at all but say things about whole classes, and particular categoricals make only indefinite reference to individuals. "Some Manitobans are nurses," for example, tells you that one or more Manitobans is a nurse, but it gives you no information about *which* Manitobans are nurses. This makes it difficult to translate arguments in which *both premises are about the same individual or individuals.* Consider the argument "Some Manitobans are nurses; they are very dedicated, therefore some Manitobans are very dedicated." The word "they" clearly refers to the group of Manitoban nurses, and the point of the argument is to say that since they are very dedicated and they are Manitobans, it follows that some Manitobans are very dedicated people. Since "nurses" is clearly the subject term of the premise "they are very dedicated," our options for translation are either the particular categorical, "Some nurses are very dedicated people," or the universal categorical, "All nurses are very dedicated people." Since our aim is to talk only about Manitoban nurses, you might think that the particular premise is better than the universal one and that the argument should look like this:

> Some nurses are very dedicated people
> <u>Some Manitobans are nurses</u>
> Some Manitobans are very dedicated people

But the difficulty is that when we translate the argument this way, the first premise does not tell you that the nurses who are dedicated are *Manitoban* nurses and the second premise does not tell you that the nurses who are Manitobans are *dedicated* nurses, and so the argument is invalid. But if you translate the first premise as "All nurses are very dedicated people" (since in the context you know that you are talking about the dedicated Manitoban nurses and can thus reasonably restrict the universe of discourse to them) the argument will turn out to be valid.

Translating statements containing proper names requires special treatment for the same kind of reason. To properly translate proper names, we need to treat the name as referring to a special class that contains all and only the things named. So to translate "Angelo is Italian," I say "All persons identical to Angelo are Italians" and since there is one and only one person in the class of persons identical to Angelo, this gets us *most* and perhaps all of what we want. It tells us that "For all the things that there are, if a thing is a member of the class of people identical to Angelo then that thing is an Italian." But it does *not* tell us that there *is* any thing that is a member of the class of people identical to Angelo. If this part of the claim to be translated is relevant to an argument involving Angelo being Italian, then we need to translate the statement as "Some Italians are people identical to Angelo." We can see this by considering the following argument: "Angelo is Italian and Angelo is an architect, therefore some architect is an Italian." This argument is clearly valid, because the conclusion, which says that there is at least one Italian who is an architect, is made true by the existence of Angelo, who is both Italian and an architect. But as in the case involving the Manitoban nurses, we cannot translate both premises as either universal or particular categoricals because in neither case will the argument be valid. Instead we need to make one premise universal and the other particular, as follows:

> Some architects are people identical to Angelo
> <u>All persons identical to Angelo are Italians</u>
> Some architects are Italians

The first premise tells us that *there is* at least one architect who is a person identical to Angelo. The second premise tells us that *if* there is a person identical to Angelo *then* that person is an Italian and between the two premises we have the information that there is at least one architect who is Italian.

The point to keep in mind when translating sentences into categorical form is that there is usually quite a lot of information implicitly available in an argument as it is informally presented and you will always lose *some* of that information in the translation, so it is important to make sure that you don't lose the information you need for assessing the validity of the argument. Very often the important information that must be preserved in the translation is information that keeps track of specific individuals mentioned in the argument. With all these considerations in mind, let us now look at some exercises involving difficulties in translation.

STUDY SETS 2

Identify the three terms, the premises, and conclusion in these arguments, translating them appropriately and putting the premises and conclusion into the standard form.

1. Bananas are delicious but rotten bananas are not so some bananas are not rotten.

2. Stephen Harper is prime minister and Stephen Harper is plump so some prime ministers are plump.

3. (In the TV show *Buffy*): Angel is a vampire with a soul and no one with a soul is totally evil so some vampires are not totally evil.

4. Men are weak and the weak always fail so some men fail.

5. The melting point of tin is 232°C and some of my pots are tin, so they melt at 232°C.

6. The monsters under your bed are afraid when Teddy is in your bed and Teddy is here in bed with you so no monsters will come out from under your bed tonight. (Hint: remember that you need to translate this using only three terms, so you will need to be creative.)

IMMEDIATE INFERENCES

CATEGORICAL STATEMENTS OF DIFFERENT FORMS THAT SHARE THE SAME TERMS ARE LOGICALLY interrelated to each other in a variety of ways involving equivalence, implication, or negation. We will look at three relations between categorical statements that are the product of manipulating the *order* of the terms, the *quantity* of the statement—whether it is universal or particular, and the **quality** of the statement—whether it is affirmative or negative. These relations are **conversion**, **contraposition**, and **obversion**. We will also look at three forms of negation, **contradiction**, **contrariety**, and **subcontrariety**. Many of these relations will only hold on the added condition that *the classes in question are not empty*, but they are nonetheless useful in establishing context and finding proper translations of arguments.

Conversion

The *converse* of a categorical statement is the new categorical statement made by interchanging the subject term and the predicate term of the first categorical statement. This procedure is called *converting* the statement. Looking back at the Venn diagrams, you can see that the diagrams for **E** and **I** categoricals are symmetrical with respect to the subject and predicate terms—if you switch the order, the diagram looks exactly the same. Since the *converse* of a categorical statement is the product of interchanging the statement's subject and predicate terms, **E** and **I** categoricals are logically equivalent to their converses (because their diagrams are symmetrical). The converse of the **E** statement "No snakes are poodles" is "No poodles are snakes" and these are equivalent claims, so an **E** statement is *logically equivalent to its converse*. And the same goes for an **I** statement: You can see *an I statement and its converse are logically equivalent*. "Some snakes are pretty things" is equivalent to "Some pretty things are snakes." Conversion thus is the ground of an immediate inference between **E** and **I** statements.

   A and **O** categoricals, however, are not equivalent to their converses. Because their diagrams are not symmetrical, interchanging the subject and predicate terms changes the diagram (see Box 6.1). It does not follow from the fact that all poodles are mammals that all mammals are poodles! Neither does it follow that if some mammals are not poodles then some poodles are not mammals.

Box 6.1

Conversion

The converse of a categorical statement is the product of interchanging the statement's subject and predicate terms.

form	statement	converse	relation
A	All S are P	All P are S	not equivalent
E	No S are P	No P are S	equivalent
I	Some S are P	Some P are S	equivalent
O	Some S are not P	Some P are not S	not equivalent

Box 6.2

Contraposition

The contrapositive of a categorical statement is the product of interchanging the statement's subject and predicate terms and replacing them with their complements.

form	statement	contrapositive	relation
A	All S are P	All non-P are non-S	equivalent
E	No S are P	No non-P are non-S	not equivalent
I	Some S are P	Some non-P are non-S	not equivalent
O	Some S are not P	Some non-P are not non-S	equivalent

Contraposition

The *contrapositive* of a categorical statement is the new categorical that results from putting the *complement* of the original subject term in the predicate place and putting the *complement* of the original predicate term in the subject place; in short, both terms are turned into their complement and their positions are switched (see Box 6.2). Remember that the complement of a class is the class of everything not in the original class, so the class of non-dogs is the complement of the class of dogs. To obtain the contrapositive of a categorical statement, first we obtain the converse by switching the order of the terms, and then we negate the terms by attaching a "non-" to both the subject and predicate terms. For example, the contrapositive of "All pickles are green things" is "All non-green things are non-pickles," which is clearly true: If all pickles are green things then all the non-green things are non-pickles, so an **A** categorical is equivalent to its contrapositive. *Contraposition* also grounds an immediate inference for **O** categoricals. For example, "Some two-legged creatures are not birds" is equivalent to "Some non-birds are not non-two legged creatures." Contraposition does not preserve truth for **E** categoricals (if "No pickles are red things" is true, it does not follow that "No non-red things are non-pickles"! Presumably there are lots of non-red things that are not pickles). Neither does it preserve truth for **I** categoricals.

Obversion

Obversion is the product of changing both the *quality* of a categorical statement—that is, changing it from negative to affirmative or affirmative to negative—and replacing the predicate term with its complement—negating it by attaching a "non-" to the predicate term. It turns out that every categorical is equivalent to its obverse. Thus the obverse of the

Box 6.3

Obversion

The obverse of a categorical statement is the product of changing the quality of the statement and replacing the statement's predicate term with its complement.

form	statement	converse	relation
A	All S are P	No S are non-P	equivalent
E	No S are P	All S are non-P	equivalent
I	Some S are P	Some S are not non-P	equivalent
O	Some S are not P	Some S are non-P	equivalent

A categorical "All cats are mammals" is "No cats are non-mammals"; the obverse of the E categorical "No snakes are mammals" is "All snakes are non-mammals"; the obverse of the I categorical "Some snakes are poisonous creatures" is "Some snakes are not non-poisonous creatures"; the obverse of the O categorical "Some parents are not men" is "Some parents are non-men"—all of these transformations preserve truth.

We can summarize these relationships using Venn diagrams (see Figures 6.6–6.9).

Figure 6.6

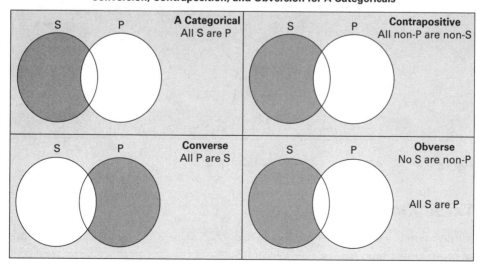

Conversion, Contraposition, and Obversion for A Categoricals

Conversion, Contraposition, and Obversion for E Categoricals

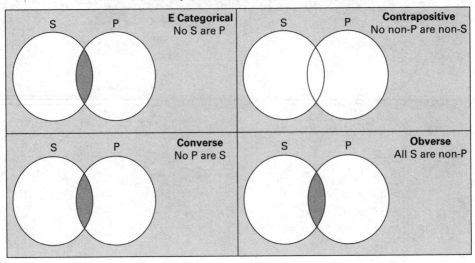

Figure 6.7

Conversion, Contraposition, and Obversion for I Categoricals

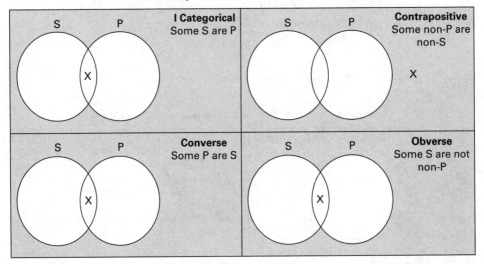

Figure 6.8

Three Kinds of Negation

We now turn to a discussion of *negation*. In *traditional* categorical logic there are three kinds of negation that form the basis for logical inference between categoricals: **contradiction**, **contrariety** and **subcontrariety**. Of these, only *contradiction* holds as a matter of logic on

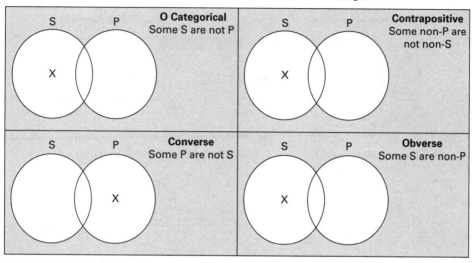

Conversion, Contraposition, and Obversion for O Categoricals

| O Categorical
Some S are not P | Contrapositive
Some non-P are
not non-S |
| Converse
Some P are not S | Obverse
Some S are non-P |

Figure 6.9

the modern account. The other two, *contrariety* and *subcontrariety*, do not hold universally in the modern form of categorical logic because they depend on the traditional assumption of universal categoricals that the terms not be empty. But because this assumption is almost always the case, in practice it is useful to discuss all three forms of negation for the light that they shed on choices for translation. But it is important to keep firmly in mind that inferences involving contraries and subcontraries can only be made in contexts in which reasoners know that the classes of things under discussion are *not empty*, and that the inferences depend materially on that knowledge.

The *contradictory* of a categorical statement is the explicit denial of the whole statement. A categorical statement and its contradiction accordingly always have opposite truth values. **A** and **O** statements are clearly contradictories: The Venn diagram of an **A** statement shows the left lune, the S non-P class, to be empty of members, but the diagram of an **O** statement shows that there is at least one non-P S thing by placing an x in that space. Similarly **E** and **I** statements are contradictories. The first denies and the second asserts that some S is P.

We discussed *contraries* in the context of the fallacy of bifurcation in Chapter 4. You will remember that two contraries cannot both be true but can both be false. Two *subcontraries*, by contrast, can both be true but at most one can be false. It turns out that *when we know that the subject classes are not empty*, universal affirmative statements and universal negative statements are contraries and particular affirmative and particular negative statements are subcontraries. For example, on the condition that pickles exist, "All pickles are blue" and "No pickles are blue" are contraries because they cannot both be true, but they can both be false. They will both be false if some pickles are blue but not all pickles are blue. Again, on the condition that pickles exist, "Some pickles are blue" and "Some pickles are not blue" cannot both be false, but both can be true.

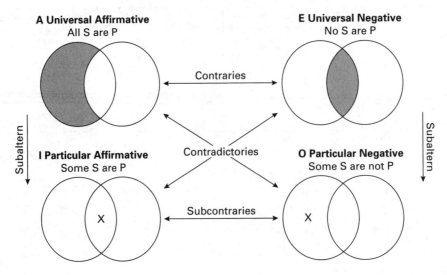

The Traditional Square of Opposition

A Universal Affirmative
All S are P

E Universal Negative
No S are P

Contraries

Subaltern

I Particular Affirmative
Some S are P

Contradictories

O Particular Negative
Some S are not P

Subaltern

X

Subcontraries

X

Figure 6.10

On the traditional interpretation of universal categoricals, there is an additional relation that grounds immediate inference, known as subalternation. Subalternation holds between **A** and **I** categoricals and between the **E** and **O** categoricals, and represents the fact that *when we know that the subject classes are not empty*, we can infer that "Some S are P" is true from the fact that all S are P, and that "Some S are not P" is true from the fact that no S are P—thus, if I know that there are ducks, I can infer that some ducks are birds from the truth that all ducks are birds, and similarly on the assumption that there are snakes, I can infer from that fact that no snakes are mammals that some snakes are not mammals.

All of these relationships are summarized in what is known as the traditional square of opposition (see Figure 6.10). The relationships summarized in it were of central importance to the development of logic for over 2,000 years. With the development of modern formal logic and the mathematics of classes, its importance has declined. Of the relations summarized by it *only contradiction holds for modern categorical logic*.

(If you have further interest in the relationship between the modern and traditional forms of categorical logic, you may wish to read the historical entry called "The Traditional Square of Opposition" in *The Stanford Encyclopedia of Philosophy* at http://plato. stanford.edu/entries/square/ on the web.)

STUDY SETS 3

Use a **T** or an **F** to mark, for each sentence, whether it is true or false.

1. _____ A and E type categorical statements are equivalent to their converses on the traditional interpretation.

2. _____ A and E categorical statements are affirmative in quality.

3. ____ **A** and **O** categoricals are contradictories.

4. ____ The subaltern of an **E** categorical, on the traditional interpretation, is an **I** categorical.

5. ____ In conversion, one interchanges the subject and predicate term.

6. ____ If "All S are P" is true then "All non-P are non-S" is true.

7. ____ If "Some S are P" is true then "Some non-P are non-S" is true.

8. ____ All four types of categoricals have the same form as their contrapositives.

9. ____ The subaltern of an **A** statement on the traditional interpretation is an **O** statement.

10. ____ If "All S are P" is true and "Some S are Q" is true then "Some P are Q" is true.

11. ____ The subcontrary of an **I** categorical is an **E** categorical.

12. ____ If "Some S are **P**" is true and "Some S are Q" is true then "Some P are Q" is true.

13. ____ In **O** statements, the subject term is distributed but not the predicate term.

14. ____ The contradictory of an **A** statement is an **O** statement.

15. ____ If "Some S are not P" is true then "Not all S are P" is true.

16. ____ **A** and **E** type categorical statements are equivalent to their contrapositives on the traditional interpretation.

17. ____ The three kinds of negation of categorical statements on the traditional interpretation are converse, obverse, and contradiction.

18. ____ The contradictory of an **A** statement is an **E** statement.

19. ____ The three kinds of negation in categorical statements on the traditional interpretation are contradiction, contrariety, and subcontrariety.

20. ____ All four types of categorical statements have the same form as their converses on the traditional interpretation.

21. ____ The three kinds of negation in categorical statements on the traditional interpretation are contrary, contradiction, and converse.

THE CATEGORICAL SYLLOGISM

WE NOW TURN TO THE THEORY OF THE SYLLOGISM. A *SYLLOGISM* IS AN ARGUMENT COMPOSED of three categorical statements, two of which are premises and the third is the conclusion. The three statements jointly contain three non-logical referring terms, each appearing in two of the three statements. The theory of the syllogism has the task of determining which syllogisms are valid. Let us consider an example:

All birds are egg layers
All ducks are birds_____
All ducks are egg layers

There are three terms, "ducks," "birds," and "egg layers," and each appears twice. The term used as the subject term of the conclusion of the syllogism ("ducks") is called the *minor* term of the syllogism as a whole. The *major* term of the syllogism is the predicate term of its conclusion ("egg layers"). The third term in the syllogism ("birds") doesn't occur in the conclusion at all, but appears in each of its premises; we call it the *middle* term. Since one of the premises of the syllogism must be a categorical statement containing its middle and major terms, we call that the *major premise* of the syllogism. The major premise is by convention written first. The other premise, which links the middle and minor terms, we call the *minor premise*. In this example, all three statements are **A** statements, which we can represent by "**AAA**." Since there are four kinds of statement, there are $4^3 (= 64)$ possibilities, traditionally called the *moods* of the syllogism. The *figure* of a categorical syllogism traditionally referred to the four possible arrangements of the middle term. The figures are represented numerically 1–4:

- Figure 1   The middle term is the subject of the first premise and the predicate of the second premise.
- Figure 2   The middle term is the predicate of both premises.
- Figure 3   The middle term is the subject of both premises.
- Figure 4   The middle term is the predicate of the first premise and the subject of the second premise.

In the example above, the figure is 1 and so the categorical syllogism was traditionally called AAA1. The combination of mood and figure was known as form. Since there are four figures for each mood and there are 64 moods, there are $64 \times 4 (= 256)$ syllogistic forms. Of these forms only a few are valid. Medieval logicians gave each form a mnemonic name to keep track of the valid ones. For example, the syllogism with the form **AAA1** is known as "Barbara," because "B<u>a</u>rb<u>a</u>r<u>a</u>" has three a's as vowels. The syllogism with the form **EAE1** is known as "C<u>e</u>l<u>a</u>r<u>e</u>nt," the syllogism with the form **AII1** is known as "D<u>a</u>r<u>ii</u>," and so on. Thus:

Celarent	Darii	Ferio
E No mammals are birds	A All swans are white	E No student is a baby
A <u>All whales are mammals</u>	I <u>Some birds are swans</u>	I <u>Some men are students</u>
E No whales are birds	I Some birds are white	O Some men are not babies

Because we will be using Venn diagrams to determine validity, we do not need to remember the small number of valid forms, nor do we need to apply the complex rules for determining validity that were necessary prior to the development of modern class logic. Venn diagrams are easy to apply and provide us with a simple and intuitive procedure for determining validity. We will now look at this procedure.

SHOWING VALIDITY WITH VENN DIAGRAMS

To show validity using Venn diagrams, we will use a *diagram with three interlocking circles* or *Trefoil*, one circle for each of the three terms of the syllogism. To show how to do this, we will use the instance of Celarent from the previous page:

No mammals are birds
<u>All whales are mammals</u>
No whales are birds

First, we graph the *major* premise, treating the *top circle* as the *middle* term, the lower left circle as the *major* term, and the lower right circle as the *minor* term. Then we graph the second, or *minor*, premise. The first two diagrams below show the two premises graphed separately; the third shows them combined as they would be after graphing both the first and the second premise on the same diagram. The third diagram shows what is made true by the conjunction of the two premises. If the conclusion is already present in the diagram after graphing the premises, then the truth of the conclusion follows from the truth of the premises and the argument is valid. If the conclusion is true, the lens made by the overlapping B and W circles will be shaded out—*and it is* (see Figure 6.11). So the argument is valid.

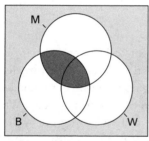
No mammals are birds

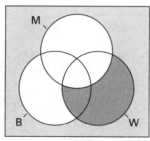
All whales are mammals

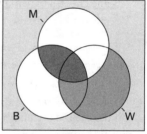
Both premises together

Figure 6.11

Let us look at another example.

Some bankers are vegetarians
<u>No anarchists are bankers</u>
Some anarchists are not vegetarians

The middle term is "bankers" so it is represented by the top circle, with the major term to the left and the minor term to the right. We graph the first premise by putting an *x* in the lens between the V and B circles. Because we don't know whether it should go inside the A circle or outside it, we put it on top of the line to express our ignorance. When we graph the second premise the lens between the B and A circles is shaded out, meaning nothing is in that space, so this pushes our *x* into the remaining space in the lens between

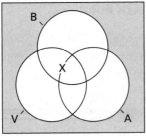

Some bankers are vegetarians

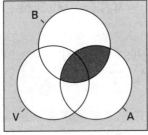
No anarchists are bankers

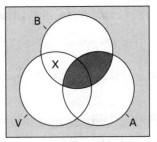
The premises together

Figure 6.12

the V and B circles (see Figure 6.12). We now look to see whether the conclusion is graphed. The conclusion is that there are some members of the class of anarchists that are not in the class of vegetarians, which implies finding an *x* somewhere in the A circle that lies outside the V circle. There is no *x* in that space, so the argument is INVALID.

We will look at one more example and then provide a set of rules for using Venn diagrams.

> Some used car salesmen are cheats
> Some cheats are bankers
> Some bankers are used car salesmen

The middle term is "cheats," so that is represented in Figure 6.13 by the top circle, the major term is represented by the left-hand lower circle, and the minor term by the right-hand lower circle. We graph the first premise by putting an *x* on the centre line in the middle of the lens formed by the C (cheats) and U (used car salesmen) circles. We graph the second premise by putting a *y* on the line in the centre of the lens formed by the C and B (bankers) circles. Figure 6.13 illustrates the result:

Figure 6.13

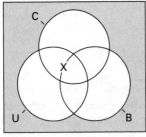
Some used car salesmen are cheats

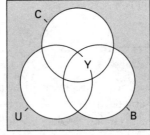
Some cheats are bankers

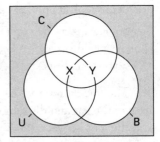
Premises combined

We can see that the argument must be invalid. The argument is invalid because although we know that there is someone (= *x*) who is a used car salesman and a cheat, we don't know that that person is a banker, and although we know that there is someone (=y) who is a cheat and a banker, we don't know that that person is a used car salesman. If we could know that *x* and *y* were *the same person* then the argument would be valid, but the premises do not authorize us in making that claim. The diagram shows us this: We don't know which side of the line the *x* in the lens between U and C is on—we don't know whether the *x* goes on the inside or the outside of the B circle because we don't know whether that person is a banker or not. Similarly for the **y**: It represents a cheat who is also a banker, but we don't know whether or not that cheating banker is also a used car salesman.

Rules for Using Venn Diagrams to Determine Validity

1. *Identify* the premises and conclusion. Determine that there are two premises and a conclusion. If there appears to be only one premise then the argument may be an enthymeme with an implicit premise, and if there appear to be three premises, the argument may be a **chained enthymeme,** in which two arguments are joined together by an implicit statement that is the conclusion of one argument and a premise in the other. We will examine cases of these two sorts in the next section.

2. *Identify* the three referring terms. The *predicate* term of the conclusion is the *major* term; the *subject* term of the conclusion is the *minor* term. (The *middle* term appears only in the two premises.) If there are *four* terms, either the argument is a fallacy of ambiguity (a fallacy of four terms) or else a chained enthymeme.

3. *Place* each statement in standard categorical form and *abbreviate* the three terms with a capital letter. *Write a dictionary* connecting the term and its abbreviation.

4. Formalize the argument by placing the abbreviated version of the *major* premise first. It is the premise that contains the *major* term. Place the abbreviated version of the *minor* premise second. Place the conclusion last under the line.

5. *Diagram the argument.* First, draw three intersecting circles, with one on top, and make sure to label them so that the lower left circle is labelled with the letter that stands for the major term, the top centre circle is labelled with the letter for the middle term, and the lower right-hand circle is labelled for the minor term. Then graph the two premises on the diagram. Use different colours or crosshatching so that you can see each premise independently. Do *not* graph the conclusion on this diagram. (If you want to graph the conclusion so that you will see how it looks, *make sure to do it on a different diagram!*) Make sure to graph particular premises by putting the *x* (or **y**) on the line if there is a line dividing the space where the *x*

(or **y**) goes. If one side of the line is shaded by the graph of a universal premise, you must move the **x** into the remaining open space. When one premise is universal and the other is particular, if you graph the universal one first you will not need to shift the **x**.

6. *Test* the argument for validity. You do this by *examining the diagram* you have made. Look to see whether the graph for the conclusion is present. If it is, the argument is formally valid; if it is not present the argument is invalid. You may wish to diagram the conclusion separately so that you can see whether shaded parts of the diagram or parts containing an "**x**" are contained in the diagram of the premises. (Of course, you should not diagram the conclusion on the same trefoil!)

Let us walk through an example to put these steps together.

All birds are egg layers
All ducks are birds
All ducks are egg layers

There are three terms, "ducks," "birds," and "egg layers," and each appears in two sentences. The *major term* of the syllogism ("egg layers") is the predicate term of its conclusion. The *middle term* of the syllogism ("birds") appears in each of its premises, but not in the conclusion. The *minor term* of the syllogism ("ducks") is the subject term of its conclusion.

The *major premise* of the syllogism is the premise containing the major term and the middle term. The *minor premise* is the premise containing the minor term and the middle term. The major premise is written *first*, the minor premise second.

To determine the *validity* of a syllogism, we graph its premises on a "trefoil" Venn diagram containing three interlocking circles, which is constructed in Figure 6.14.

Figure 6.14

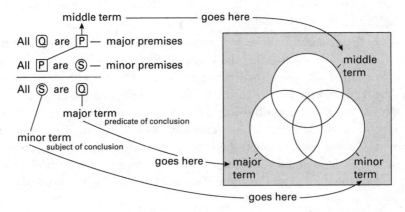

First we graph premise one and then premise two. Figure 6.15 shows each premise graphed separately and then together.

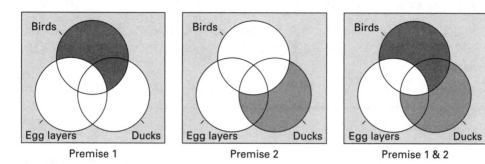

Premise 1   Premise 2   Premise 1 & 2

Figure 6.15

We can see that the argument is valid, because the "duck" circle has been blocked out everywhere outside the "egg layers" circle, so that if anything is a duck it is also an egg layer, which is what the conclusion claims.

If we drew the conclusion separately. It would look like Figure 6.16:

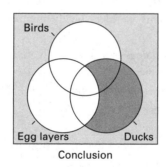

Conclusion

Figure 6.16

You can see that the graph of each premise supplies half of what is needed to graph the conclusion; together they supply all of it. The argument is **valid**.

STUDY SETS 4

<u>Part A.</u> Put these arguments in *categorical form*, using *capital letters* to abbreviate the terms used in the argument, and give a *dictionary*.

1. Sailors are not always swimmers. Swimmers always drink beer. So some sailors don't drink beer.
2. Most high school teachers are men. Some men are not dope smokers since high school teachers never smoke dope.

3. Snakes are reptiles and reptiles lay eggs, so snakes lay eggs.

4. No painters are rational since no rational being is an artist and painters are artists.

5. Mary is unhappy. Unhappy people are always maladjusted so Mary is maladjusted.

<u>Part B.</u> Put these arguments in *categorical form*, using *capital letters* to abbreviate the terms used in the argument, and give a *dictionary*. Then use Venn diagrams to determine if the arguments are valid.

1. People wearing gym shoes are allowed to play in the gym. All the grade one students are wearing gym shoes so they can play in the gym.

2. Only students get a free lunch. Martha is not a student so Martha cannot eat lunch for free.

3. All vampires drink blood. No living creatures are vampires. (So) Some blood drinkers are not alive.

4. Some dead things have souls because some vampires have souls and all vampires are dead.

5. All Greeks are liars and some philosophers are liars, so some Greeks are philosophers.

6. Some philosophy classes are very boring although all Eric's philosophy classes are exciting. So there are philosophy classes not taught by Eric.

7. Not all Canadians know the periodic table of elements, but only people who know the periodic table of elements are scientifically literate so not all Canadians are scientifically literate.

8. Anyone who likes video games is a deviant. Teenage males universally like video games so all male teens are deviants.

9. The gods are fickle and cruel. Jove is a god, so he is fickle and cruel.

10. All the reporters at the *Daily Planet* live in Metropolis. Clark Kent is a reporter at the *Daily Planet* so he lives in Metropolis.

11. All the reporters at the *Daily Planet* live in Metropolis. Lois Lane lives in Metropolis so Lois Lane is a reporter at the *Daily Planet*.

SYLLOGISTIC ENTHYMEMES

Before moving on to sentence logic, it is worth saying a few words about syllogistic enthymemes. In Chapter 1 we introduced enthymemes as follows. *An enthymeme is an argument in which a required premise is not stated explicitly but is assumed implicitly as part of the argument.* There are two kinds of syllogistic enthymemes. The first is simply a syllogism that is missing a premise that is assumed as obvious. The second is called a *chained enthymeme*, which consists of a *pair* (or more) of syllogisms in which the first has an unstated conclusion that functions as an implicit premise in the second.

Here are two examples:

Men are fools	All men are fools (or) Some men are fools
Fools waste their lives	All fools are life wasters

| People who waste their lives regret | All life wasters are regretful people |
| So men regret | All (some) men are regretful people |

Since this argument has three premises if it is to turn out to be a *chained syllogistic enthymeme*, it must be possible to reconstruct it as a pair of syllogisms where the conclusion of the first syllogism is an implicit premise in the second. We could translate the premises so that the pair could either make a claim about *all* men, as in version 1, or merely *some* men, as in version 2.

Version 1	Version 2
Syllogism 1	**Syllogism 1**
All fools are life wasters	All fools are life wasters
All men are fools	Some men are fools
All men are life wasters	Some men are life wasters
Syllogism 2	**Syllogism 2**
All life wasters are regretful people	All life wasters are regretful people
All men are life wasters	Some men are life wasters
All men are regretful people	Some men are regretful people

Here the conclusion of the first argument, that all (or some) men are life wasters, forms a premise in the second argument, producing two valid syllogisms chained together into a larger argument.

Example

Men are animals
so they need food

This argument can be reconstructed by adding the suppressed premise as the following syllogism:

All animals are food needers (*suppressed premise*)
All men are animals
All men are food needers

STUDY SETS 5

Reconstruct these enthymemes as syllogisms and test for validity.

1. All fish can swim so trout can swim.
2. The students in this class will do badly on the test because they didn't study.

3. Trout are fish and fish are tasty, so you will like eating trout. (Treat as two syllogisms where the conclusion of the first is a premise in the second.)
4. Some Canadians are bigots so don't listen to their opinions.
5. The monsters under your bed are afraid when Teddy is in your bed and Teddy is here in bed with you so no monsters will come out from under your bed tonight. (You saw this one earlier. This time you should translate it as a pair of chained syllogisms.)

ADDITIONAL STUDY SETS

LET'S FIRST REVIEW THE CATEGORICAL SYLLOGISM.

Remember that a syllogism is an argument composed of *three* categorical statements, of which *two* are premises and the *third* is the conclusion. The three statements jointly contain *three* non-logical terms referring to classes, each appearing in exactly *two* of the statements. The premises need to be in the right order and the circles in the diagram need to be properly labelled. Look at the "Birds are egg layers" example on pages 158–159 (Figures 6.14–6.16). If there are too many or too few terms, you should see if the argument is a pair of chained syllogisms or an enthymeme.

Here are four examples. Each has a different set of features that you should attend to, and that will help you do the exercises correctly.

Example 1

All leopards are big cats
All leopards have spots
so some big cats have spots

    1. Dictionary   L = leopards, middle term
                                   S = creatures with spots, major term
                                   B = big cats, minor term

    2. Notice the premises are in the wrong order.
    3. Replace the words with capital letters from the dictionary and put them in the correct order.
    4. Put the argument in proper form.
    5. Put the capital letters from the dictionary in the box by the appropriate circle.
    6. Diagram the premises.
    7. See whether the argument is valid.

Proper form of argument:

All L are S
All L are B
so some B are S

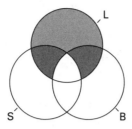

Figure 6.17

    Argument is not valid; the conclusion requires that there be an "X" in the lens made by the S and B circles.

Example 2

No Europeans are Africans
<u>All Ukrainians are Europeans</u>
so no Ukrainians are Africans

    1. Dictionary: E = Europeans, middle term
                                A = Africans, major term
                                U = Ukrainians, minor term

    2. Premises are in the correct order.
    3. Replace words with capital letters from the dictionary.
    4. Put the argument in proper form.
    5. Put the capital letters from the dictionary in the box by the appropriate circle.
    6. Diagram the premises.
    7. See whether the argument is valid.

Proper form of argument:

No A are A
<u>All U are E</u>
so no U are A

Figure 6.18

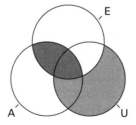

    The lens made by the U and A circles is fully blacked out as required for the conclusion to be true, so **the argument is valid**.

Example 3

No Albertans like ice cream and some Albertans like cabbage, so some people who like cabbage don't like ice cream.

1. Dictionary: A = Albertans, middle term

                              I = people who like ice cream, major term

                              C = people who like cabbage, minor term

2. Premises are in correct order but need to be regimented.

3. Replace words with capital letters from the dictionary.

4. Put the argument in proper form.

5. Put the capital letters from the dictionary in the box by the appropriate circle.

6. Diagram the premises.

7. See whether the argument is valid.

Proper form of argument:
No A are I
Some A are C
so some C are not I

Figure 6.19

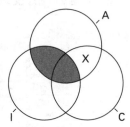

    The conclusion requires that there be an "X" within the C circle but lying outside the I circle, and there is, so **the argument is valid**.

Example 4

Elvis isn't Julia Roberts because Elvis is dead and Julia Roberts isn't.

1. Dictionary: D = dead people, middle term

J = people who are identical to Julia Roberts, major term

E = people who are identical to Elvis, minor term

2. Note: The conclusion is at front and the premises are not in correct order; also needs to be regimented.

3. Replace words with capital letters from the dictionary.

4. Put the argument in proper form.

5. Put the capital letters from the dictionary in the box by the appropriate circle.

6. Diagram the premises.

7. See whether the argument is valid.

Proper form of argument:

No J are D

<u>All E are D</u>

No E are J

Figure 6.20

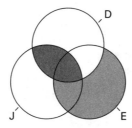

The lens made by the E and J circles is fully blacked out, so **the argument is valid**.

REVIEW OF TRADITIONAL INTERPRETATION OF CATEGORICAL STATEMENTS

LET US ALSO REVIEW THE VARIOUS RELATIONSHIPS OF IMMEDIATE INFERENCE ON THE traditional interpretation of categorical statements:

An A categorical is

■   the *equivalent* to its contrapositive and its obverse

■   the *contradictory* of the corresponding **O** categorical

■   the *contrary* of the corresponding **E** categorical

An E categorical is

- the *equivalent* to its converse and its obverse
- the *contradictory* of the corresponding **I** categorical
- the *contrary* of the corresponding **A** categorical

An I categorical is

- the *equivalent* to its converse and its obverse
- the *contradictory* of the corresponding **E** categorical
- the *subcontrary* of the corresponding **O** categorical
- the *subaltern* of the corresponding **A** categorical

An O categorical is

- the *equivalent* to its contrapositive and its obverse
- the *contradictory* of the corresponding **A** categorical
- the *subcontrary* of the corresponding **I** categorical
- the *subaltern* of the corresponding **E** categorical

STUDY SETS 6

Here are a number of different exercises.

<u>Part A.</u> Put the following statements in categorical form:

1. Knives are always dangerous.
2. Snakes cannot make conversation.
3. A few Albertans are socialists.
4. Swedes are not usually friendly.
5. Moslems just don't drink!
6. Only Baptists will be saved.
7. A few metals are magnetic.
8. He only has eyes for Margaret.
9. Success always takes perseverance.
10. If it is alcoholic Todd will drink it.
11. Mere animals never feel regret.
12. Canadians aren't usually rich.

13. Many Canadians have cancer.

14. Not everything sweet is good for you.

15. You can't be wise without study.

16. If something has wings it isn't a pig.

17. If it can fly then it has wings.

18. Not every engineer is a woman.

19. Only organic foods are safe to eat.

20. Sometimes cats are fat.

21. Parrots cannot talk.

22. Paris is in France.

23. Rectangles are not always squares.

24. Uranium is a metal.

25. Only the lonely know real pain.

26. Some fools fall in love.

27. No great lover has regrets.

28. To fail to love is a great misfortune.

Part B.

1. From a true **I** type categorical, you can infer the truth of

    A. its contrapositive and its obverse

    B. its obverse and its converse

    C. its converse and its contrapositive

    D. its contrapositive, its obverse, and its converse

    E. none of the above

2. Two categoricals are subcontraries if

    A. both can be false and both can be true

    B. both can be true but only one can be false

    C. only one can be true and both can be false

    D. if one is true the other is false

    E. none of the above

3. To make the obverse of a categorical statement, you

    A. replace the subject term by its complement and change the quality

    B. replace the predicate term by its complement and change the quality

    C. interchange the subject and predicate

D. interchange the subject and predicate terms and replace them by their complements

E. interchange the subject and predicate terms and change the quality

4. If all A are B and some C are not B, you can infer

   A. some A are C

   B. some C are not A

   C. no C are A

   D. all C are A

   E. nothing about A and C

5. From a true **A** categorical, you can infer the truth of

   A. its contrapositive and its obverse

   B. its obverse and its converse

   C. its converse and its contrapositive

   D. its contrapositive, its obverse, and its converse

   E. none of the above

6. From the square of opposition, you can see that the types of statements

   A. **A** and **O**, and **E** and **I** are contradictories

   B. **A** and **E**, and **I** and **O** are contradictories

   C. **A** and **O**, and **E** and **I** are contraries

   D. **A** and **E**, and **I** and **O** are subcontraries

   E. **E** and **O** are contraries and **A** and **I** are subcontraries

7. To make the converse of a categorical statement, you

   A. interchange the subject and predicate and change the quality

   B. replace the subject term by its complement and change the quality

   C. interchange the subject and predicate

   D. interchange the subject and predicate terms and replace them with their complements

   E. interchange the subject and predicate terms and change the quality

8. If no A are B and some C are not B, you can infer

   A. some A are C

   B. some C are not A

   C. no C are A

   D. all C are A

   E. nothing about A and C

9. From a true **I** categorical, you can infer the truth of

   A. its contrapositive and its obverse

   B. its obverse and its converse

   C. its converse and its contrapositive

   D. its contrapositive, its obverse, and its converse

   E. none of the above

10. Which categorical statements are equivalent to their contrapositives?

   A. **A** and **O** statements

   B. **A** and **E** statements

   C. **I** and **E** statements

   D. **I** and **O** statements

   E. **A** and **I** statements

11. From the square of opposition, you can see that the types of statements

   A. **A** and **O**, and **E** and **I** are contradictories

   B. **A** and **E**, and **I** and **O** are contradictories

   C. **A** and **O**, and **E** and **I** are contraries

   D. **A** and **E**, and **I** and **O** are subcontraries

   E. **E** and **O** are contraries and **A** and **I** are subcontraries

12. If no A are B and some C are B, you can infer

   A. some A are C

   B. some C are not A

   C. no C are A

   D. some A are not C

   E. nothing about A and C

13. From a true **E** categorical, you can infer the truth of

   A. its contrapositive and its obverse

   B. its obverse and its converse

   C. its converse and its contrapositive

   D. its contrapositive, its obverse, and its converse

   E. none of the above

14. Which categorical statements are equivalent to their converses?

   A. **A** and **O** statements

   B. **A** and **E** statements

C. **I** and **E** statements

D. **I** and **O** statements

E. **A** and **I** statements

<u>Part C.</u> These arguments are all enthymemes with an *implicit premise*. Identify the premises, put the resulting arguments in *categorical form*, using *capital letters* to abbreviate the terms used in the argument, and give a *dictionary*. Then use Venn diagrams to determine if the arguments are valid.

1. Some Canadians will die of cancer since so many of them smoke.

2. Robins are birds so they lay eggs.

3. Canadians have free speech so they can criticize the government.

4. Fido is a dog so he can't fly.

5. Because he's human Socrates is mortal.

6. Drugs should not be legalized because legalization would increase the number of drug addicts.

7. Because it teaches discipline practising the piano is good for children.

<u>Part D.</u> Here is a group of syllogistic arguments written in a variety of ways. Put these arguments in *categorical form*, using *capital letters* to abbreviate the terms used in the argument, making sure the premises are in the *right order*, and give a *dictionary*. Then use Venn diagrams to determine if the arguments are valid.

1. All camels are four-footed and all camels are mammals

   (so) Some mammals are four-footed.

2. Some Canadians eat high protein foods because some Canadians eat fish and fish are high in protein.

3. Wars of conquest are essentially wrong.

   Some religious wars are wars of conquest.

   Some religious wars are essentially wrong.

4. Some Romanians are not golfers.

   Romanians are Eastern Europeans.

   (so) Some Eastern Europeans are not golfers.

5. Cabbages are vegetables.

   No cabbages are conscious.

   No vegetables are conscious.

6. All good people do what is right.

People who do the right thing pay their taxes.

All good people pay their taxes.

7. Some curlers don't pay their taxes and some Canadians are curlers, so some Canadians don't pay their taxes.

8. Some sheep are not white sheep, and some sheep are not black sheep, so some black sheep are not white sheep.

9. Some cheeses are hard and all cheeses are milk products so you can infer that some milk products are hard.

10. Alberta politicians are all oilmen and oilmen are always evil-doers so all Alberta politicians are evil-doers.

11. Copper is a metal.

All metals conduct electricity.

(so) Some copper conducts electricity.

12. No reptiles are mammals.

Some animals with tails are mammals.

(so) Some tailed animals are not reptiles.

13. All punt returners are speedy.

Some punt returners are wide receivers.

(so) Some wide receivers are speedy.

14. Bananas are squishy when overripe.

Mangos are not bananas.

(so) Mangos are not squishy when overripe.

15. Some Ukrainians are welders.

Some men are welders.

(so) Some Ukrainians are men.

16. Some pool players lack souls since vampires don't have souls and some vampires play pool.

17. Residents of B.C. are frequently skiers but skiers are often not rock-climbers so many rock-climbers are not B.C. residents.

18. Killing is never permissible because killing is always evil and no evil act is permissible.

19. No reptiles are mammals.

Some animals with tails are mammals.

(so) Some tailed animals are not reptiles.

20. All real Quebecers are separatists, because real Quebecers love Quebec and people who love Quebec are separatists.

21. Some animals are mammals.

    All mammals suckle their young.

    (so) Some animals suckle their young.

22. Some dogs have tails and no humans have tails, so no humans are dogs.

23. All real Canadians love hockey and no soccer players could like hockey, so no real Canadians play soccer.

24. Many people feel oppressed by guilt. This is because feeling guilt is a kind of dysfunction and some people are dysfunctional.

Chapter 7
Sentence Logic and Consistency

In the last chapter, we studied the traditional logic of terms and learned a method of analyzing arguments by treating them as syllogisms composed of categorical statements. We saw that validity in syllogisms depends on the relationship between the terms in the categorical statements making them up. In this chapter, we will examine instead the relationships between sentences treated as units. In particular we will examine sets of sentences and consider the question of their consistency—can they be true together?

A Word about Sentence Logic

There are two standard and complementary ways of presenting sentence logic, of which we will look at one. The first way, which we will examine here, focuses on *validity* using truth tables and trees. These are procedures for assigning truth or falsity to the conclusion of an argument based on the truth or falsity of the premises. The focus is on showing validity in arguments by demonstrating that it is impossible for the premises to be true and the conclusion false. The second way, which we will not examine, focuses on *deducibility* and procedures for determining whether the conclusion of an argument can be deduced from its premises by a series of steps, each of which is known to preserve truth. The intuition here is that the conclusion *follows* from the premises by way of a series of steps. Each step in a proof should be the conclusion of an intuitively valid argument whose premises are found among the preceding steps. These steps are governed by inference rules, which are intuitively acceptable. Here is an example: You may remember from Chapter 1 that we showed

Modus Ponens ("*P* and *If P then Q* therefore *Q*") to be a valid argument form. *Modus Ponens* is a typical intuitive inference rule, so if one finds the statements *P* and *If P then Q* in a line of proof, then one can insert *Q* into the proof. The rule allows this because *Q* follows deductively from *P* and *If P then Q*. You are probably familiar with what a derivation is from high school algebra.

In a typical second-year logic course, both methods are presented and then (in a later part of the course devoted to meta-theory) it is shown that an argument is derivable by deduction only if it is valid (a property called soundness) and that it is valid only if it is derivable (a property called completeness). Logical systems like sentence logic, which are both sound and complete, are rich enough that they can provide a deduction for every valid argument that can be expressed in it. In fact, all valid arguments and only valid arguments can be derived in it. The proofs of these results in meta-theory involve considerable logical sophistication and lie well outside a course on critical thinking.

In Chapter 1, we characterized an argument as a certain sort of set of sentences, and a valid argument as one that has the property that *if the premises are true, then the conclusion must be true.* We also saw that if an argument is regimented or formalized carefully, the features that make a valid argument valid can be discerned by relatively simple methods. In the last chapter, we saw one method of regimenting arguments that has this result. A properly translated categorical syllogism can be shown to be valid or invalid by the use of a Venn diagram, because a Venn diagram is sensitive precisely to the features of a syllogism that determine its validity. In this chapter we will see another method of regimenting arguments that also allows the determination of validity by simple procedures. These procedures relate the truth or falsity of parts of arguments to the truth or falsity of the whole, treating an argument as a truth-functional structure. We will also learn some analytical skills useful in evaluation of arguments.

COMPOUND SENTENCES

IN THIS CHAPTER WE WILL BE INTERESTED IN THE ANALYSIS OF A PARTICULAR KIND OF compound sentence—the *truth-functional* compound sentence—and the role such sentences play in showing validity in arguments. The sentences we are interested in are sentences that are formed out of other, simpler sentences and whose **truth values** are related to those simpler sentences. Let's begin by considering the following two sentences:

1. John likes Mary and Bill.
2. John likes Mary or Steven.

    These sentences are compound sentences. They can be broken up into the simpler sentences connected by the words "and" and "or."

3. John likes Mary (AND) John likes Bill.
4. John likes Mary (OR) John likes Steven.

    What is of interest to us in this chapter is that the truth of sentences like 3 and 4 is precisely fixed by the truth of the simpler sentences and the truth-determining behaviour of the connecting words "and" and "or." *The truth of the compound sentence is a function of its parts* (hence the phrase "truth-functional" logic).

    We can see this more clearly by adopting a simplifying terminology. In this chapter we will use *capital letters* as abbreviations of sentences. For example:

5. M = def.   John likes Mary.
6. B = def.   John likes Bill.
7. S = def.   John likes Steven.

    Our original sentences can now be written as:

8. M and B
9. M or S

    The words "and" and "or" are part of what we will call *truth-functions.* To characterize truth-functions adequately, we need a way of talking about a sentence without saying which sentence it is. We do this by using Greek letters φ (phi), ψ (psi), χ (chi)—all rhyming with "sky"—to stand for sentence variables. A sentence variable marks a blank or a gap where a sentence can go. Thus, in:

10. φ and ψ,

if you replaced "φ" with "M" and "ψ" with "B," you would get the sentence in 8 on the previous page. Note that the use of Greek letters for variables is traditional but arbitrary; we could just have well used symbols like "♥," "♦," and "♠," or "♂," "☺," and "♫." The important thing is that a variable is a blank space into which different things can be put. If you find it confusing to think about variables using Greek letters, you might think of them instead as happy faces or as empty boxes into which you can put sentences, in which case 10 would look something like this:

11. ⬜⬜⬜⬜⬜ and ⬜⬜⬜⬜⬜,

and after you put the sentences into the boxes it would look like this:

12. John likes Mary *and* John likes Bill.

TRUTH-FUNCTIONS

WE WILL NOW INTRODUCE TWO CONCEPTS: **SENTENCE-FUNCTION** AND **TRUTH-FUNCTION**. First, sentence-function. A sentence-function is a string of English words and one or more sentence variables, which has the following property: If the sentence variables are replaced by English sentences, the whole string becomes a sentence in English. Here are some examples:

13. It's true that φ

14. Either φ or Eric is tired

15. If φ and ψ, then χ

16. Bill hopes that φ

17. φ, or φ and ψ

(Note that in 17, "φ" is repeated twice. When a sentence variable is repeated within one sentence-function it must be replaced by the same sentence at each occurrence.)

A truth-function is a sentence-function that has an additional feature: truth-functionality. The truth or falsity of the whole sentence is a function of the truth or falsity of the sentences replacing the sentence variables in it. Looking at examples 13 to 17, we can see that 13 is a truth-function because the whole sentence is true if φ is true and false otherwise. For example, if φ = "it is raining," then 13 says:

13'. It is true that it is raining,

which is true if it is raining and false if not. But if we insert "it is raining" into 14, we get

14'. Either it is raining or Eric is tired.

But this sentence is not a truth-function of "it is raining" because even though if it is raining then the sentence is true, if it is not raining the truth of the sentence is not determinable because it depends on whether or not Eric is tired. We can see immediately that 15 and 17 are truth-functional compounds because they contain only sentence variables and truth-functional words like "and," "or," and "if then." But sentence 16 is not a truth-functional compound. When we replace the variable with "it is raining," we get

16'. Bill hopes that it is raining.

Here the truth or falsity of the compound sentence is entirely a function of what Bill hopes and is not a function of whether it is raining or not. We will look at five standard truth-functions, which have the approximate natural readings: "not ___," "___ and ___," "___ or ___," "If ___ then ___," and "___ if and only if ___," for which we will use the following symbols.

The 5 Standard Truth-Functions

¬φ	: not φ	negation	(It is false that Bill is sad)
φ ∧ ψ	: φ and ψ	conjunction	(Bill is late and Mary is tired)
φ ∨ ψ	: φ or ψ	disjunction	(Bill is late or Mary is tired)
φ → ψ	: if φ then ψ	implication	(If Bill is late then Mary is tired)
φ ↔ ψ	: φ if and only if ψ	equivalence	(Bill is late if and only if Mary is tired)

TRUTH TABLES

SENTENCE LOGIC, AS WE ARE TREATING IT HERE, IS THE EXAMINATION OF ARGUMENTS TO SEE whether they are valid. In order to accomplish this we must master a number of different skills.

First, we must learn to translate sentences in English into truth-functional sentences that preserve what is central to the argument in order to regiment them for analysis. The sentences in English that we translate will always have more content and implications than we can, or would want to, translate; in this sense, the vocabulary of sentence logic is austere and restrictive. We saw in Chapter 6 just how important careful translation is in capturing the logically relevant features of a categorical syllogism. The same considerations apply here.

Second, we must learn a procedure for examining the premises together, once they are suitably regimented into truth-functional sentences, to see whether the conditions under which they are true together are conditions under which the conclusion, also suitably regimented, is true as well.

Third, to implement the procedure, we must understand fully how the five truth-functions relate to their constituents. If we do not understand the behaviour of the five truth-functions we will not be able to use our procedures reliably, and we will also be unable to select the best translations for our English sentences. These are all skills that involve other, more general critical thinking skills: attention to detail, making relevant features explicit, and the capacity to see logical structure in ordinary, non-regimented English prose. And although it may not appear obvious while we are learning these skills, they have enormously broad application outside the classroom. You will find that your capacity to discern good and bad argumentation is greatly increased, and like the skill of riding a bicycle, these skills are a permanent acquisition.

When a set of truth-functional sentences is connected by truth-functions, the truth or falsity of the resulting complex sentence is determined by the truth or falsity of the members. We make use of this fact in our analysis of arguments. In sentence logic, there are five standard truth-functions. A **truth table** indicates all the possible circumstances for truth and falsity of a statement in a convenient notation. Since every statement is either true or false, the truth table for a simple statement is

$$\frac{\varphi}{\begin{array}{c} T \\ F \end{array}}$$

Each line under the sentence variable "φ" represents a different possibility; here "T" stands for "true" and "F" stands for "false." The truth tables of the five standard truth-functions indicate the truth or falsity of the compound statement in terms of the truth or falsity of the constituent sentences. They are defined by the following truth tables.

The truth table for *negation* has only one constituent sentence, so there are only two possibilities. Negation switches the truth value from true to false or from false to true and the negation of a negated statement has the same truth value as the original statement:

φ	$\neg\varphi$	$\neg\neg\varphi$
T	F	T
F	T	F

The other four truth-functional compounds have two constituent sentences and, as a result, there are four possible combinations of truth values. The table for *conjunction* looks like this:

φ	ψ	$\varphi \wedge \psi$
T	T	T
T	F	F
F	T	F
F	F	F

This table tells us that the *conjunction* of two sentences is true whenever both constituent sentences are true, and false if one or both of the constituent sentences is false. Conjunction exactly mirrors the ordinary use of the word "and" in English.

The table for *disjunction* looks like this:

φ	ψ	φ ∨ ψ
T	T	T
T	F	T
F	T	T
F	F	F

This table tells us that the *disjunction* of two sentences is true whenever one or both of the constituent sentences is true, and is false only when both constituents are false. The word "or" has an inclusive sense and an exclusive sense in ordinary usage. Disjunction mirrors the *inclusive* use of "or" in English. The word "or" is also often used in an exclusive sense in ordinary language, where it means "one or the other *but not both*." Examples of the exclusive usage are easy to find. If someone buys two ice cream cones and says, "You can have the chocolate or the vanilla," they do not intend that you get both cones, or if a robber points a gun at you and says, "Your money or your life," you will feel ripped off if, after you give the robber your money, he shoots you. But if you think about it, exclusive "or" can be expressed by the truth-functions we have, since it means "A or B *and not* A *and* B." You should soon be able to see that we can write this statement as the compound sentence "(A ∨ B) ∧ ¬(A ∧ B)."

We need the parentheses for punctuation to prevent ambiguity. We will discuss punctuation in a moment.

The table for *implication* looks like this:

φ	ψ	φ → ψ
T	T	T
T	F	F
F	T	T
F	F	T

This table tells us that the *implication* of one statement by another is false if the first statement, the *antecedent*, is false and the second statement, the *consequent*, is true, and it is true whenever the antecedent is false or if the consequent is true. Implications are often called *conditionals*. You will remember conditionals from the discussion in Chapter 6 of the modern interpretation of universal categoricals, a conditional so called because it states that *if* the antecedent is true *then* the consequent is true as well, and so it makes a conditional truth claim. Many students find the truth table for implication very counterintuitive at first, but soon find that they get used to it. The first two lines of the truth table are obvious, the two cases where φ is true: Clearly if φ is true and ψ is true then φ → ψ is true, and clearly if φ is true and ψ is false, then φ → ψ is false, but the cases where φ is false seem less obvious. The point to keep in mind is that implication must reflect the property that premises have to the conclusion in a valid argument, namely the fact that *if* the premises are true *then* the conclusion is true. No valid argument can make a STRONGER claim than that—it cannot guarantee that the premises *are* true, for example; that is a question of how the world turns out. This means that the only thing it takes to keep an argument from being valid is the possibility of a counter-example—some possible circumstance where the premises are true and the conclusion false. One cannot produce a counter-example by making φ false, and so the two lines where φ is false make φ → ψ true by default.

Finally we will look at the fifth truth-function, *equivalence*, the table for which looks like this:

φ	ψ	φ ↔ ψ
T	T	T
T	F	F
F	T	F
F	F	T

The table shows us that two sentences are equivalent when they have *the same truth value*. (The word "equivalence" just *means* "equal in value," in this case "equal in *truth value*.") Equivalences are often called *biconditionals*. If the constituents are both true or they are both false then the biconditional sentence stating their equivalence is true, and if the constituents have different truth values then the biconditional is false. Equivalences are called biconditionals because they are equivalent to conditionals in both directions; that is,

$$(A \leftrightarrow B) \leftrightarrow ((A \rightarrow B) \land (B \rightarrow A))$$

A truth table is a kind of model of the conditions under which a compound sentence is true or false. It shows the possible circumstances under which a sentence is true and the circumstances under which a sentence is false in terms of the constituent sentences of the whole. Since a sentence analyzed in a truth table is composed of one or more constituent sentences and one or more truth-functions, the circumstances under which the sentence is analyzed are given by the various logical possibilities of truth and falsity of the constituent sentences. Each line of the truth table represents a different set of circumstances and thus represents a different assignment of truth or falsity to the constituent sentences. All the lines together exhaust the different possible assignments of truth or falsity to the constituents. As a result, a truth table represents every possible situation involving the component sentences and the truth value of each situation.

Since there are only two values assigned to each constituent (it is either *true* or it is *false*), the number of lines, n, needed for the truth table will be 2 to the m power, where m is the number of constituents (that is, $n = 2^m$). Thus if m = 1, n = 2^1 (or 2), if m = 2, n = 2^2 (or 4), if m = 3, n = 2^3 (or 8), etc., so the number of lines doubles for each additional constituent as illustrated below.

The number of lines in a truth table with n constituents is n = 2m

φ	φ ψ	φ ψ χ	φ ψ χ ω
T	T T	T T T	T T T T
F 2	T F	T T F	T T T F
	F T 4	T F T	T T F T
	F F	T F F	T T F F
		F T T 8	T F T T
		F T F	T F T F
		F F T	T F F T
		F F F	T F F F
			F T T T 16
			F T T F
			F T F T
			F T F F
			F F T T
			F F T F
			F F F T
			F F F F

ARGUMENTS USING TRUTH TABLES

WE MAY NOW CLARIFY SOME TERMS AND SHOW HOW TO DETERMINE THE TRUTH VALUE OF A compound sentence containing more than one truth-function.

- A *simple* sentence is a sentence containing no truth-functions. For example, "Bill is sad," "The room is hot," "It is raining," and "The river is swollen" are all simple sentences because they contain no truth-functions. They are assigned sentence letters and written as *p*, *q*, *r*, etc. We write a different letter for each different simple sentence.

- A *compound* sentence is a truth-functional sentence containing both simple sentences and truth-functions. For example, "It is raining *and* the river is swollen" contains two simple sentences and the truth-function "and"; it is written as "$q \wedge p$." A compound sentence may contain other compound sentences as constituents; for example, "*If* it is raining *and* the river is swollen, *then* we stay in the house" has two truth-functions and three simple sentences and is written as "$(q \wedge p) \rightarrow r$." We need to put parentheses around "$q \land p$" to show that "it is raining *and* the river is swollen" is treated as a unit (as the antecedent) by the if/then relation.

■ A **logical truth** is a sentence that is true under every possible circumstance: It can never be false. It follows that the truth table of a logical truth will contain only Ts in the column under the logical truth. Such a sentence is also called a **tautology**. The compound sentence "$p \lor \neg p$" is an example of a *tautology*.

■ A *contradiction* is a sentence that is false in every possible circumstance: It can never be true. The truth table of a contradiction will accordingly contain only Fs in the column under the contradiction. Since negation changes T to F and F to T, the negation of a contradiction is a logical truth, and the negation of a logical truth is a contradiction. This accords with ordinary intuitions, as a sentence that is always true is never false and a sentence that is always false is never true. The compound sentence "$p \land \neg p$" is an example of a contradiction.

■ An argument is *valid* if in every possible circumstance in which its premises are true the conclusion is true as well. We can express an argument as a *conditional* sentence stating that *if* the conjunction of the premises is true *then* the conclusion is true. We make such a conditional sentence by first conjoining all the premises, and second making a conditional sentence with the conjunction of the premises as the antecedent and the conclusion as the consequent. We will call this sentence the *corresponding conditional*. The **corresponding conditional** of an argument is just a compound sentence, but it is a special one because the argument is *valid* if and only if its corresponding conditional is a *logical truth*.

We have said that an argument is composed of a set of premises and a conclusion, and that a valid argument has the property that if the premises are true then the conclusion is true. Because an argument is valid if and only if its corresponding conditional is a logical truth, we can test arguments for validity by forming the corresponding conditional of an argument and doing a truth table of it. There are other tests for validity, which we will look at later in the chapter, but let us begin with this test. To apply this test, first we produce a compound sentence in which the conclusion is made conditional upon a conjunction of the premises, and has the logical form:

$$(((((\text{premise } 1) \land (\text{premise } 2)) \land (\text{premise } 3)) \land (\text{premise } 4))...) \rightarrow (\text{conclusion})$$

Then we determine whether this sentence is a tautology or logical truth. Let us look at an example:

Example: Suppose that P and Q are the constituent simple sentences of the argument and the argument is:

Premise 1	$= P \lor Q$	"either P or Q"
Premise 2	$= \neg P \rightarrow \neg Q$	"If P is false then Q is false"
(Therefore) Conclusion	$= \therefore P$	

We write the corresponding conditional of the argument as

$$((P \lor Q) \land (\neg P \to \neg Q)) \to P$$

Notice that we use parentheses for punctuation. We place each premise in parentheses, as "$(P \lor Q)$" and "$(\neg P \to \neg Q)$" and conjoin the two premises, as "$(P \lor Q) \land (\neg P \to \neg Q)$," and then put their conjunction in parentheses, as "$((P \lor Q) \land (\neg P \to \neg Q))$," making that compound the antecedent of the conditional above. So the consequent conditional says, "If the first premise *and* the second premise are true *then* the conclusion is true."

We now write the truth table as

P Q	$((P \lor Q)$	$\land$	$(\neg P$	$\to$	$\neg Q))$	$\to P$
T T	T	T	F	T	F	**T**
T F	T	T	F	T	T	**T**
F T	T	F	T	F	F	**T**
F F	F	F	T	T	T	**T**
	1	5	2	4	3	6

The numbers at the bottom indicate the order in which we assigned the rows of truth tables. We will now look at the question of how one assigns truth tables to compound sentences.

Since the column for the whole sentence contains only Ts, the sentence is logically true and a theorem. Perhaps you will be able to see that not only is the argument valid but the premises are true if and only if the conclusion is true (look at column 5 in the table, which is the truth table for the premises; it is the same as the column for "P"). In short, the biconditional

$$((P \lor Q) \land (\neg P \to \neg Q)) \leftrightarrow P$$

is also a tautology.

Notice how we have used parentheses as punctuation. When there is more than one truth-function in a sentence, punctuation is required to disambiguate the sentence. Thus the compound sentence

$$\text{"}P \lor Q \land R\text{"}$$

could mean either "$(P \lor Q) \land R$" or "$P \lor (Q \land R)$."

Using parentheses as punctuation clears up what the *scope* of each conjunct is meant to be. Anything inside a matching pair of parentheses is to be treated as a unit from outside the parentheses. The scope of a truth-function is simply what it ranges over. In a compound sentence with more than one truth-function, one of the truth-functions will have the whole compound sentence in its scope. The truth value of that function is the truth value of the whole sentence.

Let us look at how we assign truth values to a compound sentence containing two truth-functions; for example, "P ∨ (Q ∧ R)."

The truth table of "Q and R" is just the same as the definition table for "and":

Q R	Q ∧ R
T T	T
T F	F
F T	F
F F	F

But because we have three simple sentences, we need to have eight rows instead of four, like this:

P Q R	P ∨ (Q ∧ R)
T T T	T
T T F	F
T F T	F
T F F	F
F T T	T
F T F	F
F F T	F
F F F	F

You can see that the pattern T, F, F, F appears twice. We fill in the table one line at a time, looking over at the values of Q and R on the left-hand side and placing the appropriate letter on the left according to the definition table for "and." When we have filled in the whole row, we are now ready to fill in the values for "or" using the definition table:

φ ψ	φ ∨ ψ
T T	T
T F	T
F T	T
F F	F

If you look at the partly filled-in truth table above, you will see that the column under the P on the right-hand side corresponds to the column for "φ," and the column on the left-hand side under (Q ∧ R) corresponds to the column for "ψ." So we fill in the table for "or" one row at a time, like this:

P Q R	P ∨ (Q ∧ R)	
T T T	**T**	T
T T F		F
T F T		F
T F F		F
F T T		T
F T F		F
F F T		F
F F F		F

The first row corresponds to the top row of the definition table. We continue doing each row and end up with a table that looks like this:

P Q R	P ∨ (Q ∧ R)	
T T T	**T**	T
T T F	**T**	F
T F T	**T**	F
T F F	**T**	F
F T T	**T**	T
F T F	**F**	F
F F T	**F**	F
F F F	**F**	F

The column in bold shows the truth value of the compound sentence as a whole for each of the eight sets of possible truth values for P, Q, and R.

In order to do truth table analysis of arguments reliably, we need to know *in which order* to analyze the parts of the corresponding conditional and *how to put the parts together*. And before we can do that we need to know how to express an argument as its corresponding conditional.

EXPRESSING AN ARGUMENT AS ITS CORRESPONDING CONDITIONAL

To make sure we know how to apply our truth tables to the parts of the conditional sentence expressing an argument, we need to adopt a *standard procedure* for using parentheses to show the scope of each truth-function. To create the conditional sentence, we will need to take care to use parentheses to clarify the order of the conjunction of the premises. So, if an argument in standard form, with a number of premises, looks like this:

Premise 1

Premise 2

Premise 3

. . .

Premise n

Conclusion

we will begin by conjoining the first two premises, using parentheses to separate and distinguish the premises.

$$(\text{Premise 1}) \land (\text{Premise 2})$$

When we add the third premise, there is the potential for ambiguity. We **don't** want this form:

$$(\text{Premise 1}) \land (\text{Premise 2}) \land (\text{Premise 3})$$

since we could not tell what the scope of either "and" ("$\land$") was meant to be. So to keep this clear, we must introduce another set of parentheses:

$$((\text{Premise 1}) \land (\text{Premise 2})) \land (\text{Premise 3})$$

We will have to introduce another set of parentheses for every subsequent premise we conjoin to the rest. And for any further premises:

$$(((\text{Premise 1}) \land (\text{Premise 2})) \land (\text{Premise 3})) \ldots \land (\text{Premise n})$$

This procedure is in itself somewhat arbitrary, but we need a *standard procedure* to keep clear the relation between the conjuncts and so that truth tables may be done consistently. We adopt the rule that we always begin by grouping together the first two premises by putting parentheses around them, and then simply add each subsequent premise, grouping the third together with the conjunction of the first two, and then the fourth with that, etc. Finally, we need to include the conclusion of the argument in this sentence, making it conditional upon the conjunction of all the premises. Since the conclusion is conditional upon the *whole* set of premises, we place a further set of parentheses around the premises, insert the conditional symbol ("$\rightarrow$"), and add the conclusion.

$$((((\text{Premise 1}) \land (\text{Premise 2})) \land (\text{Premise 3})) \ldots \land (\text{Premise n})) \rightarrow (\text{Conclusion})$$

We are now in a position to do a truth table evaluating an argument, using the procedure just demonstrated for compound sentences.

DOING TRUTH TABLES

WHEN A COMPOUND SENTENCE CONTAINS TWO OR MORE TRUTH-FUNCTIONS, ONE ALWAYS has the whole compound sentence as its scope. This truth-function shows the *general form* of the sentence. One can always determine the general form of a sentence by the placement of parentheses. Compare a) and b):

a) ¬(P → Q),   here the general form is "¬φ" [i.e., ¬□]

b) ¬P → Q,   here the general form is "φ → ψ" [i.e., □ → ■]

In a), the "¬" serves to negate the whole sentence inside the parentheses; it says of the sentence "P → Q" that it is not true. But in b), the "¬" negates only "P" and the whole sentence states that the sentence "not-P → Q" is true; by convention we don't bother to put parentheses around the "P" because negation does not connect two sentences, it simply negates the one it is operating on. So when you see compound sentences containing a "¬" it always negates what it is immediately in front of. When a compound sentence has two or more truth-functions, we need to find the one with the *widest* scope. It will be the one whose associated parentheses cover the whole sentence.

Once we have identified the general form of the sentence, we look inside it to see if it contains sentences involving truth-functions. Thus we see that in a) the sentence "φ" itself has the general form of "ψ→χ." We continue this process of finding the general form of parts of the original sentence until the constituent sentences are all simple sentences; that is, constituent sentences that do not contain truth-functions. Let us look at a) again. We found first that

¬(P → Q) has the form   ¬φ   [i.e., ¬ □],

and then we found that "¬φ"'s constituent, "φ," has the form "ψ→χ," where both "ψ" and "χ" are filled with simple sentences. We do a truth table of a) by first doing a truth table of φ, and then, since we have the values for φ, by doing a truth table of ¬φ. We do these line by line using the definition tables for the truth-functions.

Step 1:

P Q	P → Q
T T	T
T F	F
F T	T
F F	T

Step 2:

P → Q	¬(P → Q)
T	F
F	T
T	F
T	F

But, we don't need to write the second truth table separately. Instead, we make a single table, and do both steps on it. Like this:

P Q	¬(P → Q)
T T	F T
T F	T F
F T	F T
F F	F T
	↑ ↑
	Step 2 Step 1

(We use the table for "P → Q" in step one to produce step two.)

Let us look at an example, this time of a biconditional:

Example   ¬(P ∧ Q) ↔ (¬P ∨ ¬Q)

The table for this sentence requires six steps: two for the left-hand side, three for the right, and one for the whole. First, we do the table for the "¬P" (step 1) and "¬Q" (step 2), then we do the table for "(¬P ∨ ¬Q)" (step 3) using the first two tables. Next, we do the table for "P ∧ Q" (step 4), and then, using the result, the table for "¬(P ∧ Q)" (step 5). Finally, using the table for "¬(P ∧ Q)" and "(¬P ∨ ¬Q)" we do the table for the whole sentence (step six). The following truth table assembles all six steps into a single tabular form:

P Q	¬(P ∧ Q) ↔ (¬P ∨ ¬Q)
T T	F T **T** F F F
T F	T F **T** F T T
F T	T F **T** T T F
F F	T F **T** T T T
	↑ ↑ ↑ ↑ ↑ ↑
Step	5 4 6 1 3 2

First we did steps one and two using the definition table for "¬," then using those two tables we did step three, using the definition table for "∨." **Then** we moved over to the other side and did step four, using the definition table for "∧" and then using column four, we did step five, using the definition table for "¬." At this point we had a table for each side (tables three and five); step six was comparing tables three and five to get table six using the definition table for "↔." The sentence had all Ts in the final column and so it is a tautology or logical truth. While this sounds complicated, it gets easy very quickly!

STUDY SETS 7

<u>Part A.</u> Here are the five standard argument forms we looked at in Chapter 1.

First translate the logical terms of these arguments into our standard truth-functions and then turn them into the corresponding conditionals. Now do their truth tables. Since these are all valid arguments, if you do the truth tables correctly you will see that they are tautologies.

1. *MODUS PONENS*	2. *MODUS TOLLENS*	3. HYPOTHETICAL SYLLOGISM
if P then Q	if P then Q	if P then Q
P	not Q	if Q then R
∴ Q	∴ not P	∴ if P then R

4. DISJUNCTIVE SYLLOGISM

P or Q
not P
∴ Q

5. CONSTRUCTIVE DILEMMA

if P then Q
if R then S
P or R
∴ Q or S

<u>Part B.</u> Here are some logical equivalences that express important logical laws. They are worth studying because they express important biconditional relationships between various truth tables. Try doing truth tables of them. Since they are all tautologies, if you do your truth tables correctly your tables will show this.

DOUBLE NEGATION	$P \leftrightarrow \neg\neg P$
DeMORGAN'S THEOREMS	$\neg(P \vee Q) \leftrightarrow (\neg P \wedge \neg Q)$
	$\neg(P \wedge Q) \leftrightarrow (\neg P \vee \neg Q)$
COMMUTATIVE LAWS	$(P \vee Q) \leftrightarrow (Q \vee P)$
	$(P \wedge Q) \leftrightarrow (Q \wedge P)$
	$(P \leftrightarrow Q) \leftrightarrow (Q \leftrightarrow P)$
ASSOCIATIVE LAWS	$(P \vee (Q \vee R)) \leftrightarrow ((P \vee Q) \vee R)$
	$(P \wedge (Q \wedge R)) \leftrightarrow ((P \wedge Q) \wedge R)$
	$(P \leftrightarrow (Q \leftrightarrow R)) \leftrightarrow ((P \leftrightarrow Q) \leftrightarrow R)$
DISTRIBUTIVE LAWS	$(P \wedge (Q \vee R)) \leftrightarrow ((P \wedge Q) \vee (P \wedge R))$
	$(P \vee (Q \wedge R)) \leftrightarrow ((P \vee Q) \wedge (P \vee R))$
CONTRAPOSITION	$(P \rightarrow Q) \leftrightarrow (\neg Q \rightarrow \neg P)$
EXPORTATION	$((P \wedge Q) \rightarrow R) \leftrightarrow (P \rightarrow (Q \rightarrow R))$
MATERIAL IMPLICATION	$(P \rightarrow Q) \leftrightarrow (\neg P \vee Q)$
EQUIVALENCE	$(P \leftrightarrow Q) \leftrightarrow ((P \rightarrow Q) \wedge (Q \rightarrow P))$
	$(P \leftrightarrow Q) \leftrightarrow ((P \wedge Q) \vee (\neg P \wedge \neg Q))$
TAUTOLOGY	$P \leftrightarrow (P \wedge P)$
	$P \leftrightarrow (P \vee P)$

Part C. Do truth tables for these sentences.

1. $(P \wedge Q) \leftrightarrow (Q \wedge P)$

2. $(P \to Q) \vee Q$

3. $(P \wedge Q) \leftrightarrow (Q \wedge P)$

4. $(((P \to Q) \to P) \to Q)$

5. $((P \wedge Q) \vee R) \to ((P \vee R) \wedge (Q \vee R))$

6. $(P \to Q) \to (Q \to P)$

7. $\neg P \to (P \vee \neg P)$

8. $(((P \to Q) \wedge (Q \to R)) \wedge P) \to R$

9. $((P \vee \neg Q) \wedge Q) \to P$

TRANSLATION

IN THIS SECTION, WE LOOK AT HOW TO TRANSLATE ENGLISH SENTENCES INTO SL (SYMBOLIC logic) and how to translate SL sentences into English. The steps of translation are essentially simple, although it is always important to pay careful attention to context when you are translating the premises in an argument. Basically, we have to identify which truth-functions are appropriate to use and which simple sentences they connect, paying attention to the scope of the truth-functions. In the following examples going from English to SL, we will proceed through five steps:

1. Identify the truth-functions in the sentences to be translated.

2. Identify the simple sentences in the sentences to be translated.

3. Write a dictionary of simple sentences, assigning a letter to each sentence starting (for example) with "P."

4. Replace the English truth-functions with their SL counterparts, using parentheses and starting with the truth-function having the widest scope.

5. Replace the simple sentences with the sentence letters you have assigned in your dictionary.

Example 1
Bill likes cats, and if they like him he gives them milk

1. There are two truth-functions, "$\wedge$" and "$\to$", in the sentence.

2. There are three simple sentences:
"Bill likes cats"
"Cats like Bill"
"Bill gives cats milk"

3. We assign the simple sentences capital letter in a dictionary:

P = def.   Bill likes cats
Q = def.   They like them
R = def.   He gives them milk

4. The truth-function "∧" has wider scope than "→", so first we get
(Bill likes cats) ∧ (if they like him he gives them milk) and then:
(Bill likes cats) ∧ ((They like him) → (He gives them milk))

5. Finally we replace the English sentences with their abbreviations to get

$$P \wedge (Q \rightarrow R).$$

Example 2
If Bill stops at the store while he is on his walk I will be mad

1. There are two truth-functions, "→" and "∧" (in the present context the word "while" has the truth-functional value of "and"; frequently it means "at the same time as," but nothing here hangs on that additional content).

2. There are three simple sentences:
Bill stops at the store
Bill is on his walk
I will be mad

3. We make a dictionary:

P = def.   Bill stops at the store
Q = def.   Bill is on his walk
R = def.   I will be mad

4. The truth-function "→" has wider scope than "∧," so first we get
(Bill stops at the store while he is on his walk) → (I will be mad)   and then
((Bill stops at the store) ∧ (He is on his walk)) → (I will be mad)

5. By substitution we get

$$(P \wedge Q) \rightarrow R.$$

Going from SL to English is roughly the reverse; the steps we follow are:

1. Make a dictionary, assigning an English sentence to each sentence letter.

2. Replace the sentence letters with the sentences in your dictionary.

3. Rewrite the SL truth-functions in English.

4. Alter the sentence as much as is needed to make it sound natural.

Example 1
(P → Q) ∨ ¬P

1. Dictionary: Dogs eat meat = def. P
   Dogs have fleas = def. Q

2. ((dogs eat meat) → (dogs have fleas)) ∨ (¬dogs eat meat)

3. If dogs eat meat then dogs have fleas, or dogs don't eat meat.

4. Either dogs don't eat meat, or—if they do—then they have fleas.

Example 2
¬(P ∧ ¬P)

1. Dictionary: Dogs eat meat = def. P

2. ¬((dogs eat meat) ∧ (¬dogs eat meat))

3. It is false that both dogs eat meat and dogs don't eat meat.

4. Dogs don't both eat meat and not eat meat.

As these examples probably show, you will have very little use for translating in this direction, so you should concentrate on mastering translation from English to symbolic notation. The only time that translating back into English really is likely to matter is in the context of an actual argument, which you have already translated from English, and so the meanings of simple sentences will already be fixed by that context.

STUDY SETS 8

<u>Part A.</u> Translate from English to SL using this dictionary:

P = Mary hates Bill,
Q = Mary invites Bill to dinner,
R = Mary burns the roast
   (Note that you should assume that if Mary hates Bill she doesn't like him.)

1. If Mary hates Bill, she won't invite him to dinner.

2. Mary hates Bill so if she invites him to dinner she will burn the roast.

3. Mary burns the roast or she doesn't, but she likes Bill.

4. If Mary burns the roast and likes Bill, she won't invite him to dinner.

5. If Mary invites Bill to dinner and she likes him then she won't burn the roast.

6. Either Mary invites Bill to dinner and burns the roast, or she doesn't burn the roast but either she doesn't invite him to dinner or doesn't like him.

Part B. Using the dictionary you have from part A, translate these sentences from SL into English (don't expect your translations to make too much sense):

1. $P \land (P \leftrightarrow Q)$
2. $(P \lor Q) \land (Q \rightarrow R)$
3. $(P \lor (P \land R)) \rightarrow Q$
4. $\neg(P \land (\neg Q \lor P))$

DIFFICULTIES IN TRANSLATION

YOU WILL REMEMBER FROM CHAPTER 6 THAT WHEN WE WERE TRYING TO TRANSLATE THE premises of arguments expressed in ordinary language into categorical form, we needed to regiment the argument in a way that made it possible for us to use the formal procedures we had available, so that we could evaluate the argument. And we also saw that when we attempted to express the premises and conclusion in categorical form, we needed to draw on knowledge about the context to help guide our choice of translations. This is also true in sentence logic, although the resources for translation are somewhat different. In any case, not all the logical words in natural English are truth-functions. If they were, translation would be a breeze. But they are not; in fact, most of the logical words in natural language are much richer in meaning and so only approximate truth-functions. This poses difficulties for adequate translation into SL. In one of the examples above we translated "while" as "∧" (or "and"), but "while" doesn't mean exactly the same thing as "and." "While" means different things in different contexts, but it always is equivalent to "and" *plus something more*. Sometimes "while" means "at the same time as," and sometimes it means something like "on the other hand." The question you need to ask yourself in translation is whether the *something more* meant by the English term is part of what is crucial in the analysis of the argument. To see this, consider these two examples:

1. Mary danced *while* she worked. If she danced she was happy. So she must have been happy.
2. Mary danced *while* she worked. She dined *after* she worked. So she danced *before* she dined.

In the first argument, translating "while" as "and" is correct, because the argument rests only on the part of the meaning of "while," which means "and." What you need to know is that she danced; from that you get she was happy by *Modus Ponens*. In the second argument, translating "while" as "and" is not correct, because the argument rests on the *difference* between "at the same time as" and the pair "after" and "before." You need to know *when* she danced, not just *that* she danced, so translating "while" as "and" is not appropriate. So when you are translating an English sentence, you need to know not only what it means but also what role it plays in the argument before you know just how to translate it.

Another problem in translation is determining which simple sentences to recognize as the ones playing a role in an argument. Consider this argument:

3. Mary hates Bill if she burns the roast. But she doesn't burn the roast so she must like him.

Should we translate this using three simple sentences: "Mary hates Bill," "She burns the roast," and "She likes him," or should "She likes him" be treated as "¬(She hates him)"? If you treat "She likes him" as the negation of "She hates him," the argument turns out to be valid, but if you treat it as an independent simple sentence, the argument doesn't turn out valid, so in the context the first option is correct.

Translating sentences using "→" poses special difficulties. As we saw in Chapter 6, words like "therefore," "so," and "because" often make references not only to what does happen but what would happen or might happen or must happen given certain counterfactual conditions. The truth-function "→" is not an adequate translation for these purposes; it means "if __ then __" and nothing else. These other purposes involve non-truth-functional relationships, which can be regimented with logical machinery only with very complex logical techniques that are beyond the scope of this course. Doing translation is a *skill*, a critical thinking skill. To do it well, you need insight into logical relationships that may be subtle and hard to express. You get better at it as you practise. As you practise you gain a more powerful insight into the logical structure of the language you speak. As a result, your ordinary processes of reasoning will improve. Below is a list of translations that often work. They do not always work. Whether they work will depend on the context of the argument of which they are a part.

¬ :	("it is false that"; "it is not the case that")
Dogs don't like fish:	¬(Dogs like fish)
Dogs never bite:	¬(Dogs sometimes bite)
It isn't as if he is poor:	¬(He is poor)
∧ :	("and")

Although it was raining, he went out in his shirt:
(It was raining) ∧ (He went out in his shirt)

He jumped and sang:	(He jumped) ∧ (He sang)
She hid but he found her:	(She hid) ∧ (He found her)
Mary is a German woman:	(Mary is German) ∧ (Mary is a woman)

(Note that context is likely to be important here; the important part in a given argument may be simply that Mary is a woman or that Mary is German or that she is German and a woman).

∨ :	"or"
He is a liar or a fool:	(He is a liar) ∨ (He is a fool)

We will not win the lottery unless we buy a ticket:
(We buy a ticket) ∨ (We will not win the lottery)

As we noted before, in English "or" can mean "either P or Q, but not both" (*exclusive* "or"), or "either P or Q or both" (*inclusive* "or"). In SL "∨" always means the *inclusive* "or." To get *exclusive* "or" we must say: "(P ∨ Q) ∧ ¬(P ∧ Q)."

→:	("if ___ then___")
If Bill is sad then Mary is mad:	(Bill is sad) → (Mary is mad)
Mary is mad *if* Bill is sad:	(Bill is sad) → (Mary is mad)
Assuming you are right it is 8 o'clock:	(You are right) → (It is 8 o'clock)

Note that the antecedent of a conditional is always the term preceded by "if," whether it comes first or at the end.

↔:	("if and only if" or "if," "exactly when," "just if," "just in case," etc.)
Mary is sad just in case Bill is glum:	(Mary is sad) ↔ (Bill is glum)
Mary is sad if Bill is and Bill is sad if Mary is:	(Mary is sad) ↔ (Bill is sad)

STUDY SETS 9

Part A. Translate into SL:

1. Mary is a terrific dancer and so is Bill.

2. No sick animals may enter the country.

3. Bill's sick plant needs water.

Part B. Translate these arguments:

1. Barbara is mad at Phil. If Phil is sick or Barbara is mad at him then he will skip school. Therefore Phil skips school.

2. Lola is sick or Gerry is hungry. If Trina is angry then Gerry can't eat. If Gerry is hungry then Gerry can eat. But Lola isn't sick. So Trina isn't angry.

3. Either the bird flies away or the snake eats it. If the snake catches her eye, the bird will be paralyzed with fear. So if the snake catches her eye it will eat the bird.

4. If I give Mary a lift, Bill will be mad. But if I don't, she will get wet from the rain. If I let Mary get wet from the rain, Bill will be mad. So (either way) Bill will be mad.

5. Don't drink if you can't hold your liquor. If you drink, don't drive home. If you go to the party you will drink. So if you can't hold your liquor, either don't go to the party or don't drive home.

Part C. Do truth tables of these sentences in SL:

1. $((P \wedge Q) \vee \neg Q) \rightarrow P$
2. $(P \wedge Q) \rightarrow (R \rightarrow (P \vee Q))$
3. $(P \vee (Q \wedge R)) \rightarrow (\neg P \rightarrow Q)$
4. $(P \rightarrow (\neg P \rightarrow (\neg P \rightarrow P)))$

TRUTH TREE TECHNIQUE

WE HAVE LOOKED AT TESTING ARGUMENTS FOR VALIDITY BY DOING TRUTH TABLES OF THEIR corresponding conditionals. While every valid argument has a corresponding conditional with a logical truth, there is a practical barrier to the universal use of truth tables. Truth tables can quickly become unwieldy to construct as the number of simple sentences in the sentence to be analyzed goes up. The number of possible situations represented in a truth table is 2^n, where n is the number of simple sentences. (A conditional containing 10 simple sentences thus needs a truth table with 1,024 rows—15 simple sentences would require 32,768 rows!) You should be able to convince yourself that a chain argument with premises "P," "P $\rightarrow$ Q," "Q $\rightarrow$ R," "R $\rightarrow$ S," and so on will validly support a conclusion that is the consequent of the last if/then statement: the first two premises *imply "Q," and Q and the third premise imply "R,"* and so on. *In short, we have a chain of* Modus Ponens arguments, each of which we know to be valid.

The **truth tree** technique is very similar to truth table analysis except that it graphs the various possible situations of truth and falsity on a tree instead of in a table. A tree can represent a very large number of possibilities economically, so it is much more practical to analyze complex conditionals using truth trees than by truth tables.

Truth tree technique is a method of testing whether a set of sentences (i.e., a complex conjunctive sentence) is consistent. The basic fact it depends on is this: If a set of sentences is consistent, then the sentences can be true together in some situations. A tree is an attempt to describe such a situation using sentences that are as short as possible. In sentence logic, this means using only simple sentences and their negations, and complex sentences are unpacked into their simple parts on the tree. A tree is constructed in a series of steps. First, we write down the sentences to be analyzed. Second, we take any one of those sentences and try to describe which simple sentences would have to be true for each part of it to be true.

> Example: "(P∧Q)" — both "P" and "Q" must be true
>
>   "(P∨Q)" — one of "P" and "Q" (or both) must be true

Third, we write those atomic sentences below the sentence to be analyzed. We connect them to it by a vertical line if there is only one way it can be true and we connect them by a branching pair of lines if there are two (see Figure 7.1).

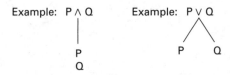

Figure 7.1

Fourth, if a sentence contains three possibilities, first we divide it into a pair (one of which will contain a compound sentence) and then after graphing the pair, we graph the compound member of the pair (see Figure 7.2).

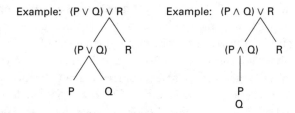

Figure 7.2

In general, when a compound sentence contains a number of truth-functions, we graph it serially in order of wideness of scope, as in Figure 7.3.

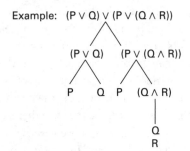

Figure 7.3

Truth trees are just a variant of truth tables, so we can derive rules for truth trees from the defining truth tables for each of the basic truth-functions.

CONSTRUCTING TRUTH TREES FROM TRUTH TABLES

TRUTH TREES GRAPH ONLY THE CONDITIONS UNDER WHICH SENTENCES (OR SETS OF SENTENCES) are *true*. But truth trees and truth tables agree exactly in their accounts of the truth conditions of sentences. It is easy to construct truth tree definitions from truth tables. On the line (or lines) under the sentences under analysis, we write down a representation of the circumstances that the truth of the sentence would require.

Negation: We need three truth trees for atomic sentences, their negation, and their double negation. They look like this:

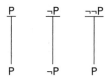

Figure 7.4

We derive them from the truth table for ¬like this:

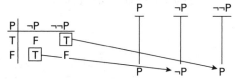

Figure 7.5

Conjunction: The tables for *and* and *not-and* look like this:

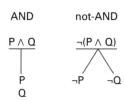

Figure 7.6

Since there is only one way for an *and* statement to be true, there is only a single line graphing its truth conditions. There are three ways the negation of an *and* statement can be true—corresponding to the three rows where the *and* statement is false. However, since two of those ways reflect conditions when P is false (and since Q is true in one case and false in the other, its truth value doesn't matter) and two represent conditions when Q is false (and since P is true in one case and false in the other, P's truth value doesn't matter), we can graph all three cases with two lines, one on which P is false and the other on which Q is false:

Relation of truth trees to truth tables for "∧": in each case,
we put on the line what it takes to make the statement true.

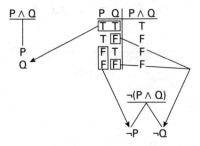

Figure 7.7

Disjunction: Here is how we construct the trees for *or* and *not-or*:

Relation of truth trees to truth tables for "∨": in each case,
we put on the line what it takes to make the statement true.

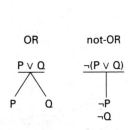

Figures 7.8 and 7.9

Implication: Here is how we construct the trees for *if __ then* and *not-if __ then*:

Relation of truth trees to truth tables for "→": in each case,
we put on the line what it takes to make the statement true.

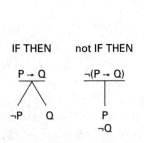

Figures 7.10 and 7.11

Equivalence: Here, finally, are the two trees for equivalence or *if and only if* and its negation. Remember that two statements are equivalent if they have the same truth value and not equivalent if their truth values are different:

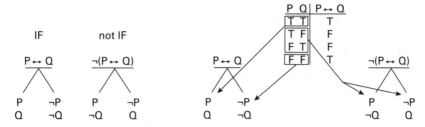

Relation of truth trees to truth tables for "↔": in each case, we put on the line what it takes to make the statement true.

Figures 7.12 and 7.13

We have now seen how to graph single sentences. Remember, however, that our objective is to graph a set of sentences to see whether they are *consistent*. Suppose we have graphed one sentence; how do we go about graphing the next sentence? We do this exactly as before but we add the new graph to the bottom of *each line* of the graph that is already there. Thus, for example, if this is the situation after graphing one sentence,

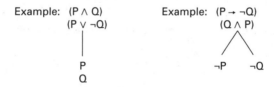

Figure 7.14

then we graph the second sentence as follows:

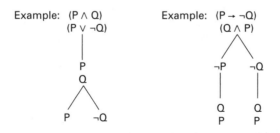

Figure 7.15

We have now graphed both sentences and are now in a position to see whether the set of compound sentences is consistent. We do this by tracing down each line in turn. If the constituent sentences in a line are inconsistent—if the set of constituent sentences occurring on a line contains both an instance of any simple sentence "φ" and an instance of its negation "¬φ"—we know that that line cannot represent a possible way to make the set of sentences true together so we draw a line under that line closing it off. If all the lines are closed off, then there is no way the compound sentences being analyzed can be true together and they are inconsistent. In the cases above we get:

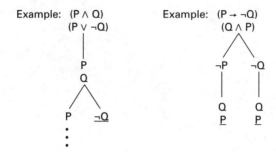

Figure 7.16

The test of consistency in a line is very simple: *If a line contains both an instance of "φ" and "¬φ" then it is inconsistent; otherwise, it is consistent.*

When you are graphing larger sets of sentences, you proceed exactly as before, with this proviso: Once a line is closed you do not need to graph the next sentence under that line. It is closed off since it is already inconsistent. Let us look at two examples involving three sentences.

Example 1
Graph the set {(P ∧ Q), ((Q ∨ R) → ¬P), (P → R)}

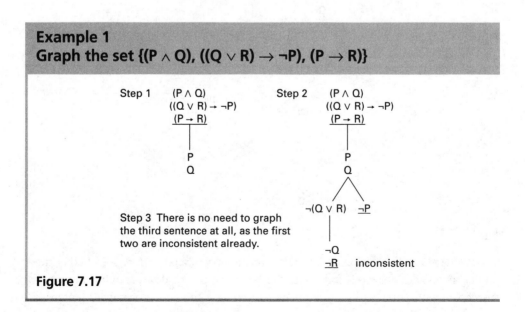

Figure 7.17

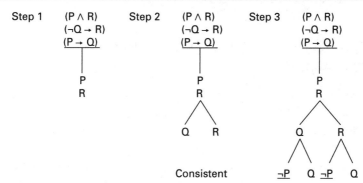

Example 2
Graph the set {(P → Q), (¬Q → R), (P∧R)}

Step 1

(P ∧ R)
(¬Q → R)
(P → Q)

|
P
R

Step 2

(P ∧ R)
(¬Q → R)
(P → Q)

|
P
R
/ \
Q   R

Consistent

Step 3

(P ∧ R)
(¬Q → R)
(P → Q)

|
P
R
/ \
Q   R
/ \   / \
¬P Q ¬P Q

Figure 7.18

STUDY SETS 10

Part A. Do truth tables for these:

1. $(P \wedge (Q \vee R)) \rightarrow (P \wedge Q)$
2. $(P \vee (P \wedge Q)) \rightarrow (Q \rightarrow P)$
3. $(((R \wedge Q) \wedge (Q \vee R)) \wedge P) \rightarrow R$
4. $((P \wedge (P \rightarrow Q)) \wedge ((P \vee Q) \rightarrow Q)) \rightarrow Q$

Part B. Translate to SL and prove using truth tables or truth trees:

1. Either Mary hid her coat, or she lost it but isn't telling. If she lost it Bill will be mad. But Bill will be mad too if she is hiding it. Either way Bill will be mad.

2. Freddy is a pig. If Freddy is a pig and Dotty isn't, their love is unnatural. But since Dotty is a pig, it is OK.

3. Blind Bill is sad. Mad Mary is glad. If Mary is glad because Bill is blind then Mary is mad and so Bill is sad.

4. Push either the red knob or the green knob. If you don't push the red knob then turn the orange handle. Don't push the green knob unless the light is on. If you push the red knob and pull the brown cord the light goes off. So either you pull the brown cord or the light is on.

5. If I have a headache I take Aspirin. I only take Aspirin with food in my stomach. And if I eat Mary will eat too. But Mary doesn't eat. So I don't have a headache.

Part C. Do truth trees of these sets:

1. $\{(P \wedge Q); (Q \rightarrow (R \vee P)); ((\neg P \vee P) \rightarrow \neg R)\}$
2. $\{(P \rightarrow Q); (Q \rightarrow R); (R \rightarrow S); (P \rightarrow \neg S)\}$

3. $\{(P \land (Q \lor R)); (P \to Q); (Q \lor T); (\neg T \to \neg P)\}$

4. $\{((P \land Q) \lor R); (\neg P \to R); Q\}$

5. $\{(P \land \neg Q); (Q \lor (P \land \neg R)); (R \to (S \land \neg T)); (S \land R)\}$

EVALUATING ARGUMENTS BY TRUTH TREE TECHNIQUE

THERE ARE TWO WAYS THAT TRUTH TREE TECHNIQUES COULD BE USED TO EVALUATE AN argument. The *first* would be to construct a tree of the set of premises. You would then look at all the open lines and *if the conclusion is contained in all of them, then the argument is valid*. The difficulty with this method is that if the conclusion is a complex sentence it is difficult to tell whether it is contained in the open lines. The *second* method, which is much more practical and is presented in this book, is the *method of counter-example*. If you remember, an argument of the form

$$(((\text{premise 1}) \land (\text{premise 2})) \land \ldots \land (\text{premise n})) \to \text{conclusion})$$

is valid if it has no counter-example. This means that the attempt to construct a counter-example to a valid argument will yield an inconsistent set of sentences. One constructs a counter-example by conjoining the premises with the negation of the conclusion. One can then show that an argument is valid by using truth tree technique to show that the counter-example set is inconsistent. Let us look at three examples:

Example 1
Consider *Modus Ponens*: $(P \land (P \to Q)) \to Q$

The counter-example set is $\{P, (P \to Q), \neg Q\}$
    and the resulting tree is:

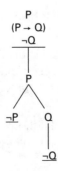

Figure 7.19

The tree has no open lines, so the counter-example set is inconsistent; the argument has no counter-example and is thus **valid**. Using truth trees makes even quite complex arguments easy to test for validity, as the next two examples show us.

Example 2
$(((P \land Q) \land (Q \rightarrow (R \lor S))) \land (\neg S \rightarrow \neg R)) \rightarrow (P \land S)$

The counter example set is:
$$\{(P \land Q); (Q \rightarrow (R \lor S)); (\neg S \rightarrow \neg R); \neg(P \land S)\},$$
and the truth tree is:

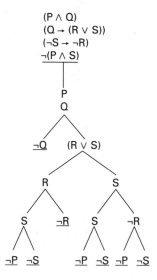

Figure 7.20

The tree has no open lines, so the counter-example set is inconsistent; the argument has no counter-example and is thus **valid**.

Example 3
$((((P \wedge Q) \wedge \neg(R \vee S)) \wedge (T \rightarrow S)) \wedge \neg(P \wedge T)) \rightarrow \neg T$

The tree of the counter-example set is:

$$\{(P \wedge Q); \neg(R \vee S); (T \rightarrow S); \neg(P \wedge T); T\},$$

and the truth tree is:

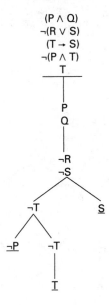

(P ∧ Q)
¬(R ∨ S)
(T → S)
¬(P ∧ T)
T

P
Q

¬R
¬S

¬T   S

¬P   ¬T

I

Figure 7.21

Once again the counter-example set is inconsistent, so the argument is valid. Notice how simple the diagram is compared to a truth table of the argument's corresponding conditional: "$((((P \wedge Q) \wedge \neg(R \vee S)) \wedge (T \rightarrow S)) \wedge \neg(P \wedge T)) \rightarrow \neg T$." That truth table would have five simple sentences, and so 2^5 (or 32) rows and 11 truth-functions to graph. Notice also that the first premise states that both P and Q are true and the fourth premise states that P and T are not both true; the conclusion that T is false follows straight away from those two premises alone. You will be able to check this for yourself.

STUDY SETS 11

<u>Part A.</u> Graph the following sets of sentences to show whether or not they are consistent.

1. $\{(P \wedge Q); (Q \rightarrow \neg R); (R \leftrightarrow P)\}$

2. $\{(P \wedge \neg Q); (\neg Q \rightarrow (P \wedge R)); (R \vee \neg P)\}$

3. {P; (Q → ¬P); ¬Q}

4. {(P ∧ (Q ∧ R)); ¬(R ∨ Q); (P → ¬Q)}

Part B. Show whether the arguments expressed by these conditionals are valid by making truth trees of their counter-example sets.

   1. ((P → Q) ∧ (Q → R)) → (P → R)

   2. (((P ∨ Q) → R) ∧ (Q ∧ ¬R)) → ¬P

   3. (P → ¬(P → Q)) → (¬Q → P)

   4. ((P ∧ ¬(Q ∨ R)) ∧ ¬(P → ¬R)) → (¬P → Q)

   5. (((P ∨ Q) → R) ∧ ((S ∨ T) → U)) → ((P ∧ S) → (R ∧ U))

Part C. Translate the following arguments and test them for validity using the method of counter-example:

   1. Either Bill or Peter fed the cat. The cat was mad because she got dog food. She got Pampers cat food if Peter fed her. Therefore, Bill fed the cat.

   2. If the boss is tired and you make a mistake he snaps at you. You made a mistake but he didn't snap at you, so he wasn't tired.

   3. If I take his pawn with my knight, he will either take my knight or move his bishop to the space my knight is guarding now. If he takes my knight, I will lose a good piece, but his queen will be exposed. If he moves his bishop, my queen will be exposed. But if I don't take his pawn with my knight, my queen will be exposed anyway. So either his queen or mine will be exposed.

ADDITIONAL STUDY SETS FOR PART III

Part A. Test these conditionals by truth table.

   1. [((P → Q) ∨ (Q∧ ¬P)) → ¬(P∧ ¬Q)]

   2. [(((P → ¬Q) ∧ (Q ∨ ¬R)) ∧ (P →(R ∨ Q))) → ¬P]

Part B. Test these sets for consistency with truth trees.

   1. (P ∧ ¬Q); (¬Q → (S ∨ P)); (¬P→ ¬R); (S → R); (¬P ∨ ¬R)

   2. (R ∧ ¬Q); (P ∨ (Q ∨ ¬R)); (R → (S ∨ ¬T)); ¬(S ∧ R); (P ∧ T)

Part C. Test the arguments associated with these conditionals for validity by counter-example method.

   1. (((P ∨ Q) → R) ∧ ((R ∧ ¬S) → ¬T) ∧ ((P ∧ ¬S) ∨ (¬S ∧ Q)) ∧ (T ∨ U)) → U

   2. (((P ∧ Q) → S) ∧ (S → ¬R) ∧ (¬S ∨ ¬P) ∧ (Q →¬T) ∧ R) → ¬T

Part D. Translate these arguments into symbols and test for validity by the method of counter-example.

1. If time travel were possible then you could go back in time, marry your grandparent, and have a child who is your own parent. If you had a child who was your own parent then you would be the child of your child. But if you were the child of your child you would be the cause of your own existence. But if you are not God then you can't be the cause of you own existence. But you are not God . . . so time travel is impossible.

2. God is good if God exists, and if God is good everything is without flaw. If there is pain in the world it has a good reason or else it is a flaw. So if God exists and there is pain in the world it has a good reason.

3. Either you are free or determined by your circumstances. If you are free then you are responsible for your acts, but if you are determined you are not. If you are depressed and responsible for your acts then you will regret it. But if you are determined then regret is inevitable. So if you are depressed you will regret it.

4. Either there is objective right and wrong or else morality is merely relative. If some things are objectively right then it is wrong to act immorally. If morality is merely relative then helping the poor is no better than killing babies. But it is better to help the poor, so it is wrong to act immorally.

5. If Lois wants to be fit she goes to the gym. People don't care about their health unless they want to be fit, and Lois does care about her health. So Lois goes to the gym.

Part E. Do these truth tables.

1. P Q (Q ∧ (P ∨ Q)) → Q

   T T
   T F
   F T
   F F

2. P Q R ((Q → ¬R) ∧ (P → Q) ∧ (P ∨ ¬R)) → P

   T T T
   T T F
   T F T
   T F F
   F T T
   F T F
   F F T
   F F F

3. P Q ((P → ¬Q) ∧ (Q ∨ ¬P)) → Q]

T T
T F
F T
F F

4. P Q R ((¬Q → R) ∧ (¬Q ∨ P) ∧ (¬P → ¬R)) → P

T T T
T T F
T F T
T F F
F T T
F T F
F F T
F F F

5. P Q ((¬Q → P) ∧ ¬P) ↔ ¬(Q → P)

T T
T F
F T
F F

6. P Q R ((R → P) ∧ (Q ∨ R) ∧ (Q → P)) → P

T T T
T T F
T F T
T F F
F T T
F T F
F F T
F F F

7. P Q $((\neg P \lor (P \lor Q)) \land Q) \to (\neg P \to Q)$

T T

T F

F T

F F

Part F. Translate these arguments and test for validity by the method of counter-example.

1. If living were always better than dying and people knew it then people would not commit suicide. But people do commit suicide. So living isn't always better than dying or else people are misinformed.

2. If Bill is a ghoul then he isn't a vampire. Bill doesn't drink human blood and he isn't un-dead. He would drink blood and be un-dead if he were a vampire. So Bill must be a ghoul.

3. If Eric is a duck then ducks can talk or your philosophy professor is a duck. Ducks can't talk and your philosophy professor doesn't look like a duck. If your philosophy professor doesn't look like a duck then either he isn't a duck or some ducks look like people. But ducks don't look like people, so Eric isn't a duck.

4. The world shows a fitness of its parts to their functions. If it shows such a functional fitness it must be the product of intelligent design. There must be a designer if it is the product of intelligent design. Only God could design a world [hint: treat this as an if-then sentence]. Therefore God must exist.

5. If global warming continues then the oceans will rise. Millions will die needlessly in floods if the oceans rise. Unless all of us cut back on our wasteful use of energy, global warming will continue. We are too selfish to cut back on our use of energy. So, millions will die.

6. If the Liberals won then either most Canadians liked the Liberals or most people distrusted the Conservatives. Either most people trusted the Conservatives or the NDP did well. If the NDP did well then the Liberals lost unless most people distrusted the Conservatives. Most Canadians didn't like the Liberals so unless the NDP did well most people distrusted the Conservatives.

Part G. Test these sets for consistency using truth trees.

1. $P \land R$

   $\neg Q \to \neg P$

   $P \to Q$

2. $P \land Q$

   $Q \to R$

   $P \land S$

   $\neg S \lor R$

   $\neg R$

3. $P \rightarrow (Q \rightarrow R)$
$Q \lor S$
$P \rightarrow S$
$\neg Q \rightarrow \neg S$

4. $P \land Q$
$P \rightarrow R$
$\neg Q \lor S$
$(R \land S) \rightarrow T$
$T \rightarrow U$

5. $P \rightarrow T$
$R \rightarrow S$
$\neg T \lor R$
$S \rightarrow Q$
$\neg Q \land P$
$\neg U$

6. $P \land T$
$\neg T \lor R$
$S \lor \neg P$
$S \rightarrow U$
$U \rightarrow \neg R$

Glossary

Ambiguity (lexical, structural; see fallacy list in Chapter 5) Ambiguity is the condition of having more than one interpretation or meaning. Ambiguity can arise in two basic ways. The first is lexical ambiguity or **equivocation**, in which a word or phrase has more than one lexical definition and so can be understood in more than one way; alternatively, two different words that look or sound the same may become confused and lead to fallacious inference. The second basic way is *structural* ambiguity or **amphiboly**, in which a string of words in a sentence has more than one legitimate grammatical interpretation and so can be understood in more than one way.

Antecedent A **conditional statement** asserts a relation between two statements of which it is made, stating that if the antecedent (first) **statement** is true then the **consequent** (second) statement is also true. For example, in the conditional statement "if it is raining then you will get wet," "it is raining" is the antecedent and "you will get wet" is the consequent.

Argument An argument in the broad sense is a social exchange between several reasoners who advance claims and then support them with reasons. In a narrow sense argument is a set of **statements** in which it is claimed that the **truth** or likelihood of the **premises** support the **conclusion**.

Argument pattern Logical arguments usually occur in characteristic patterns. These patterns represent the formal relationships the **premises** have to each other in light of which they support the **conclusion**. An argument pattern is a formal structure that many different **arguments** fit.

Categorical logic The traditional logic of terms, developed by Aristotle, covering a theory of the **syllogism** and a theory of immediate **inference**.

Chain argument (kind of **enthymeme**) A chain **argument** (or chained enthymeme) is two or more arguments that are joined together by one or more implicit statements that form the **conclusion** of one argument and a **premise** in the next.

Claim The assertion of a sentence; the claim that it is true.

Classification Classification is a kind of division according to a rule: A group of individuals is divided into subgroups by a rule that sorts them by a set of common properties.

Complement The complement of a class is everything in the **universe of discourse** that is not a member of that class.

Conclusion A claim or **statement** made in an **argument** its **premises** are intended to support. The aim of giving an argument is to rationally persuade an audience that a **conclusion** is true or likely if its **premises** are.

Conditional probability (*see* **probability**) The conditional probability of a **statement** is its probability given another statement; "the conditional probability of q given p is x," written as $\Pr(q/p) = x$.

Conditional statement A conditional **statement** asserts a relation between the two statements of which it is composed, stating that if the **antecedent** (first) statement is true then the **consequent** (second) statement is also true. For example, the statement "if it is raining then you will get wet" is a conditional.

Consequent A **conditional statement** asserts a relation between two statements of which it is made, stating that if the **antecedent** (first) statement is true then the consequent (second) statement is also true. For example, in the conditional statement "if it is raining then you will get wet," "it is raining" is the antecedent and "you will get wet" is the consequent.

Constructive dilemma (*see* **argument patterns**) Constructive dilemma is a valid argument pattern that takes the form

> If P then Q
> If R then S
> P or R
> ∴ Q or S

Context The context of a **statement** or **argument** is the set of background conditions that are **implicitly** assumed to hold. We often need to make some aspect of the context **explicit** to fully reconstruct the meaning of an argument.

Contradiction, contradictory This term has two related meanings. A single **statement** is called a contradiction when it is a statement that is false under every possible interpretation; its **negation** is a **logical truth**. Contradiction is also a kind of relational negation; it is the relation that two statements have when they are contradictory to each other. Two statements are contradictory if each is the **explicit** negation of the other so that if the first is true the second is false and if the second is true the first is false.

Contraposition (in **immediate inference**) In the traditional logic of terms, the contrapositive of a categorical statement is the new categorical that results from putting the *complement* of the original subject term in the predicate place and putting the *complement* of the original predicate term in the subject place; in short, both terms are turned into their complement and their positions switched.

Contrariety, contrary Contrariety is a kind of relational **negation**; it is the relation that two **statements** have when they are *contraries* of each other. Two statements are *contraries* if both can be false but at most one can be true; for example, "today is Friday" and "today is Wednesday." In **categorical logic**, the relation of contrariety depends on the subject terms having reference; for example, on the condition that pickles exist: "All pickles are blue" and "No pickles are blue" are contraries because they cannot both be true but they can both be false.

Conversion (in **immediate inference**) In the traditional **logic** of terms, the converse of a **categorical statement** is made by interchanging the statements' subject and predicate terms. This procedure is called conversion.

Corresponding conditional The corresponding conditional of an **argument** is a sentence of the form: "If the conjunction of the **premises** is true then the conclusion is true"; its value is that the argument is **valid** if and only of its corresponding conditional is a **logical truth**.

Counter-example A counter-example of an **argument** is a situation in which the **premises** are true and the **conclusion** is false. If an argument is **valid,** there is no possible counter-example and the **statement** produced by conjoining the premises with the **negation** of the conclusion is a **contradiction**.

Critical thinking Thinking that is disciplined by being guided by principles of good method.

Deductive (argument) A deductive argument is one whose **conclusion** can be derived from its **premises** by procedures that preserve **truth**; in short, a deductive argument is one the truth of whose conclusion follows from the truth of the premises.

Definition The definition of a term is a **statement** that specifies what the term means.

Definition, argument from An argument from definition is an **argument** in which the conclusion is presented as following simply by **definition** or by the meanings of the words used in the argument.

Disjunctive Syllogism (*see* argument patterns) Disjunctive Syllogism is a valid argument pattern taking the form

    P or Q
    <u>Not P</u>
    ∴ Q

Enthymeme An **argument** in which a required **premise** is not stated **explicitly** but is assumed **implicitly** as part of the argument.

Epistemic From the word "epistemology," which means the study of belief and knowledge. An epistemic consideration is one that bears on the question of whether what is under discussion is known or else reasonable to believe. An epistemic reason for a **statement** is a reason for belief; that is, a reason for taking the statement to be true.

Equivocation A form of **ambiguity** in which a word or phrase has more than one lexical **definition** and so can be understood in more than one way. Alternatively, two different words that look or sound the same may become confused and lead to fallacious **inference**.

Exemplar (instance, instantiation) An exemplar, or instance or instantiation of a general term or **argument,** is a particular that meets the conditions of the term or argument; a dog is an exemplar of the term "dog."

Explicit (*see* **implicit**) Information required to make an **argument valid** may not actually be stated but merely assumed. To show the relevance of that information, we have to make the information **explicit** by adding a sentence that states the information clearly.

Fallacy (*see* fallacy list in Chapter 5) A fallacy is an **argument** that violates one or more of the conditions of a **cogent argument**.

Falsity (falsehood) A **statement** is false if things are not as the statement says they are. To assert that a sentence—for example, "it is raining"—is false, it suffices to assert the **negation** of the sentence (because "it is raining" is false if and only if it is not raining). The negation of a falsehood is a **truth**.

Generalization A **statement** concerning a class of things stating that all or some number of members of that class have some feature.

Hypothetical Syllogism (*see* argument patterns) Hypothetical syllogism is the valid argument pattern having the form

If P then Q
If Q then R
∴ if P then R

Implicit (*see* **explicit, premise, enthymeme**) An implicit **statement** is a statement that is assumed to be true in some **context** but is not explicitly stated.

Indicative sentence An indicative sentence is one that when uttered makes a **truth** claim; that is, is either true or false.

Inductive (inductive **argument**, inductive **inference**, inductive strength) An inductive *argument* makes a general claim on the strength of a set of particular **statements**. Inductive arguments are not true in virtue of their form but because the **generalization** is made true by the way the world is. An inductive *inference* is the mental act of drawing an inductive **conclusion** from a set of particular **premises**. Inductive *strength* is the degree to which the premises support the likelihood of the conclusion.

Inference An inference is a mental act or piece of **reasoning** that culminates in a **conclusion**.

Instance *See* **exemplar**

Invalid (*see* **valid**) An **argument** is invalid if has **a counter-example**. One can show that an argument is invalid by constructing a counter-example or by showing that its **negation** is valid.

Justification Justification is a relation with grounds. To say that a **conclusion** is justified is to say that the **premises** provide adequate grounds for asserting the conclusion.

Logic Logic is the systematic study of **arguments**.

Logical truth A logical truth is a **statement** that is true under every interpretation; it is impossible for a logical truth to be false and its **negation** is a **contradiction**.

Mill's methods Mill's methods are a set of five inductive rules for discovering causal relationships between natural phenomena. They are called Mill's methods because John Stuart Mill was the first to formulate them explicitly. These methods are, respectively, the method of agreement, the method of difference, the joint method of agreement and difference, the method of residue, and the method of concomitant variation (see Chapter 4).

Modus Ponens (*see* **argument patterns**) *Modus Ponens* is the valid argument pattern having the form

If P then Q
P
∴ Q

Modus Tollens (*see* **argument patterns**) *Modus Tollens* is the valid argument pattern having the form

If P then Q
Not Q
∴ not P

Necessary A statement that is necessary is never false.

Necessary condition (*see* **sufficient condition**) A **necessary** condition of a **statement** must be satisfied for the statement to be true.

Necessary truth A necessary truth is the same as a logical truth or tautology.

Negation The negation of a **statement** is the statement formed by denying, or asserting the **falsity** of, the original statement. Negation is a logical operation on a statement that changes the **truth value** of that statement from true to false or from false to true. The negation of a **truth** is a **falsehood** and the negation of a falsehood is a truth.

Obversion (in **immediate inference**) In the traditional logic of terms, the obverse categorical statement is the product of changing the **quality** of the statement and replacing the statement's predicate term with its **complement**.

Premise A premise is a claim made in an **argument** to ground or support the **conclusion**.

Proof A proof is a procedure that demonstrates the **truth** of a **conclusion**; alternately, a proof is the set of **statements** that are the product of such a demonstration

Quality In the traditional **logic** of terms, the *quality* of a categorical **statement** is the character (affirmative or negative) of the relationship it affirms between its subject and predicate terms. It is an affirmative statement if it states that the class designated by its subject term is included, either as a whole or only in part, within the class designated by its predicate term, and it is a negative statement if it wholly or partially excludes members of the subject class from the predicate class.

Quantifier A quantifier is a logical word expressing number, for example "all," "some," "seven," "a few."

Reasoning A mental process in which the mind is moved to endorse **statements** because they appear to be justified by other statements the person accepts.

Refutation by counter-example A procedure in logic whereby an **argument** is shown to be **invalid** by the construction of a genuine **counter-example** in which the **premises** are true and the **conclusion** false.

Relevance A word with very general application, indicating the bearing that one thing has on something else.

Scope The word "scope" has several uses, each of which indicates the range or extent of something that is in question. In sentence logic, the scope of a **truth-function** is indicated by parentheses and shows what sentences the truth-function covers.

Soundness, sound Soundness is the property of being sound; a sound **argument** is a **valid** argument that has true **premises**.

Standard form The standard form of an **argument** is a way of regimenting it to show the relation between **premises** and **conclusion**. For example, the argument "You are tired and tired people should sleep so *you should sleep*" has the standard form

Premise 1	You are tired
Premise 2	Tired people should sleep
Conclusion	You should sleep

Statement A sentence used to make a claim (which can be true or false).

Subcontrariety, subcontrary (*see* **contrary**) Subcontrariety is a kind of relational **negation**; it is the relation two statements have when they are *subcontraries* of each other. Two subcontraries can both be true but at most one can be false; for example, "some dogs are black" and "some dogs are not black." In categorical **logic**, the relation of subcontrariety depends on the subject terms having reference (in the case of the example, that there are dogs).

Sufficient condition (*see* **necessary condition**) A sufficient condition is one that, if satisfied, assures the **statement's truth**.

Syllogism A syllogism is a very general **argument pattern** that involves two **premises** and a **conclusion** and three terms. In the traditional **logic** of terms, a syllogism is an argument composed of three categorical **statements**, two of which are premises and the third is the conclusion. The three statements jointly contain three nonlogical referring terms each appearing in two of the three statements (see Chapter 6).

Tautology Another term for **logical truth**.

Truth A **statement** is true if things are as the statement says they are. To assert that a sentence—for example, "it is raining"—is true it suffices to assert the sentence (because "it is raining" is true if and only if it is raining). The **negation** of a truth is a **falsehood**.

Truth-function (and **sentence-function**) A sentence-function is a string of English words and one or more sentence variables, which has the following property: If the sentence variables are replaced by English sentences, the whole string becomes a sentence in English. A truth-function is a sentence-function that has an additional feature: truth-functionality. The **truth** or **falsity** of the whole sentence is a function of the truth or falsity of the sentences replacing the sentence variables in it.

Truth table A truth table is a tabular model of the conditions under which a compound sentence is true or false. Since a sentence analyzed in a truth table is composed of one or more constituent sentences and one or more **truth-functions**, the circumstances under which the sentence is analyzed are given by the various logical possibilities of **truth** and falsity of the constituent sentences. Each line of the truth table represents a different set of circumstances and thus represents a different assignment of truth or falsity to the constituent sentences. All the lines together exhaust the different possible assignments of truth or falsity to the constituents.

Truth tree A truth tree is a graphic representation of the various possible conditions under which a compound sentence is true or false in terms of the of **truth** and falsity of its component simple sentences.

Truth value In **logic, statements** are evaluated as either true or false. These two possibilities are the possible truth values of the sentence.

Universe of discourse The universe of discourse in a situation is the set of all the things there are in the universe under discussion. This universe of discourse is typically either just reality or else a stipulated domain under discussion, such as "all the people in this room."

Validity, valid An **argument** is valid if and only if it there is no possible situation in which the **premises** are true and the **conclusion** is false. Validity is the property of a valid argument.

Venn diagram A method of representing the properties of sets useful in diagramming categorical statements and determining validity in categorical syllogisms, named for John Venn, its inventor.

Answers to Selected Study Sets

PART I
Chapter One

Study Sets 1

Part A.

2. **What time is it?**
   Question (NOT a statement)

4. **I hate you.**
   Statement (Makes a claim)

6. **Either Rome is the capital of Italy or it isn't.**
   Disjunction of **two statements** (Makes a claim, which, as it turns out, is always true)

8. **Pay attention, you lazy lout!**
   Order, but *presupposes* the truth of the claim "You are a lazy lout"

Part B.

2. **The moral law demands that we pursue, and ultimately attain, moral perfection. But we can't reasonably expect to reach moral perfection in this life. Therefore, we must postulate, or suppose, that there is another life in which this demand of the moral law can be met.**
   Pr. The moral law demands that we pursue, and ultimately attain, moral perfection.

   Pr. We can't reasonably expect to reach moral perfection in this life.

   C. We must postulate, or suppose, that there is another life (in which this demand of the moral law can be met).

4. **Martha bought vodka and Frank bought wieners. Between them they bought vodka and wieners.**
   Pr. Martha bought vodka

   Pr. Frank bought wieners

   C. Between them they bought vodka and wieners

6. **No computer can think. To think requires one to understand the meanings of statements. To understand the meanings of statements one needs to be conscious. But no computer could be conscious.**
   Pr. To think requires one to understand the meanings of statements

   Pr. To understand the meanings of statements one needs to be conscious

Pr. No computer could be conscious

C. No computer can think

8. **The secretary isn't answering the phone and that is part of her job. So either she isn't there or she isn't doing her job.**
   P. The secretary isn't answering the phone which is her job

   C. Either she isn't there or she isn't doing her job

10. **If I have a headache I take Aspirin. I only take Aspirin with food in my stomach. And if I eat Mary will eat, too. But Mary doesn't eat. So I don't have a headache.**
    Pr. If I have a headache I take Aspirin.

    Pr. I only take Aspirin with food in my stomach.

    Pr. If I eat Mary will eat too.

    Pr. Mary doesn't eat.

    C. I don't have a headache

Study Sets 2 (no answers for parts A, B and C)

Part D.

2. **If Ottawa is in Manitoba then it is near Brandon. Ottawa isn't in Manitoba because it isn't near Brandon.**
   This argument is an instance of *Modus Tollens*

   IF Ottawa is in Manitoba THEN it is near Brandon

   NOT (Ottawa is near Brandon)

   NOT (Ottawa is in Manitoba)

   or   If P then Q
         not Q
         not P

4. **The Senators play in either Ottawa or Montreal. They must play in Ottawa because they don't play in Montreal.**
   This argument is an instance of Disjunctive Syllogism

   The Senators play in Ottawa OR The Senators play in Montreal

   NOT (The Senators play in Montreal)

   The Senators play in Ottawa

   or   P or Q
         not Q
         P

6. **If you are tall you can reach the cookies and you can eat some if you can reach them so if you are tall you can eat some cookies.**
This argument is an instance of Hypothetical Syllogism

IF you are tall THEN you can reach the cookies

IF you can reach the cookies THEN you can eat some cookies

IF you are tall THEN you can eat some cookies

or   if P then Q
        <u>if Q then R</u>
        if P then R

Chapter Two

Study Sets 3

Part A.

2. **Divide your marble collection into the multi-coloured solids, the clear coloured, the clear colourless with swirls inside, the clear colourless without swirls inside.**
Scheme = multicoloured solids; clear coloured, clear colourless with swirls inside, and clear colourless without swirls. The distinctions are **clear** and **exclusive;** whether or not the scheme is exhaustive depends on what kind of solids you have—there is no category for single-coloured solids so if you have any single-coloured solids then the scheme is not exhaustive. As a taxonomy of marbles it is therefore **inadequate.**

4. **Friends (be nice), people who can hurt you (be nice), everyone else (screw them).**
Scheme = friends, people who can hurt you, everyone else. The scheme is **exhaustive,** since the "everyone else" category guarantees no one is left out. The scheme is **not exclusive,** since a person could both be a friend and could hurt you. It is **not particularly clear** since it is not obvious how you know whether a person fits in any category. It is **overly simplistic (and so not adequate)** for the task of determining how to treat others.

6. **(Kinds of animals): Pets, vermin, game, work animals, food animals.**
This scheme is **not exhaustive** since there may be animals in no category. It is **unclear** whether game and food animals are distinct (if "food animals" means "domestic animals raised for food" and "game" means "wild animals hunted for food" then they are distinct). This scheme is nevertheless **useful descriptively** since it reflects distinct ways that humans treat animals with which they have dealings.

8. **(Pre-season list for the coach): Last year's returning players, kids with attitudes, losers,**

kids who are promising but need more skills, kids I can't tell about yet.
The scheme is **neither exhaustive nor exclusive.** It is not exhaustive since there may be players who fit in no category (example: new players with great skills); it is not exclusive (example a returning player could fit in other categories as well).

Part C. (No answers for part B)

2. **A kite is a toy consisting of a light frame with paper or other thin material stretched upon it, to be flown in a strong wind by means of a string attached and a tail to balance it.**
Generally good definition: it captures the essential characteristics of a kite; (However, one might quibble about whether all kites are toys)

4. **"Homophobe" means a person who has an irrational hatred or fear of homosexuality.**
Generally good—this is **simply the standard definition** of the meaning of the word.

6. **A paddle is a stout pole shaped into a wide and flat blade at one end held freehand and used to propel a boat through water.**
Generally good – this is **simply the standard definition** of the meaning of the word.

8. **"Rectangle" means a two-dimensional figure with four sides.**
Inadequate definition; too broad: all rectangles are two-dimensional figures with four sides but they must also have right angles so not all two dimensional figures with four sides are rectangles.

10. **"Cello" means a stringed musical instrument made of wood.**
Too broad: since many stringed musical instruments made of wood are not cellos (for example, violins); (also **too narrow** since not all cellos are made of wood—though most are).

Study Sets 4

2. **Mary didn't study for the test tomorrow; I guess she is going to fail.**
Mary didn't study for the test tomorrow

People who don't study for tests (are likely to) fail them (implicit premise)

Mary is (likely) going to fail

4. **I'm sorry, I cannot sell you any beer. I am not permitted to sell to underage kids.**
You are under age (implicit premise)

I am not permitted to sell beer to people who are underage

I cannot sell you any beer

6. **Boxing should be banned in Canada because it is dangerous.**

Boxing is dangerous

Dangerous sports should be banned (implicit premise)

Boxing should be banned

8. **Don't ever buy a Taurus. It's a Ford!**
A Taurus is a Ford

Don't ever buy a Ford (implicit premise)

Don't ever buy a Taurus

Additional Study Sets for Part I

2. **If an argument has true premises and a false conclusion, then it is invalid.**
TRUE

4. **If an argument has a counter-example, it is invalid.**
TRUE

6. **No valid argument has false conclusions.**
FALSE

8. **Every sound argument has a true conclusion.**
TRUE

10. **All valid arguments have true premises.**
FALSE

12. **If an argument has true premises and a true conclusion, then it is valid.**
FALSE

14. **All unsound arguments have false premises.**
TRUE

Part B.

2. **An argument that is valid may have**
d. all of the above.

4. **An argument is sound if and only if**
d. is a valid argument with true premises

6. **An argument with true premises and a true conclusion may be**
d. all of the above

Part C.

2. **"Cat" means a small long-haired feline animal.**
too narrow

4. **"Psychologist" means a person who practises the art of psychology.**
circular

6. **"Dusk" means twilight as the evening darkens.**
acceptable

8. **A circus is a show with clowns, happening in a tent.**
too narrow (and too broad)

10. **"Soldier" means a person who serves in the army.**
too broad

12. **"Sexy" means causing men to find one very attractive.**
too narrow

14. **"Poodle" means a very small curly-haired show dog.**
too broad

16. **"Politician" means a person who nobly serves his country as a lawmaker.**
slanted

18. **"Guard" means one of the players stationed in the back court.**
too narrow

20. **"Mac and cheese" is a delicious dish containing cheese.**
slanted and circular

22. **"Tennis" means a game played with racquets and a net.**
too broad

24. **A shovel is a long-handled tool for moving snow.**
too narrow

Part D.

2. **The kids said they were hungry so Stella took them to Burger King.**
The kids said they were hungry (so they were hungry)

Hungry people need to eat (implicit premise)

People can eat at Burger King (implicit premise)

Stella took them to Burger King

4. **A square circle must be logically impossible. God can do anything that is logically possible but God can't make a square circle.**
God can do anything which is logically possible

God can't make a square circle

(so making) A square circle must be logically impossible

6. **Shanghai is the size of New York so it is much bigger than Saskatoon.**
Shanghai is the size of New York

New York is much bigger than Saskatoon (implicit premise)

---

so Shanghai is much bigger than Saskatoon

8. **People don't trust the Liberals. This means that Dion will probably lose the election because people just won't vote for a leader they don't trust.**

People don't trust the Liberals

Dion is the leader of the Liberals (is a Liberal) (implicit premise)

people just won't vote for a leader they don't trust

Dion will probably lose the election

10. **Mary didn't study for the final exam. So, of course, she will fail the class.**

Mary didn't study for the final exam

People who don't study will fail the class (implicit premise)

So, of course, she will fail the class

12. **Never hit your child. Health professionals have shown that hitting children fosters rage and self-loathing in them.**

Health professionals have shown that hitting children fosters rage and self-loathing in them.

Don't foster rage and loathing in your child (implicit premise)

Never hit your child.

Part E.

2. **If the banks are still open, then I'd better hurry downtown. But the banks are closed, so I guess there's no need to hurry.**
Modus Tollens

4. **We'll need to go for groceries either Thursday or Saturday. If we go Saturday, we'll be late for the opera. If we go Thursday, we'll have to miss *Star Trek*. So it looks like we will either be late for the opera or miss *Star Trek*.**
Constructive Dilemma

6. **The Saskatchewan Roughriders are better than the Argonauts and the Blue Bombers stink compared to the Argonauts so the Roughriders are better than the Blue Bombers.**
Syllogism; depends on the transitivity of "better than" (read: "The Blue Bombers stink compared to the Argonauts" as "The Argonauts are better than the Blue Bombers.")

PART II
Chapter Three

Study Sets 1

2. **Our X-ray unit will give you an examination for tuberculosis and other diseases, which you**
will receive free of charge. (Public service announcement)
Amphiboly (ambiguity of cross-reference suggests you get free diseases)

4. **The owners of this laundromat should be arrested for indecency. Look at the sign over the washers: "People using washers must remove their clothes when the machines stop."**
Amphiboly (suggests that people should remove the clothes that they are wearing rather than the clothes that they are washing)

6. **The font so generously presented by Mrs. Smith will be placed in the east end of the church. Babies may now be baptized at both ends.**
Amphiboly (ambiguity of cross-reference suggests ends of babies rather than ends of the church)

8. **I will not do this act because it is not right. I know it isn't right because my conscience advises me against it, and my conscience tells me so because the act is wrong.**
Circular Argument (conclusion states the same thing as the premises)

10. **Since every third child born in New York is a Catholic, Protestant families living there should have no more than two children.**
There is an *equivocation* (of two senses of "every third": "one third of class" vs. "every third member of the class"), but one may also see this as a case of *division* (where of the property "every third child is a Catholic" as true of the whole collection but not of all sub-groups of the collection).

12. **The Bible tells us to return good for evil. But Fred has never done me any evil, so it will be all right to play a dirty trick or two on him.**
Accent (on "evil" suggests "only evil" instead of "even evil")

14. **Richard Hudson is the most successful mayor the town has ever had because he's the best mayor of our history.**
Circular, "the most successful mayor the town has ever had" is has approximately the same meaning as "the best mayor of our history."

16. **(From *Alice in Wonderland*) "In that direction," the Cat said, "lives a Hatter and in that direction lives a March Hare. . . . They're both mad." "But I don't want to go among mad people," Alice remarked. "Oh, you can't help that," said the Cat: "we're all mad here. I'm mad. You're mad." "How do you know I'm mad?" said Alice. "You must be," said the Cat, "or you wouldn't have come here." (. . . Alice didn't think that proved it at all.)**
Circular

18. I like chocolate the best since it's my favourite kind of ice cream.
Circular

20. Good steaks are rare these days, so don't order yours well-done.
Equivocation (on "rare" = "hard to find" and "cooked little")

22. You should support the God-given right of parents to raise their children according to their own beliefs.
Complex question, the claim presupposes what is at issue.

24. Of course things like bribery are illegal; if such actions were not illegal, then they would not be prohibited by law.
Circular, to be illegal is to be prohibited by law

Chapter Four

Study Sets 2

Part A.

2. What is the probability that the two dice have a combined total of eight on your next throw?
There are 36 possible throws and five add up to 8 (6 + 2, 5 + 3, 4 + 4, 3 + 5, 2 + 6) so the probability is 5/36 (about 14 per cent)

Part B.

2. If he brings you the wrong book and then gets you another (also randomly picked) what is the probability that the second book is your psych text?
1/4

4. If in the beginning he had brought you three books, what is the chance that one of them would have been your psych text?
3/5

Part C.

2. What is the probability of selecting a red card or a black ace?
There are 26 red cards and two black aces, so 28/52

4. (Without replacing the first card) what is the probability of selecting first a spade and then a red face card?
13/52 times 26/51 = 338/2652 = 1/34 (almost 12.7 per cent)

6. (Without replacing the any cards) what is the probability of selecting first a spade and then a diamond and then another spade?
13/52 times 13/51 times 12/50 = 2028/132600 (about 16 per cent)

8. What is the probability of selecting an ace and, after returning it to the deck, selecting a second ace?
4/52 times 4/52 = 1/169 about 0.6 per cent

Part D.

2. Japanese high school students work harder than Canadian students. They spend more time in school and they have more homework. So they will be better at Canadian History than Canadians when the enter university.
Whether or not Japanese students will be better at what they have studied, it is unlikely that they will have studied Canadian History much or at all so the conclusion is quite unsupported. We could make the argument clearer by finding out what the various students studied in high school.

4. In a study of anabolic steroid use among male university students, 27 (about 3 percent) of males reported using steroids. Of these, 13 were competitive athletes at their schools, 10 were bodybuilders, and 4 reported wanting to improve their personal appearance. We concluded that students in athletic programs were more likely to take steroids than other students.
The sample size is considerable since presumably 900 male students were participants; 13/27 is almost half the positive reports and if the participants were randomly chosen, it is very unlikely at a normal school that anywhere near half the students would be in athletic programs, so on these assumptions (and the assumptions that all students were equally forthcoming) the conclusion is reasonably strong. Testing these assumptions would give us better evidence.

6. It snowed on Halloween last year in Edmonton, and the year before, and two years before that. It is likely to snow on Halloween in Edmonton this year.
Given what we know about the geographical location of Edmonton, and the fact that Halloween is pretty late in the fall, the fact that it has snowed three years out of four on Halloween is strong evidence that snow is at least likely. The argument would be improved if we knew how frequently it tends to snow generally in the fall in Edmonton— the fact that the date is Halloween of course has nothing to do with the chance of snow; the chance is a product of the time of year alone.

8. My friend Bill votes NDP. So does my friend Mary. In fact almost all my friends vote NDP. The NDP are sure to win the next election.

This is not supported and is an example of a typical fallacy, due to a form of cognitive bias resulting from what is called the *availability heuristic* in which people base their predictions of the frequency of an event or a proportion within a population having some feature, on how easily an example comes to mind. One's friends, or the people one works with, are quite likely to be rather like oneself. If you are a lawyer you will know lots of lawyers; if you are a restaurant server you will likely know many other servers. In particular one's friends are likely to share core beliefs, so the fact that most of your friends vote NDP is a good predictor that you vote NDP but not that most people will.

10. On four different occasions in the last month, dead animals were found in parks in Winnipeg. All were dogs, and all had been suffocated and their tails cut off. The police think all were committed by one person.

The event kind in question is very unusual. Dogs are not usually suffocated and left in a park—at the very least this is a criminal act, indeed it suggests psychological problems in the perpetrator. Then on top of this their tails are cut off, an act which is not connected with the cause of death. So the kind of act fits the bill of a single agent who has very unusual mental problems. So the conclusion is reasonably well supported.

Study Sets 3

Part A.

2. Bill ate beans, rice, and cantaloupe; Mary ate beans, rice, corn, and ham; Phil ate beans, corn, cantaloupe, and cheese; Tom ate rice, cantaloupe, and cherries. Everyone got sick except Phil.

Everyone who got sick ate rice. Phil didn't get sick and didn't eat rice. At least one person ate thing that Phil ate. = joint method

4. Sandy drank a beer, ate two pickles, and had chips and ice cream. Kieran ate three pickles, ate chips, and drank a beer. Howard drank a beer and ate chips and ice cream, Lois drank a beer, ate two pickles, and had ice-cream. Kieran got really sick, Lois and Sandy felt queasy and ill and Howard was fine.

How sick people got correlated with the number of pickles they ate; this suggests the method of concomitant variation.

6. Part of the damage in the accident was due to hitting the tree. Another part was clearly caused by the car rolling over before it hit the tree. But some of the damage seems to have been caused by something else. Perhaps we should look for evidence of a bomb.

Since there are damages that don't appear to be caused by the tree or rolling we must look for a third cause: the method of residue

8. Many of the kids at St. Albert school would smoke marijuana outside the school. School authorities correlated observed smoking and absenteeism, and discovered that when Bill Dodd or Ricky Jalapeia missed school for more than a day or two the number of kids smoking marijuana would decline.

The only difference between heavy smoking days and light smoking days was the presence or absence of Bill and Ricky at school. Method of difference

Study Sets 4

2. Most people who smoke marijuana will eventually try cocaine, because in study after study, a majority of cocaine addicts admitted to smoking marijuana before taking cocaine.

False Cause: mere correlation (compare: replacing "smoking marijuana" with "drinking milk")

4. Doctors don't really know any more than you or I do. This is the third case of faulty diagnosis I have heard of this month.

Hasty Generalization (medical diagnosis requires specialized knowledge but it is also fallible so a few mistaken diagnoses does not imply a general lack of knowledge among doctors)

6. We have just found out that Mary did not get into Harvard or the University of Toronto, so now she must abandon her hopes of going to a truly superior university.

Bifurcation (there are other "truly superior" universities)

8. A mob is no worse than the individuals who make it up.

Hasty Generalization is a possibility but so is composition.

10. You seem to have very discriminating tastes! Tell me, do you give top preference to California wines or to Okanagan wines?

Bifurcation (there are other kinds of wine that you might like better)

12. Bill Hotstuff is on the best team in the league so he must be a wonderful hockey player.
From this section: Sweeping Generalization, but Division is really a better diagnosis (team being best does not imply member of team is best)

14. *Jell-O* brand pudding pops are the tastiest and most nutritious snack you can get for your child today: Bill Cosby says so.
Authority (Bill Cosby is a famous TV "doctor" but is not known to be a nutrition expert)

Chapter Five

Study Sets 5

2. No, if you don't mind losing a tire, going off the road, and maybe killing yourself, you don't need a new tire.
Force or Fear (makes you fear not to buy a new tire)

4. A vote for my opponent is a vote for war.
Force or Fear (makes you fear to vote for him)

6. The Cadillac Eldorado. Life is too short to put it off for long.
Mob Appeal since it appeals to your snobbery

8. I'm on probation, Professor. If I don't get a good grade in this course I won't be able to stay in school. Please, could you let me have at least a C?
Pity (is supposed to make me sympathize with your plight)

10. There is no point in listening to Jolene's views about religion; she is an atheist if I ever saw one.
Abuse & Poisoning the Well (personal attack since it implies that it is bad to be an atheist)

12. Most women think guys who drink espresso are sexy. So, all you guys, get out there and drink espresso.
Mob appeal (appeal to your desire (if you are a guy) to be thought sexy; since there is no reason to think that this is any kind of serious generalization)

Study Sets 6

Study Sets 6 are for group work in class; no answers are provided here.

Additional Study Sets for Part II

Part A.   Here is a set of *fallacies of ambiguity*. Identify each one and in a few words explain why it is an instance of that fallacy.

2. Diamonds are rarely found in this country, so be careful not to misplace your wedding ring.
Equivocation ("rarely found" does not mean "hard to find if lost" but rather "an uncommon natural resource")

4. The NDP was booted out of government in last provincial election in Saskatchewan, so NDPer Pat Atkinson must have lost her race here in Saskatoon Broadway.
Division (The party as a whole had a difficulty which one of the party members need not have had)

6. On a church bulletin: It would be a great help toward keeping the churchyard tidy if we all followed the example of those who clip the grass on their own graves.
Amphiboly (ambiguity of cross-reference suggests that the dead cut the grass on their own graves)

8. The marriage of Ms. Bianca and Mr. Conrad, which was announced in yesterday's paper, was a mistake and we wish to correct it.
Amphiboly (the announcement was a mistake not the marriage)

10. Farm folk call the evening meal "supper" and city people "dinner." Therefore we must arrest those farm folk for cannibalism before they eat any more city people.
Amphiboly (the grammar suggests that farm folk eat city folk as food for dinner)

12. Nothing is better than peaches and ice cream! A crust of bread is better than nothing. Obviously, then, a crust of bread is better than peaches and ice cream.
Equivocation: four terms

Part B.

2. The owners shouldn't negotiate a settlement with the members of the NHL players' association. Those players are the most overprivileged, overpaid collection of prima donnas in sports today.
Question-Begging Epithets (best) and Abuse

4. God must exist, since if everyone believed that there was no God then we would have no reason not to obey the law and the world would be in chaos.
Irrelevant Thesis (tries to show why everyone must **believe** that God exists not why God exists, which is what is at issue)

6. Consider why you should accept Jesus into your heart as your personal saviour. Do you want to go to hell? You have a choice, salvation or endless suffering. If you accept Jesus and change your life you will be saved. If you don't, you will go to hell. (Notice that this fallacy is, in addition

to being a fallacy of presumption, also *force or fear*, which is a fallacy of relevance. The question is, which fallacy of presumption is it?)
Bifurcation (better) and Force or Fear

8. I'm not hoarding. I am only stocking up on everything before the hoarders get it all.
Special Pleading (they "hoard" but I merely "stock up")

10. You can argue all you want that democracy in Canada only gives the illusion of popular control over the government, but I don't buy it. I was brought up to believe in our democratic system.
Irrelevant Thesis (how you were brought up has no bearing on the truth of the conclusion)

12. No genuine religion could ever lead to bigotry, hatred, or conflict. But every so-called religion history has ever seen has done just that. So clearly there has never been a genuine religion, nor is there now.
Special Pleading (poor example)

14. When people get severe migraine headaches, they get nauseous and feel faint, so nausea makes you feel faint.
False Cause: spurious correlation (sinus headaches cause both nausea and feeling faint)

16. Chelsea told me that I'm her best friend so I must be since Chelsea would never lie to her best friend.
Begging the Question (my reason for believing that X is true is that X is true)

18. When Joe drinks he is no fun to be around. He is unhappy, he hates his job and Marcia picked up with another guy. Really, Joe should stop drinking. Drinking makes him a real bummer, man.
False Cause (The **direction of causation** is not determined: does drinking make Joe's life a mess or does the mess in Joe's life make him drink?)

20. A farmer can never make much money from growing wheat. Either he grows a lot of it and the price is too low, or he grows a little and doesn't have much to sell.
Bifurcation (there are other possibilities)

22. Recent studies show that the death rate in Canadian hospitals is considerably higher than the overall Canadian death rate. Obviously Canadian hospitals are not providing proper care.
Hasty Generalization (the circumstances which put people in the hospital—that they are ill— blocks makes it a special case and blocks the generalization)

Part C.

2. I am sure you will agree that this is an excellent class and that you are learning a great deal. If you don't, I will have to conclude that you are stupid and give you a bad grade.
Force or Fear

4. This theory, as you should know, was introduced by a godless atheist with known communist sympathies. There cannot be much to it.
Abuse

6. God must have created the universe. Have you noticed that no scientist or evolutionist has been able to explain where the power for the "big bang" came from?
Ignorance

8. We should support city council's bid for a nuclear reactor to be built in the city. Surely if there were any economic or safety problems they would know about them and be against the proposal.
Authority and Ignorance (the members of city council are not authorities on nuclear power and so their lack of concern is not a valid sign of security)

Part D.

2. "There has been a major accident and we have closed this street to regular traffic so we cannot allow you to drive your ambulance down it."
C   Sweeping generalization; ambulance blocks generalization

4. Students who get help from tutors get lower scores on average than students who don't. This shows that tutors are a waste of time.
B   Spurious correlation; poor ability is a common cause of both the need for tutor and bad grades

6. It really doesn't cost much for the government to pay for the medicare costs of a sick person. It's just a few thousand dollars a year on average. So medicare can't be a big factor in the national budget.
C   Composition; what is true of each sick person is not true of whole group

8. "There are two types of people in this world: the rich and the suckers. Do you want to get rich, or are you happy to remain a sucker?"
E   Bifurcation; there are other possibilities

10. Some people argue that sport fishing is wrong because fish can feel pain and they suffer. But that is nonsense. Fishing is a wonderful sport. It's relaxing and fun for the whole family and you get to eat what you catch!
D   Appeal to ignorance; arguer changes subject

12. At a certain point a car gets old enough and breaks down so frequently that it is no longer reasonable to fix it and we junk it. In the same way when a person gets old and decrepit enough he or she should be mercifully put to death.

D   False analogy; old cars and old persons are not relevantly similar

14. You don't need to ask Joseph what he thinks about the Holocaust. You know what he will say—he's Jewish.

E   Poisoning the well; tries to discount opponent's testimony due to circumstantial feature

Part E.

2. It doesn't seem that there is any room for debate here. Either we start selling cigarettes to boost our profit margin or we drift into bankruptcy when we can't pay our bills. So which would you prefer?

D   Bifurcation; there are more alternatives than these two

4. Buses use much more gasoline than automobiles, so the proposal that we all take the bus to work instead of driving a car is completely irresponsible. We would use so much more gas if we did that.

D   Composition; feature of individual buses not shared by the collection of all buses

6. Look, you don't need to take Father Bob's remarks about gay marriage seriously. He's a priest. He has to be against it or he gets in trouble with the Church.

C   Poisoning the well; reference to being a priest undercuts Father Bob's reply

8. An intelligent and well-read person like you shouldn't have any difficulty understanding how reasonable and important it is to support our town's school budget in the referendum

D   Mob appeal; flatters the audience to produce agreement

10. In Toronto it has been found that there is a significant correlation between the number of fire trucks spraying water on a fire and the financial losses due to the fire. The extra trucks clearly make the damage worse.

A   Spurious correlation; third factor (seriousness of fire) causes both cost and number of trucks

12. Don't let worry kill you off—let the Church help.

D   Amphiboly; Suggests the church will kill you instead of worry

14. My professor Eric Dayton is always spouting off about superstition and obviously is an atheist. I had better keep quiet about my religious beliefs so he won't be tempted to fail me.

C   Force or fear; Appeals to fear of being harmed as a reason

---

PART III
Chapter Six

Study Sets 1

Part A.

2. **Lead is malleable**
   type A

4. **Rectangles are sometimes squares**
   type I

6. **Uranium is radioactive**
   type A

8. **Some dogs bite children**
   type I

10. **Some students at the University of Manitoba are not Canadians**
    type O

Part B.

2. **Mustangs are Fords**
   A   All M are F

4. **Students often bike to school**
   I   Some S are P (people who bike to school)

6. **Some polar bears do not live in Canada**
   O   Some P are not D (dwellers in Canada)

8. **Everything worth doing is worth doing well**
   A   All T are W (or All things worth doing are things worth doing well

10. **Detroit isn't beautiful**
    E   No P (places identical to Detroit) are B

Study Sets 2

2. **Stephen Harper is prime minister and Stephen Harper is plump so some prime ministers are plump.**
   The terms: A = persons identical with Stephen Harper, B = persons identical with the Prime Minister, C = plump persons. Premises: "All persons who are identical with Stephen Harper are persons identical with the prime minister" (All A are B), and "Some persons identical with Stephen

Harper are plump persons" (Some A are C); conclusion: Some persons identical with the prime minister are plump persons" (Some B are C). Because the conclusion is particular, one of the premises must be as well.

4. **Men are weak and the weak always fail so some men fail.**
The terms: M = men, W = weak creatures, F = creatures that fail. The second premise ("the weak always fail") is clearly universal (an **A** statement) and the conclusion is particular (an **I** statement), so the first premise ("men are weak") will have to be translated as a particular premise (**I** statement) or else the argument cannot be valid, so the premises are: Some men are weak creatures (Some M are W); All weak creatures are creatures that fail (All W are F), and the conclusion should be Some men are creatures that fail (Some M are F)

6. **The monsters under your bed are afraid when Teddy is in your bed and Teddy is here in bed with you so no monsters will come out from under your bed tonight. (Hint: remember that you need to translate this using only three terms, so you will need to be creative.)**
There are several ways to make this argument amenable to translation as a single syllogism. Thinking of events or times is one way. If the three terms are P = times when monsters under your bed won't come out, Q = Times when Teddy is in your bed and R = Times identical to tonight, then the argument could be rewritten as: Premise 1: All times when Teddy is in your bed are times when monsters under your bed won't come out, and Premise 2: All times identical to tonight are times when Teddy is in your bed, conclusion: All times identical to tonight are times when monsters under your bed won't come out. This translation assumes that monsters won't come out when they are afraid to come out, and that they are afraid of Teddy; so the translation is not perfect but it *does* preserve the validity of the argument.

Study Sets 3

2. __F__ **A** and **E** categorical statements are affirmative in quality.

4. __F__ The subaltern of an **E** categorical, on the traditional interpretation, is an **I** categorical.

6. __T__ If "All S are P" is true then "All non-P are non-S" is true.

8. __T__ All four types of categoricals have the same form as their contrapositives.

10. __T__ If "All S are P" is true and "Some S are Q" is true then "Some P are Q" is true.

12. __F__ If "Some S are P" is true and "Some S are Q" is true then "Some P are Q" is true.

14. __T__ The contradictory of an **A** statement is an **O** statement.

16. __F__ **A** and **E** type categorical statements are equivalent to their contrapositives on the traditional interpretation.

18. __F__ The contradictory of an **A** statement is an **E** statement.

20. __T__ All four types of categorical statements have the same form as their converses on the traditional interpretation.

Study Sets 4

Part A.

2. **Most high school teachers are men. Some men are not dope smokers since high school teachers never smoke dope.**

hs teachers = H	No H are D
men = M	Some H are M
dope smokers = D	Some M are not D

4. **No painters are rational since no rational being is an artist and painters are artists.**

painters = P	No R are A
rational beings = R	All P are A
artists = A	No P are R

Part B.

2. **Only students get a free lunch. Martha is not a student so Martha cannot eat lunch for free.**

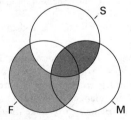

F = people getting free lunch
S = students
M = people identical to Martha

All F are S
No M are S
No M are F   VALID

4. **Some dead things have souls because some vampires have souls and all vampires are dead.**

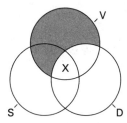

D = dead things

V = vampires

S = possessors of souls

Some V are S
All V are D
Some D are S   VALID

6. **Some philosophy classes are very boring although all Eric's philosophy classes are exciting. So there are philosophy classes not taught by Eric.**

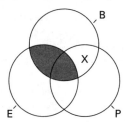

P = philosophy classes

B = boring classes

E = Eric's classes

No E are B
Some P are B
Some P are not E   VALID

8. **Anyone who likes video games is a deviant. Teenage males universally like video games so all male teens are deviants.**

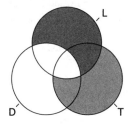

L = people who like video games

D = deviants

T = teenage males

All L are D
All T are L
All T are D   VALID

10. **All the reporters at the *Daily Planet* live in Metropolis. Clark Kent is a reporter at the *Daily Planet* so he lives in Metropolis.**

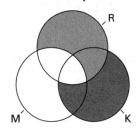

R = reporters at the *Daily Planet*

M = people who live in Metropolis

K = people identical to Clark Kent

All R are M
All K are R
All K are M   VALID

Study Sets 5

2. **The students in this class will do badly on the test because they didn't study.**

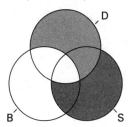

There are a number of ways to translate this depending on whether you want to say that all or only some students will do badly and whether or not you treat "study" or "don't study" as your middle term. I have assumed that we have an A statement, in which case the missing information is that people who don't study will do badly

S = the students in Phil 140

B = people who will do badly on the test

D = people who don't study

All S are D
All D are B   Implicit premise
All S are B   VALID

4. **Some Canadians are bigots so don't listen to their opinions.**

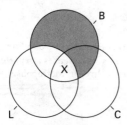

We need to add an implicit premise with the information that we don't need to listen to the opinions of bigots

L = people we don't listen to

C = Canadians

B = bigots

Some C are B

<u>All B are L</u>   Implicit premise

Some C are L

In graphing this syllogism we graph the first premise by putting the "X" on the line dividing the lens between C and B and then the second by filling in the crescent made by the part of B outside of L. This bumps the "X" into L and so the argument is VALID

Study Sets 6

Part A.

2. **Snakes cannot make conversation.**
   No snakes are conversationalists
   No S are C

4. **Swedes are not usually friendly.**
   Some Swedes are not friendly
   Some S are not F

6. **Only Baptists will be saved.**
   All people who will be saved are Baptists
   All P are B

8. **He only has eyes for Margaret.**
   E = people he has eyes for (and)
   M = people identical to Margaret
   All E are M [an unusual case for "only"]

10. **If it is alcoholic Todd will drink it.**
    All alcoholic drinks are things that Todd will drink
    All A are T

12. **Canadians aren't usually rich.**
    Some Canadians are not rich people
    Some C are not R

14. **Not everything sweet is good for you.**
    Some sweet things are not things that are good for you
    Some S are not G

16. **If something has wings it isn't a pig.**
    No winged things are pigs
    No W are P

18. **Not every engineer is a woman.**
    Some engineers are not women
    Some E are not W

20. **Sometimes cats are fat.**
    Some cats are fat
    Some C are S

22. **Paris is in France.**
    All places identical to Paris are places in France
    All P are F
    (or if you need the fact that there *is* a place called Paris);
    Some places identical to Paris are places in France
    Some P are F

24. **Uranium is a metal.**
    All instances of uranium are instances of metal
    All U are M

26. **Some fools fall in love.**
    Some fools are people who fall in love
    Some F are L

28. **To fail to love is a great misfortune.**
    All failures to love are great misfortunes
    All F are M

Part B.

2. **Two categoricals are subcontraries if**
   B.   Both can be true but only one can be false

4. **If all A are B and some C are not B, you can infer**
   B.   Some C are not A

6. **From the square of opposition, you can see that the types of statements**
   A.   A and O, and E and I are contradictories

8. **If no A are B and some C are not B, you can infer**
   E.   Nothing about A and C

10. **Which categorical statements are equivalent to their contrapositives?**
    A.   A and O statements

12. **If no A are B and some C are B, you can infer**
    B.   Some C are not A

14. **Which categorical statements are equivalent to their converses?**
    C.   I and E statements

Part C.

2. Robins are birds so they lay eggs

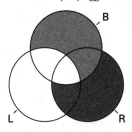

The implicit premise is "all birds lay eggs," and as the major premise it goes first.

The dictionary is:

B = birds (Middle term)
L = egg layers (Major term)
R = robins (Minor term)

The proper form of the argument is:

All B are L   (implicit premise)
<u>All R are B</u>
All R are L

Since the entire part of the R circle lying outside of the L circle is blacked out the argument is VALID.

4. Fido is a dog so he can't fly

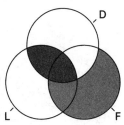

The implicit premise is "no dogs are flying things," and as the major premise it goes first.

The dictionary is:

D = dogs (Middle term)
F = beings identical to Fido (Minor term)
L = flying things (Major term)

The proper form of the argument is:

No D are L (implicit premise)
<u>All F are D</u>
No F are L

The lens between F and L is filled in: the argument is VALID.

6. Because he's human Socrates is mortal

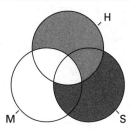

The implicit premise is that "Socrates is human,"

The dictionary is:

H = human (Middle term)
S = beings identical to Socrates (Minor term)
M = mortal beings (Major term)

The proper form of the argument is:

All H are M
<u>All S are H</u>
All S are M

The diagram is just like that of Question 2: the argument is VALID.

Part D.

2. Some Canadians eat fish
fish are high in protein
(so) Some Canadians eat high-protein foods
Premises in wrong order! The translation is tricky!

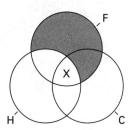

The dictionary is:

F = people who eat fish (Middle term)
C = Canadians (Minor term)
H = people who eat high protein food (Major term)

The proper form of the argument is:

All F are H
<u>Some C are F</u>
Some C are H

There is an "X" in the lens between H and C circles, so the argument is VALID.

4. **Some Romanians are not golfers.**
Romanians are Eastern Europeans.
(so) Some Eastern Europeans are not golfers.

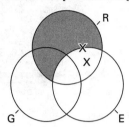

The dictionary is:

R = Romanians (Middle term)
E = Eastern Europeans (Minor term)
G = golfers (Major term)

The proper form of the argument is:

Some R are not G
All R are E
Some E are not G

There is an "x" in the E circle outside the G circle so the argument is VALID.

6. **All good people do what is right.**
People who do the right thing pay their taxes.
All good people pay their taxes.

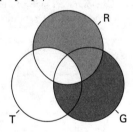

Premises in wrong order!

The dictionary is:

R = people who do what is right (Middle term)
G = good people (Minor term)
T = people who pay their taxes (Major term)

The proper form of the argument is:

All R are T
All G are R
All G are T

The two premises between them black out the part of G outside of the T circle: the argument is VALID.

8. **Some sheep are not white sheep, and some sheep are not black sheep, so some black sheep are not white sheep.**

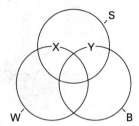

The dictionary is:

S = sheep (Middle term)
B = black sheep (Minor term)
W = white sheep (Major term)

The proper form of the argument is:

Some S are not W
Some S are not B
Some B are not W

Since X and Y are on the lines we do not know whether there is an "X" which is in the B circle and outside the W circle; the argument is INVALID.

10. **Alberta politicians are all oilmen and oilmen are always evil-doers so all Alberta politicians are evil-doers.**

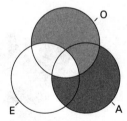

Premises in wrong order!

The dictionary is:

O = oilmen (Middle term)
B = Alberta politicians (Minor term)
E = evil people (Major term)

The proper form of the argument is:

All O are E
All B are O
All B are E

This argument has the same diagram as exercise 6, and is **valid**.

12. **No reptiles are mammals.**
Some animals with tails are mammals.
so some tailed animals are not reptiles.

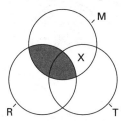

The dictionary is:

O = mammals (Middle term)
T = tailed animals (Minor term)
R = reptiles (Major term)

The proper form of the argument is:

No R are M
Some T are M
Some T are not R

There is an X in T outside of R so the argument is VALID.

14. **Bananas are squishy when overripe.**
Mangos are not bananas.
(so) Mangos are not squishy when overripe.

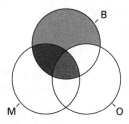

The dictionary is:

B = bananas (Middle term)
M = mangos (Minor term)
O = things that are squishy when overripe (Major term)

The proper form of the argument is:

All B are O
No M are B
No M are O

The lens between M and O is not fully blacked out so the argument is INVALID (things besides bananas could be squishy when overripe)

16. **Some pool players lack souls since vampires don't have souls and some vampires play pool.**

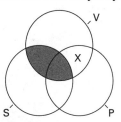

Premises in wrong order!

The dictionary is:

V = vampires (Middle term)
P = pool players (Minor term)
S = possessors of souls (Major term)

The proper form of the argument is:

No V are S
Some V are P
Some P are not S

Notice that despite a different arrangement of premises the diagram is the same as exercise 12 and is VALID.

18. **Killing is never permissible because killing is always evil and no evil act is permissible.**

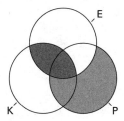

Premises in wrong order!

The dictionary is:

E = evil acts (Middle term)
K = killings (Minor term)
P = permissible acts (Major term)

The proper form of the argument is:

No E are P
All K are E
No K are P

This argument is VALID.

20. **All real Quebecers are separatists, because real Quebecers love Quebec and people who love Quebec are separatists.**

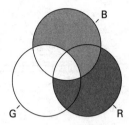

The dictionary is:

P = people who love Quebec (Middle term)
R = real Quebecers (Minor term)
S = separatists (Major term)

The proper form of the argument is:

All P are S
All R are P
All R are S

This argument is clearly VALID.

22. **Some dogs have tails and no humans have tails, so no humans are dogs.**

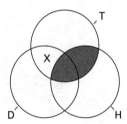

The dictionary is:

T = tail possessors (Middle term)
H = humans (Minor term)
D = dogs (Major term)

The proper form of the argument is:

Some D are T
No H are T
No H are D

The lens between D and H is not fully blacked out so the argument is INVALID.

24. **Many people feel oppressed by guilt. This is because feeling guilt is a kind of dysfunction and some people are dysfunctional.**

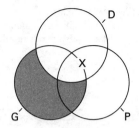

The dictionary is:

D = feelers of a dysfunction (Middle term)
P = people (Minor term)
G = feelers of guilt

The proper form of the argument is:

All G are D
Some P are D
Some P are G

This argument is INVALID. We do not know which side of the line D and G the "X" is on; There may be more than one kind of dysfunction and so although we know that some people feel a dysfunction, we do not know that the dysfunction they feel is guilt.

Chapter Seven

Study Sets 7

<u>Part A.</u>

2. The corresponding conditional of *Modus Tollens* is $((P \rightarrow Q) \wedge \neg Q) \rightarrow \neg P$ and the truth table is:

P Q	$((P \rightarrow Q) \wedge \neg Q)) \rightarrow \neg P$				
T T	T	F F	**T**	F	
T F	F	F T	**T**	F	
F T	T	T F	**T**	T	
F F	T	T T	**T**	T	

4. The corresponding conditional of Disjunctive Syllogism is $((P \vee Q) \wedge \neg P) \rightarrow Q$, and the truth table is:

P Q	$((P \vee Q) \wedge \neg P)) \rightarrow Q$			
T T	T	F F	**T**	
T F	T	F F	**T**	
F T	T	T T	**T**	
F F	F	F T	**T**	

Part C. (no answers for Part B)

2.

P Q	$(P \rightarrow Q) \vee Q$	
T T	T	**T**
T F	F	**F**
F T	T	**T**
F F	T	**T**

4.

P Q	$(((P \rightarrow Q) \rightarrow P) \rightarrow Q)$		
T T	T	T	**T**
T F	F	T	**F**
F T	T	F	**T**
F F	T	F	**T**

6.

P Q	$(P \rightarrow Q) \rightarrow (Q \rightarrow P)$		
T T	T	**T**	T
T F	F	**T**	T
F T	T	**F**	F
F F	T	**T**	T

8.

P Q R	$(((P \rightarrow Q) \wedge (Q \rightarrow R)) \wedge P) \rightarrow R$				
T T T	T	T	T	T	**T**
T T F	T	F	F	F	**T**
T F T	F	F	T	F	**T**
T F F	F	F	T	F	**T**
F T T	T	T	T	F	**T**
F T F	T	F	F	F	**T**
F F T	T	T	T	F	**T**
F F F	T	T	T	F	**T**

Study Sets 8

Part A.

2. $P \wedge (Q \rightarrow R)$

4. $(R \wedge \neg P) \rightarrow \neg Q$

6. $(Q \wedge R) \vee (\neg R \wedge (\neg Q \vee P))$

Part B.

2. Either Mary hates Bill or she invites him to dinner but if she invites him to dinner she will burn the roast.

4. It isn't true both that Mary hates Bill and that either she doesn't invite him to dinner or she hates him.

Study Sets 9

2. No sick animals may enter the country.
This could be translated many ways: as P as ¬P as or as $P \rightarrow \neg Q$, depending on your choice of dictionary.

Part B.

2. Lola is sick or Gerry is hungry. If Trina is angry then Gerry can't eat. If Gerry is hungry then Gerry can eat. But Lola isn't sick. So Trina isn't angry.

Lola is sick = A	$A \vee B$
Gerry is hungry = B	$C \rightarrow \neg D$
Trina is angry = C	$\underline{B \rightarrow D}$
Gerry can eat = D	$\neg A$
	$\therefore \neg C$

4. If I give Mary a lift, Bill will be mad. But if I don't, she will get wet from the rain. If I let Mary get wet from the rain, Bill will be mad. So (either way) Bill will be mad.

I give Mary a lift	= X	$X \rightarrow Y$
Bill will be mad	= Y	$\neg X \rightarrow Z$
she will get wet	= Z	$\underline{Z \rightarrow Y}$
		$\therefore Y$

Part C.

2.

P Q R	$((P \wedge Q) \rightarrow (R \rightarrow (P \vee Q)))$			
T T T	T	**T**	T	T
T T F	T	**T**	T	T
T F T	F	**T**	T	T
T F F	F	**T**	T	T
F T T	F	**T**	T	T
F T F	F	**T**	T	T
F F T	F	**T**	F	F
F F F	F	**T**	T	F

4.

P	$(P \rightarrow (\neg P \rightarrow (\neg P \rightarrow P)))$				
T	**T**	F	T	F	T
F	**T**	T	F	T	F

Study Sets 10

Part A.

2.

P Q R	$(P \lor (P \land Q)) \to (Q \to P)$			
T T T	T	T	**T**	T
T T F	T	T	**T**	T
T F T	T	F	**T**	T
T F F	T	F	**T**	T
F T T	F	F	**T**	F
F T F	F	F	**T**	F
F F T	F	F	**T**	T
F F F	F	F	**T**	T

4. Notice that the first two conjuncts of the sentence entail Q by *Modus Ponens*; since a deductive argument is monotonic, the argument must be valid:

$$((P \land (P \to Q)) \land ((P \lor Q) \to Q)) \to Q$$

Part B.

2. **Freddy is a pig. If Freddy is a pig and Dotty isn't, their love is unnatural. But since Dotty is a pig, it is OK.**

Freddy is a pig = P   premise 1   P

Dotty is a pig = Q   premise 2 $(P \land \neg Q) \to \neg R)$

Their love is natural = R   premise 3   <u>Q</u>

                           conclusion ∴ R

(If you check you will see that this argument is NOT valid.)

4. **Push either the red knob or the green knob. If you don't push the red knob then turn the orange handle. Don't push the green knob unless the light is on. If you push the red knob and pull the brown cord the light goes off. So either you pull the brown cord or the light is on.**

Push the red knob = R   premise 1   R ∨ G

Push the green knob = G   premise 2   ¬R → O

Turn orange handle = O   premise 3   G → L (note!)

The light is on = L   premise 4   <u>(R ∧ B) 6 → ¬L</u>

Pull the brown cord = B   conclusion ∴ B ∨ L

Part C.

2.

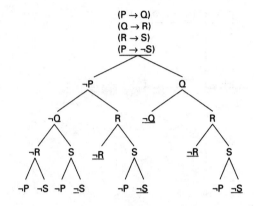

4.

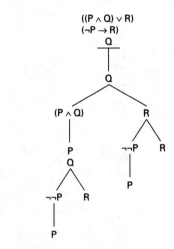

Study Sets 11

2.

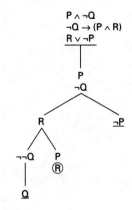

Consistent

4.

P ∧ (O ∧ R)
¬(R ∨ Q)
P → ¬Q
———
P
Q
R
|
¬R
¬Q

Only the first two sentences are needed to make the set inconsistent.

Part B.

2.

pr   (P ∨ Q) → R
pr   Q ∧ ¬R
¬con ¬¬P

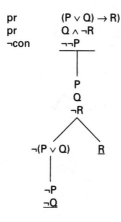

P
Q
¬R
¬(P ∨ Q)   R
¬P
¬Q

Valid

4.

pr   P
pr*   ¬(Q ∨ R)
pr*   ¬(P → ¬R)
¬con ¬(¬P → Q)

|

P

|

¬P
Q

Valid; the '*'ed premises are not needed

Part C.

2.

pr   (X ∧ Y) → Z
pr   (Y ∧ ¬Z)
¬con ¬¬X

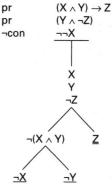

X
Y
¬Z
¬(X ∧ Y)   Z
¬X   ¬Y

DICTIONARY PROOF
The boss is tired = X
You make a mistake = Y
He snaps at you = Z
FORMALIZED
(X ∧ Y) → Z
(Y ∧ ¬Z)
¬X
No lines remain open so this argument is valid

Additional Study Sets for Part III

Part A.

2. [(((P → ¬Q) ∧ (Q ∨ ¬R)) ∧ (P →(R ∨ Q))) → ¬P]

P Q R	(((P → ¬Q) ∧ (Q ∨ ¬R)) ∧ (P → (R ∨ Q))) → ¬P
T T T	F F F T F F T T **T** F
T T F	F F F T T F T T **T** F
T F T	T T F F F F T T **T** F
T F F	T T T T T F F F **T** F
F T T	T F F T F F T T **T** T
F T F	T F F T T F T T **T** T
F F T	T T F F F T T T **T** T
F F F	T T T T T T T F **T** T

Part B.

2. $(R \land \neg Q)$; $(P \lor (Q \lor \neg R))$; $(R \to (S \lor \neg T))$;
   $\neg(S \land R)$; $(P \land T)$

$(R \land \neg Q)$	1
$(P \lor (Q \lor \neg R))$	Not needed
$(R \to (S \lor \neg T))$	3
$\neg(S \land R)$	4
$(P \land T)$	2

R
¬Q
P
T

¬R $(S \lor \neg T)$

S   <u>¬T</u>

<u>¬S</u>   <u>¬R</u>

Part C.

2. $(((P \land Q) \to S) \land (S \to \neg R) \land (\neg S \lor \neg P) \land$
   $(Q \to \neg T) \land R) \to \neg T$

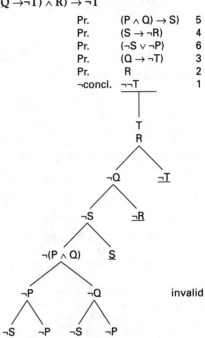

Pr.	$(P \land Q) \to S)$	5
Pr.	$(S \to \neg R)$	4
Pr.	$(\neg S \lor \neg P)$	6
Pr.	$(Q \to \neg T)$	3
Pr.	R	2
¬concl.	¬¬T	1

T
R

¬Q   <u>¬T</u>

¬S   <u>¬R</u>

$\neg(P \land Q)$ <u>S</u>

¬P   ¬Q

¬S   ¬P   ¬S   ¬P

invalid

2. **God is good if God exists, and if God is good everything is without flaw. If there is pain in the world it has a good reason or else it is a flaw. So if God exists and there is pain in the world it has a good reason.**

Dictionary: G = God is good

E = God exists

F = All is without flaw

P = There is pain in the world

R = There is a good reason for the existence of pain

Pr.	E → G	2
Pr.	G → F	3
Pr.	(P → (R ∨ ¬F)	4
¬concl.	¬P ∧ E) → R	1

¬R
P
E   Valid

¬E   G

¬G   F

¬P   (R ∨ ¬F)

R   ¬F

4. **Either there is objective right and wrong or else morality is merely relative. If some things are objectively right then it is wrong to act immorally. If morality is merely relative then helping the poor is no better than killing babies. But it is better to help the poor, so it is wrong to act immorally.**

Dictionary   O = There is objective right and wrong

R = everything is relative

W = it is wrong to act immorally

H = helping the poor is no better than killing babies

Pr.	O ∨ R	4
Pr.	O → W	3
Pr.	R → H	5
Pr.	¬H	1
¬concl.	¬W	2

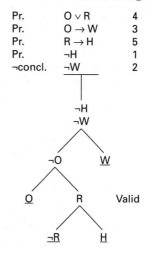

¬H
¬W

¬O   W

O   R   Valid

¬R   H

Part E.

2.

P Q R	(((Q → ¬R) ∧ (P → Q)) ∧ (P ∨ ¬R)) → P	
T T T	F F F T F T F T	
T T F	T T T T T T T T	
T F T	T F F F F T F T	
T F F	T T F F F T T T	
F T T	F F F T F F F T	
F T F	T T T T T T T F	INVALID
F F T	T F T T F F F T	
F F F	T T T T T T T F	

4.

P Q R	((¬Q → R) ∧ (¬Q ∨ P) ∧ (¬P → ¬R)) → P	
T T T	F T T F T T F T F T	
T T F	F T T F T T F T T T	
T F T	T T T T T T F T F T	
T F F	T F F T T F F T T T	
F T T	F T F F T F T F F T	VALID
F T F	F T F F T F T T T T	
F F T	T T T T T F T F F T	
F F F	T F F T T F T T T T	

P Q R	((R → P) ∧ (Q ∨ R) ∧ (Q → P)) → P					
T T T	T	T	T	T	T	T
T T F	T	T	T	T	T	T
T F T	T	T	T	T	T	T
T F F	T	F	F	F	T	T
F T T	F	F	T	F	F	T
F T F	T	T	T	F	F	T
F F T	F	F	T	F	T	T
F F F	T	F	F	F	T	T

VALID

Part F.

2. If Bill is a ghoul then he isn't a vampire. Bill doesn't drink human blood and he isn't un-dead. He would drink blood and be un-dead if he were a vampire. So Bill must be a ghoul.

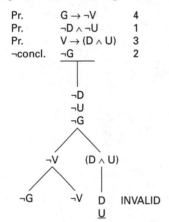

Pr.	G → ¬V	4
Pr.	¬D ∧ ¬U	1
Pr.	V → (D ∧ U)	3
¬concl.	¬G	2

Dictionary:
 G = Bill is a ghoul
 V = Bill is a vampire
 D = Bill drinks blood
 U = Bill is un-dead

This argument is pretty obviously invalid because even though it shows that Bill is not a vampire, and it is true that if he is a ghoul he isn't a vampire, it is also true that if he is a regular person or a chipmunk then he isn't a vampire (and isn't a ghoul either!)

4. The world shows a fitness of its parts to their functions. If it shows such a functional fitness it must be the product of intelligent design. There must be a designer if it is the product of intelligent design. Only God could design a world [hint: treat this as an if-then sentence]. Therefore God must exist.

Dictionary:
 F = The world shows fitness, etc.
 P = The world is the product of intelligent design
 D = There is a designer
 G = God exists

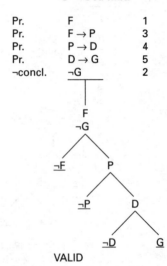

Pr.	F	1
Pr.	F → P	3
Pr.	P → D	4
Pr.	D → G	5
¬concl.	¬G	2

VALID

6. If the Liberals won then either most Canadians liked the Liberals or most people distrusted the Conservatives. Either most people trusted the Conservatives or the NDP did well. If the NDP did well then the Liberals lost unless most people distrusted the Conservatives. Most Canadians didn't like the Liberals so unless the NDP did well most people distrusted the Conservatives.

Dictionary:
 W = The Liberals won
 L = Canadian liked the Liberals
 C = Canadians trusted the Conservatives
 N = The NDP did well

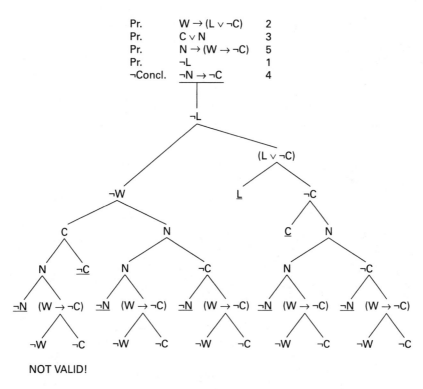

Pr.	$W \rightarrow (L \vee \neg C)$	2
Pr.	$C \vee N$	3
Pr.	$N \rightarrow (W \rightarrow \neg C)$	5
Pr.	$\neg L$	1
¬Concl.	$\neg N \rightarrow \neg C$	4

NOT VALID!

Part G.

2.

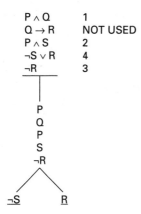

$P \wedge Q$	1
$Q \rightarrow R$	NOT USED
$P \wedge S$	2
$\neg S \vee R$	4
$\neg R$	3

4.

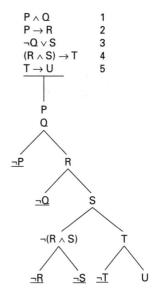

$P \wedge Q$	1
$P \rightarrow R$	2
$\neg Q \vee S$	3
$(R \wedge S) \rightarrow T$	4
$T \rightarrow U$	5

6.

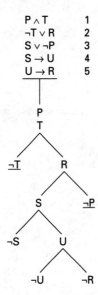

$P \wedge T$ 1
$\neg T \vee R$ 2
$S \vee \neg P$ 3
$S \rightarrow U$ 4
$U \rightarrow R$ 5

P
T

¬T   R

S   ¬P

¬S   U

¬U   ¬R

Index

A

ambiguity, 47
    equivocation, 47, 50
    amphiboly, 47, 50–53
analogy, 79–84
Archimedes, 81
argument. *See also* Aristotelian
    logic; sentence logic
    from definition, 31–32
    chain argument. *see*
        enthymeme
    cogent, 8–9, 39
    deductive, 10
    in a broad sense, 7
    in a narrow sense, 9–10
    inductive. *see* induction
    logical, 9–10
    patterns, 4–18, 34, 188
Aristotle, 131
Aristotelian logic, 131
    categorical statement,
        131–133
    complement, 132, 134
    contraposition, 148
    copula, 132, 138
    contrariety, 151
    conversion, 147
    enthymemes in, 160–161
    immediate inference in,
        146–152
    major term, 154
    middle term, 154
    minor term, 154
    modern interpretation of,
        140, 152
    obversion, 148–149
    problem of empty terms,
        140–143
    quantity in, 132, 139
    quality in, 132, 139
    singular reference in, 139,
        144–146
    subcontrariety, 151

syllogism, 153–154
    the traditional square of
        opposition, 152
    testing for validity in,
        155–159
    translation into, 136–139,
        140–146
    universe of discourse,
        133–134
    Venn diagrams, 133–136
authority, 102

B

belief, 6–35, 43
    aim of, 36
bias, 109–111

C

classification, 25–26
complement. *see* Aristotelian logic
conditional probability. *see*
    probability
conjunction problem, 75–77
consequent. *see* conditional
    statement
conspiracy theory, 104–105
constructive dilemma. *see*
    argument patterns
contradiction, 94, 151, 181
contraposition. *see* Aristotelian
    logic
contraries, 93–94
    see also Aristotelian logic
conversion. *see* Aristotelian logic
copula. *see* Aristotelian logic
corresponding conditional, 181
counter-example, 15–17
critical thinking, 3, 35, 130

D

deductive argument, 129–130
definition, 27–29
    argument from, 31–32

disjunctive syllogism *see*
    argument patterns
Doyle, Arthur Conan, 88

E

empty terms. *see* Aristotelian
    logic
enthymeme, 32–33, 160–161
    and material inference,
        67–69
    see also Aristotelian logic
equivocation *see* ambiguity

F

fallacy, 39–118
    abuse, 111
    accent, 53–56
    amphiboly, 47, 50–53
    appeal to authority,
        100–102
    appeal to force or fear, 113
    appeal to ignorance,
        103–106
    appeal to pity, 112–113
    begging the question, 60
    bifurcation, 93–95
    causal fallacies, 96–100
    complex question, 62–63
    composition, 56–58, 92
    division, 58–59, 93
    equivocation, 47, 50
    false cause, 96–97
    false analogy, 80, 95–96
    hasty generalization, 92–93
    hypostatization, 59
    inductive fallacies, 75–107
    irrelevant thesis, 106–107
    mere correlation, 97–98
    mob appeal, 112
    personal attack, 111
    poisoning the well, 111
    post hoc ergo propter hoc, 97
    review of, 116–117